# *Beginner's* FRENCH

## Catrine Carpenter

Advisory Editor: Paul Coggle
University of Kent at Canterbury

D1493108

TEACH YOURSELF BOOKS

Catrine Carpenter was born in France and is now a lecturer at Brighton Polytechnic. She has an MA in Media Assisted Language Learning and Teaching and has wide experience in writing and publishing teaching materials.

To Geoff Lees, Violaine and Edward

# Acknowledgement:

My very warm thanks to Elspeth Broady for her extensive help during the writing of this book.

Long-renowned as *the* authoritative source for self-guided learning – with more than 30 million copies sold worldwide – the *Teach Yourself* series includes over 200 titles in the fields of languages, crafts, hobbies, sports, and other leisure activities.

*British Library Cataloguing in Publication Data*
Carpenter, Catrine
  Teach Yourself beginner's French
  I. Title
  448

  ISBN 0 340 55578 5

*Library of Congress Catalog Card Number:* 92-81681

First published in UK 1992 by Hodder Headline Plc, 338 Euston Road, London NW1 3BH

First published in US 1992 by NTC Publishing Group, 4255 West Touhy Avenue, Lincolnwood (Chicago), Illinois 60646 – 1975 U.S.A.

Typeset by Transet Typesetters Ltd, Coventry.
Printed in England by Cox & Wyman Ltd, Reading, Berkshire.

| Impression number | 17 | 16 | 15 | 14 | 13 | 12 | 11 | 10 | 9 | 8 |
|---|---|---|---|---|---|---|---|---|---|---|
| Year | | 1999 | 1998 | 1997 | 1996 | 1995 | 1994 | | | |

# CONTENTS

About the course ..................................................... 1
Pronunciation Guide ................................................ 5
1 Bonjour  *Hello* ................................................ 9
   Simple questions ............................................. 12
   Refusing politely in French ............................... 13
   Calling the waiter's attention ........................... 13
   Being courteous .............................................. 13
   How to learn vocabulary ................................... 13

2 C'est combien?  *How much is it?* ..................... 17
   Numbers up to 10 .......................................... 19
   A, an ........................................................... 20
   The – **Le, la, l', les** – The definite article .......... 20
   Have you a/the ...? ........................................ 21
   Some, any .................................................... 21
   One/a/an ..................................................... 22
   How much is it? ............................................ 22
   How to organise your learning ........................... 22

3 Je m'appelle ... et vous?  *My name is ... and you?* .... 26
   Numbers 10 – 20 ........................................... 27
   Regular verbs ending in **-er** .......................... 29
   Two important verbs: to have, to be .................... 30
   The negative form .......................................... 30
   Agreement of adjectives .................................. 30
   Using capital letters ...................................... 31
   What, which ...? ........................................... 31
   Saying how old you are ................................... 31
   When to use **tu**; when to use **vous** ............ 32
   Be active in your learning ............................... 32

4 Vous habitez où?  *Where do you live?* ............... 37
   Numbers 20 – 70 ........................................... 38
   How to ask simple questions ............................. 40
   Is it ...?, Is that ...? ..................................... 40
   Is there ...? Are there ...? ............................... 40
   Some likely answers: Yes there is ... No there isn't .... 40
   More answers: Yes I have ... No I haven't ... ......... 41
   Other questions ............................................ 41

My, your, his ... ..................................................41
Create every opportunity to speak ..........................42

**5 Quelle heure est-il** *What time is it?* ....................45
Days of the week ...............................................46
Numbers 70 – 90 ...............................................47
Months of the year ............................................47
Saying what you want/want to do .........................48
Asking what you can do; asking for help ................49
Three different ways to ask a question ...................49
Questions starting with 'what' ..............................49
Verbs ending in **-ir** and **-re** ...........................50
Giving the date .................................................50
Telling the time .................................................51
To do, to make .................................................52
To take ...........................................................52
Experiment while learning ...................................52

**6 Pour aller à ...?** *The way to ...?* ........................56
Numbers 90 upwards ..........................................58
Asking the way and giving directions .....................59
To go, to leave .................................................59
Understanding directions .....................................60
When to use **à** when to use **en** .......................61
When **à** is followed by **le, la, l', les** ...............61
Locating the exact spot .......................................62
1st, 2nd, 3rd ... ...............................................62
Self-evaluation .................................................63

**7 C'est comment** *What is it like?* .........................69
Colours ...........................................................71
This, that, these, those .......................................73
Saying precisely what you want ............................73
How adjectives work ..........................................74
Making comparisons ...........................................76
Learning to cope with uncertainty .........................76

**8 Vous aimez le sport?** *Do you like sport?* ............81
Asking and saying what you do as a hobby ..............84
Likes and dislikes ..............................................84
Pronouns: it, him, her, them ................................85
More negatives .................................................85
When to use **savoir**; when to use **connaître**: to know ..........86
What's the weather like? ......................................86
Learn from errors ..............................................87

**9 Qu'est-ce qu'il faut faire?** *What should I do?* ............91
   Asking for assistance ................................................93
   Two very useful verbs: to be able to, to want ......................94
   Giving and understanding instructions ............................94
   Learn to guess the meaning ........................................97

**10 A l'avenir** *In the future* ...................................101
   Name of the seasons ..............................................102
   Saying what you usually do, using reflexive verbs ...............104
   Saying what you need .............................................104
   Stating your intentions ..........................................105
   The pronoun **y**: there .........................................105
   More useful verbs: to go out, to come ...........................106
   Using capital letters ............................................106
   When to use **visiter**, to visit in French .....................106
   Assess yourself and keep up with grammar ........................107

**11 Les courses** *Shopping* ....................................112
   Shops in France ..................................................112
   Food shopping ....................................................114
   At the market ....................................................116
   Shopping for other things ........................................117
   In a clothes shop ................................................118

**12 Se reposer, dormir** *Resting, sleeping* ....................121
   Choosing a hotel .................................................121
   Looking for a hotel ..............................................124
   Checking in ......................................................125
   Complaining ......................................................126
   At the campsite ..................................................127
   The French alphabet ..............................................128
   Writing letters: .................................................130
   Booking accommodation ............................................130
   The confirmation .................................................131

**13 Bien manger, bien boire** *Eating and drinking well* ...132
   Eating well ......................................................132
   Ordering a snack .................................................135
   At the restaurant ................................................138

**14 Les transports publics** *Public transport* .................142
   The Paris underground ............................................144
   Taking a taxi ....................................................145
   Travelling by bus ................................................147
   French railways ..................................................149
   At the information office ........................................149

**15**  **Faire du tourisme**  *Sightseeing* ............................... 152
    Getting information on things to see ........................ 153
    Visiting ..................................................... 155
    Going on an excursion ....................................... 157

**16**  **Sortir**  *Going out* ............................................ 160
    Where to go ................................................. 161
    Booking a seat .............................................. 164
    Booking a tennis court ...................................... 165

**17**  **Bonne route**  *Safe journey* .................................. 169
    French roads ................................................ 169
    Driving in France ........................................... 172
    Parking ..................................................... 175
    Do you know the French highway code? ........................ 176
    Filling up the car with petrol .............................. 177
    Broken down ................................................. 179

**18**  **L'argent**  *Money* ............................................. 184
    French banks ................................................ 185
    Coins and banknotes ......................................... 187
    Getting small change ........................................ 188
    Changing money .............................................. 189
    Error in the bill ........................................... 190

**19**  **Les problèmes**  *Coping with problems* ....................... 193
    Chemists in France .......................................... 194
    Making an appointment ....................................... 197
    Phoning in France ........................................... 199
    At the police station ....................................... 201

    **Réponses** ................................................ 205
    **Numbers** ................................................. 212
    **Vocabulary**
      French–English ............................................ 213
      English–French ............................................ 225
    **Index** ................................................... 233

# About the course

Teach Yourself Beginner's French is the right course for you if you are a complete beginner or wanting to make a fresh start. It is a self-study course which will help you to understand, read and speak most of the French you will need on holiday or a business trip.

## Two key elements

The book has two parts. The first ten units introduce you to the basic structures and grammatical points you'll need in everyday situations. Units 1–10 should be taken in order as each builds on the previous one.

Units 11–19 deal with everyday situations such as shopping, eating, booking a room, travelling and give you the opportunity to put into practice the language you've acquired in the first part. These units may be taken in any order.

The course is best used together with the accompanying 90-minute audio cassette, but is not dependent upon it. You are recommended to obtain and use the cassette if possible. The recorded dialogues and audio exercises give you plenty of practice in understanding the basic language; they will help you develop an authentic accent and increase your confidence in saying simple phrases. Readers without the cassette will find that some units include one activity that cannot be done with the book alone, but in such cases the material is always adequately covered by the other activities in the unit.

## *About Units 1–10*

Each unit covers approximatively ten pages.

The first page tells you what you are going to learn and there is an easy exercise **Essayez** which gets you speaking straight away.

**Mots-clefs** contain the most important words and phrases from the unit. Try to learn them by heart. They will be practised in the rest of the unit and the later units.

**Dialogue.** Listen to the dialogue once or twice without stopping the tape or read through it without looking anything up; try to get the gist of it. The notes underneath each dialogue will help you to understand it. Then, using the pause button on your cassette recorder, break the dialogue into manageable chunks and try repeating each phrase aloud. This will help you acquire a more authentic accent.

**The** sections marked with the ❇ symbol help you to develop your own 'techniques' to become a better learner, giving you tips on how to master the grammar, learn the vocabulary, improve your listening and reading skills and develop confidence in speaking.

**Explications.** In this section, you may want to start by reading the example(s) then work out the grammatical point or you may prefer to read the **Explications** first and see how the rule applies. Once you feel confident about a particular grammar point, try to create your own examples.

**Activités.** Each activity, in this section, allows you to practise one of the points introduced in the **Explications** section. In some activities you will need to listen to the cassette. It is not essential to have the cassette in order to complete this course, as most of the activities are not dependent on it. However, listening to the cassette will make your learning much easier.

**Petit test.** At the end of each unit you can test yourself on the last two or three unit(s). In Units 9 and 10 you are given a chance to test yourself on Units 1 to 10 with **Grands tests**.

## About Units 11–19

Each unit covers approximately eight pages.

**The first page** tells you what you are going to learn. There is also a checklist of structures which you have already learnt and will be practising in the unit. You'll also find in many units a short text in French about the topic.

**Mots-clefs** contains the basic vocabulary you'll need when coping, in real life, with practical situations such as checking into a hotel, ordering a snack, asking for a train timetable, going on an excursion.

**Dialogues.** There are several short dialogues, each dealing with a different aspect of the topic. Remember to listen to the dialogues first and use the pause button to practise the new words and phrases out loud.

**Activités.** The activities are mostly based on authentic French material. Here you can develop a feel for how things work in France, as well as practising your reading skills. You will then have more confidence to cope with the real situations.

**Petit test.** (As in Units 1–10.)

## Réponses

The answers to all the **Activités, Essayez, Pratiquez, Petits tests, Grands tests** can be found at the back of the book.

## Be successful at learning languages

1 **Do a little bit every day,** between 20 and 30 minutes if possible, rather than 2 or 3 hours in one session.
2 **Try to work towards short-term goals** e.g. work out how long you'll spend on a particular unit and work within this time limit.
3 **Revise and test yourself regularly** using the **Petit test** at the end of each unit and the two **Grand tests** in Units 9 and 10.
4 **Make use of the tips** given in the book and try to say the words and phrases out loud whenever possible.
5 **Try every opportunity to speak the language.** Attend some classes to practise your French with other people, get some help from a French speaker or find out about French clubs, societies etc.
6 **Don't worry too much about making mistakes.** The important thing is to get your meaning across and remember that making mistakes in French will not stop a French person understanding you. Learning can be fun particularly when you find you can use what you have learnt in real situations.

## *At the back of the book*

At the back of the book is a reference section which contains:

p.205 **Réponses**
p.212 **Numbers**
p.213 **A French-English Vocabulary** list containing all the words in the course.
p.225 **An English-French Vocabulary** list with the most useful words you'll need when expressing yourself in French.
p.233 **An Index** to enable you to look things up in the book.

# About symbols and abbreviations

This indicates that the cassette is needed for the following section.

This indicates dialogue.

This indicates exercises – places where you can practise using the language.

This indicates key words or phrases.

This indicates grammar or explanations – the nuts and bolts of the language.

This draws your attention to points to be noted.

This refers you to another page giving further information on a point.

| (m) | masculine |
| (f) | feminine |
| (sing) | singular |
| (pl) | plural |
| (lit) | literally |

# ———— Pronunciation guide ————

 **1 How to sound French**

Here are a few rules that will help you to sound French right from the beginning:

1   In French, unlike in most English words, it is the last part of the word that bears a heavy stress:
res-tau-**rant**, o-**range**, ca-**fé**, té-lé-**phone**

2   French words that are spelt like English words are almost always pronounced differently:
**pardon, important, parking, sandwich, ticket**

3   In general consonants at the end of a word such as **d g p s t x z**, and the letter **h**, are silent.
vou**s** anglai**s** nui**t** dame**s** messieu**r**s **h**ôtel

**2 French sounds**

Here is the list of the **French vowels** with a rough English equivalent sound. You'll see that an accent on an **e** or an **o** changes the way the letter is pronounced.

|   |   | *rough English sound* |   |
|---|---|---|---|
| a à |   | cat | madame |
| e | 1 | above | le ne |
|   | 2 | best (before two consonants or x) | merci |
|   | 3 | may (before z, r) | parlez |
| é |   | may | café |
| è ê |   | pair | père fête |
| i î y |   | police | merci dîner typique |
| o |   | dot | olive |

— 5 —

| | | |
|---|---|---|
| u | a sound not found in English. First say **oo**, but then keeping the lips in that position try saying **ee** | **u**ne, d**u** |
| ai | as **è ê** above | l**ai**t |
| ô au eau | pronounced as **o** but with rounded lips | h**ô**tel **au**tobus beauc**ou**p |
| eu oeu | sir | l**eu**r s**oeu**r |
| oi | the **wa** sound at the beginning of **one** | bons**oi**r |
| ou | moo | v**ou**s |

Many **consonants** are similiar to English, with a number of exceptions and variations:

### rough English sound

| | | |
|---|---|---|
| ç | sit | **ç**a fran**ç**ais |
| ch | shop | **ch**ic |
| g | leisure (before **i, e**) | Bri**g**itte |
| gn | onion | co**gn**ac |
| h | not pronounced | **h**ôtel **h**ôpital |
| j | leisure | **j**e bon**j**our |
| l ll | yes (often when **i** precedes **l, ll**) | fi**ll**e trava**il** |
| qu | care | **qu**estion |
| r | pronounced at the back of the throat with the tongue touching the bottom teeth | **r**at Pa**r**is |
| s | desert (between vowels) | mademoi**s**elle |
| t | (before **ion**) pass | atten**t**ion |
| th | tea | **th**é |
| w | 1  what | **w**hisky |
| | 2  van | **w**agon-restaurant |

Here are the **nasal sounds** formed usually with vowels followed by **m** or **n**. Speak through your nose when you pronounce them and listen carefully to the cassette.

| | | |
|---|---|---|
| ein im | } bang (stop before the g) } | fr**ein** **im**portant |
| in ain | | v**in** tr**ain** **im**possible |

| en  an | long (stop before the g) | encore Jean |
| on | as above but with lips pushed foward | pardon |
| un  um | similar to **ein  im  in  ain** | parfum un |

### 3 How to link the sounds together

To make the words run more smoothly the final consonants of words which are usually silent are sounded when the next word starts with a vowel or **h** e.g. **très_important** (trayzimportan). This is called a liaison. In some cases, as above, liaisons are essential; in other cases they are optional. To help you recognise when the liaisons are essential they'll be indicated with a linking mark (_) in Units 1–10.

When making liaisons all French people:
1  pronounce **s** and **x** like **z**: les_oranges deux_heures
2  pronounce **d** and **t** like **t**, but the **t** of **et** (and) is never sounded: le grand_homme  c'est_ici  un café et une bière
3  link **n** in the nasal **un** when the next words starts with a vowel or a silent **h**: un_enfant  un_hôtel

### 4 A few tips to help you acquire an authentic accent

It is not absolutely vital to acquire a perfect accent. The aim is to be understood; here are a number of techniques for working on your pronunciation:

1  Listen carefully to the cassette or native speaker or teacher. Whenever possible repeat aloud imagining you are a native speaker of French.
2  Tape record yourself and compare your pronunciation with that of a native speaker.
3  Ask native speakers to listen to your pronunciation and tell you how to improve it.
4  Ask native speakers how a specific sound is formed. Watch them and practise at home in front of a mirror.
5  Make a list of words that give you pronunciation trouble and practise them.

**6** Study the sounds on their own then use them progressively in words, sentences and tongue-twisters.

Try this one! **Panier-piano, panier-piano, panier-piano** (panier is a basket in French). Check the pronunciation with the **Pronunciation Guide** ➡️ 🅿 5.

**☑️5 And now practise ...**

Starting with **Paris** go round France anticlockwise saying aloud each of the 14 towns. Pause after each town and check your pronunciation with the cassette. If you haven't got the cassette, check your pronunciation with the **Pronunciation Guide** ➡️ 🅿 5.

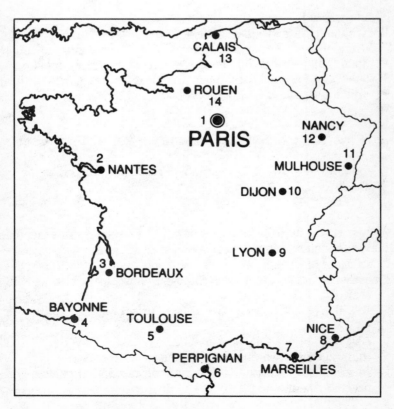

CALAIS 13

●ROUEN 14

1◉ **PARIS**

NANCY 12●

2 ●NANTES

MULHOUSE● 11

DIJON ●10

LYON ●9

3 ●BORDEAUX

BAYONNE ●4

TOULOUSE 5●

NICE 8●

7● MARSEILLES

PERPIGNAN ●6

# 1

# BONJOUR
*Hello*

## In this unit you will learn

- how to say hello and goodbye
- how to exchange greetings
- how to observe basic courtesies
- how to ask people to speak more slowly

## Avant de commencer  Before you start

Read the introduction to the course on ➡️ P 1–8. This gives some useful advice on studying alone and how to make the most of the course.

Different people have different ways of learning: some need to know rules for everything, others like to feel their way intuitively. In this unit you'll be given the opportunity to find out what works best for you so look out for the symbol ✴

Make sure you've got your cassette 📼 next to you as you'll need it to listen to the **Pronunciation Guide** and **Dialogues** sections. If you don't have the cassette, use the **Pronunciation Guide** in the book.

✴ Remember that studying for 20 minutes regularly is better than occasionally spending two hours in one go.

1 Listen to the **Dialogues** once or twice without the book (read them if you haven't got the cassette).

2 Go over each one, bit by bit, in conjunction with the **Mots-clefs** and notes underneath the dialogues.

3 Read the section **Explications** very carefully and study it.

4 Read the tips on **How to learn vocabulary** and **How to pronounce**.

5 Go back to the **Dialogues** and **Mots-clefs** for more listening and studying, this time using the pause button on the cassette-recorder and repeating aloud after the cassette.

6 Do the **Activités,** check your answers in **Réponses** and test yourself with **Petit test.**

## Essayez Try

Can you think of any French words you know such as the words for hello and thank you? Say them aloud, and then look at the section **Mots-clefs** to check the answers.

# Mots-clefs
# Key words and phrases

| | |
|---|---|
| bonjour | good morning, afternoon, hello |
| bonsoir | good evening (after 5.00p.m.) |
| bonne nuit | good night (when going to bed) |
| au revoir | goodbye |
| bonjour Madame | good morning (Madam) |
| bonjour Mademoiselle | good morning (Miss) |
| bonsoir Monsieur | good evening (Sir) |
| au revoir Messieurs-dames | goodbye ladies and gentlemen |
| oui | yes |
| non merci | no thank you |
| merci | thank you |
| merci beaucoup | thank you very much |
| s'il vous plaît | please |
| d'accord | OK |
| pardon | sorry (to apologise), excuse me |
| comment ça va? | how are things? |
| ça va | fine |
| très bien merci | very well thank you |
| et vous? | and you? |

| | |
|---|---|
| pardon? | sorry? (you want something repeated) |
| vous parlez_anglais? | do you speak English? |
| parlez plus lentement | speak more slowly |

✳ ➡️📕 7 When you see a linking mark between two words, sound the last letter of the first word as though it were attached to the next word: **vous parlez_anglais?**

## Dialogues

Listen to the tape and hear people practising saying hello and greeting each other in French. Press the pause button after each sentence and repeat aloud.

### Dialogue 1  Saying hello

Jane      Bonjour Messieurs-dames.

Michel   Bonjour Mademoiselle.
Jane      Bonjour Monsieur.

Roger    Bonsoir Madame.
Nathalie Bonsoir Monsieur.

Roger    Comment ça va, Jane?
Jane      Très bien et vous?
Roger    **Moi aussi,** ça va bien.

### Dialogue 2  Saying goodbye

Michel   Au revoir Madame et … merci beaucoup.
Nathalie Au revoir Monsieur.

### Dialogue 3  When things get difficult …

Jane      Pardon Monsieur, vous parlez_anglais?
Garçon   Ah non, **je regrette** …

| | |
|---|---|
| Garçon | Bonjour Madame. Qu'est-ce que vous désirez? |
| Nathalie | Parlez plus lentement, s'il vous plaît. |
| Garçon | D'accord ... Qu'est-ce que vous désirez? |

| | |
|---|---|
| **moi** | me, I |
| **aussi** | also, too |
| **garçon** | waiter |
| **je regrette** | I'm sorry |

## ❇ *How to pronounce*

1  As a general rule don't pronounce **d g p s t x z** at the end of a word e.g: beaucoup vous nuit plaît.

2  The letter **e** often gets swallowed as in **mad'moiselle**.

3  The stress, in French, is on the last part of the word: par-**don** mer-**ci** mad'-moi-**selle** mon-**sieur**.

4  ç placed before **o**, **u**, **a** is pronounced **s** as in *sit*: garçon, ça va?

5  The **s** in monsieur is pronounced as **ss** in *pass*.

# Explications
# Explanations

## 1  Simple questions

The simplest way of asking something in French is to raise your voice on the last syllable (part of a word):

Vous parlez anglais? ↑
Pardon?
Ça va?

Now practise saying par**don?** ↑ (to have something repeated) and **pardon** ↓ (to apologise or attract someone's attention).

## 2 Refusing politely in French

If you want to refuse something in France, you can say **non merci** or **merci** on its own.

## 3 Calling the waiter's attention

Although **garçon** is the word for waiter, today you would usually say **Monsieur** to attract his attention. For a waitress, you say **Madame** or **Mademoiselle** as you think fit or just look expectant and say **s'il vous plaît.**

## 4 How to be courteous

In France when you're talking to someone you don't know very well, it's polite to add **Monsieur, Madame, Mademoiselle** particularly after short phrases like **oui, non, bonjour,** or **merci.**

The French shake hands with friends and acquaintances every time they meet or say goodbye. Kissing (on both cheeks) is reserved for family and close friends.

## *How to learn vocabulary*

There are several ways of learning vocabulary. Find out the way that works best for you; here are a few suggestions:

1 Say the words aloud as you read them.

2 Write the words over and over again.

3 Listen to the tape several times.

4 Study the list from begining to end then backwards.

5 Associate the French words with similiar sounding words in English. (e.g. **parlez** with *parlour*, a room where people chat.)

6 Associate the words with pictures or situations.
e.g. **bonjour, bonsoir** with shaking hands.

**7** Use coloured pencils to underline/group the words in a way that will help you to remember them.

**8** Copy the words on to small cards or slips of paper, English on one side, French on the other. Study them in varying order giving the French word if the card comes out with the English on top, and vice versa.

# Activités
# Activities

**1** How would you say *hello* in the situations below? Remember to add **Monsieur, Madame, Mademoiselle**. Write your answer underneath each picture.

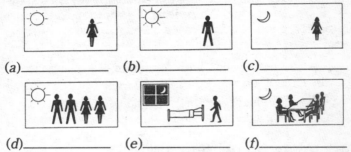

(*a*)_____ (*b*)_____ (*c*)_____

(*d*)_____ (*e*)_____ (*f*)_____

**2** You're arriving late at a hotel one evening; greet the person behind the reception desk by choosing the right box below.

| Au revoir Madame | | Bonsoir Monsieur |

| Pardon? | | Bonjour Messieurs-dames |

**3** A person at the bus stop asks you a question that you do not hear properly. What do you say? Choose (*a*), (*b*) or (*c*).

(*a*) **s'il vous plaît**     (*c*) **pardon?**
(*b*) **non merci**

4 You are staying the night with some friends. It's late and you decide to go to bed. You say:

| Au revoir | Comment ça va? | Bonne nuit |

5 You meet up with a French speaking colleague. How do you ask *How are you?*

C o m m e n t ça v a?

The answer is *very well thank you*. What is it in French?

T _ _ _ b _ _ _ _ _ _ _ i

6 Use the clues to complete the grid. When you've finished, the vertical word will be what you say if you step on someone's foot!

(a) The French translation for *please*.
(b) Your answer to a friend who asks how you are.
(c) *Goodbye.*
(d) Calling the waitress's attention.
(e) Greeting someone after 5 pm.
(f) Refusing politely.

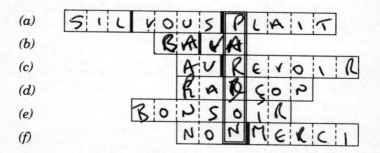

(a) S I L V O U S P L A I T
(b) B A V A
(c) A U R E V O I R
(d) R A R Ç O P
(e) B O N S O I R
(f) N O N M E R C I

**7** Choose the appropriate word or group of words.

| | | |
|---|---|---|
| (*a*) How would you greet several people? | (i) | Bonjour Madame. |
| | (ii) | Au revoir Madememoiselle. |
| | (iii) | Bonjour Messieurs-dames. |

| | | |
|---|---|---|
| (*b*) How would you refuse politely? | (i) | D'accord. |
| | (ii) | Non merci. |
| | (iii) | Pardon. |

| | | |
|---|---|---|
| (*c*) To ask someone if s/he speaks English you say: | (i) | Parlez plus lentement. |
| | (ii) | Au revoir Messieurs-dames. |
| | (iii) | Vous parlez_anglais? |

| | | |
|---|---|---|
| (*d*) To wish someone good night you say: | (i) | Bonjour. |
| | (ii) | Bonsoir. |
| | (iii) | Bonne nuit. |

Remember to check your answers at the end of the book. If you have a number of wrong answers ➡ 🄿 13 as it gives useful tips for learning key words and phrases, then do the exercises again.

## ☑*Petit test   Mini test*

You've arrived at the end of Unit 1. Now you know how to say thank you and exchange greetings and you've also learnt a little about French sounds. How would you:

**1** Say hello to your friend?
**2** Ask someone to slow down when speaking French? (Don't forget to add *please* at the end.)
**3** Apologise as you step on someone's foot?
**4** Say you agree?

You'll find the answers to **Petit test** in **Réponses** at the end of the book. If they are correct you are ready to move to Unit 2. If you found the test difficult, spend more time revising Unit 1.

# 2

## C'EST COMBIEN?
*How much is it?*

### In this unit you will learn

- how to count up to ten
- how to ask for something
- how to say how much you want
- how to ask the price

### Avant de commencer

In this unit we will show you that it is nearly always possible to ask for what you want with just two words, **je voudrais** (*I would like*) and **s'il vous plaît** at the end.

The dialogue is short but there are a lot of new words including useful things you may need in France. Try to learn the words by heart using one of the techniques described in Unit 1 in the section **How to learn vocabulary.**

### ✅ Essayez

You are in a **pâtisserie** (*a cake shop*) in France to buy a **baguette** (*French stick*). How would you greet the woman behind the counter? How would you ask for a French stick?

# Mots-clefs

## A dire   *To say*

| | |
|---|---|
| un café | a coffee/a café |
| un thé | a tea |
| un coca-cola | a coca-cola |
| un franc | a franc |
| un journal | a newspaper |
| un plan | a map, plan |
| une baguette | a French stick |
| une bière | a beer |
| une chambre | a room |
| une pharmacie | a chemist's |
| une station-service | a petrol station |
| le timbre | the stamp |
| la carte postale | the postcard |
| la gare | the station |
| l'hôtel (m) | the hotel |
| l'hôpital (m) | the hospital |
| l'eau minérale (f) | the mineral water |
| l'addition (f) | the bill |
| les toilettes | the toilets |
| je voudrais | I would like |
| vous_avez ...? | do you have ...? |
| ça | this/that |
| du pain | some bread |
| du vin | some wine |
| de la limonade | some lemonade |
| de l'aspirine (f) | some aspirins |
| des sandwiches | some sandwiches |
| c'est combien? | how much is it? (lit. it is how much?) |
| un kilo | one kilo |
| un demi-kilo | half a kilo |
| un paquet | one pack |
| une bouteille | one bottle |
| une boîte | one tin, box |

## A comprendre   *To understand*

| | |
|---|---|
| fermé | shut |
| je n'en_ai pas | I haven't got any |
| avec ça? | will that be all? (lit. *with that?*) |
| c'est tout? | is that all? |

## Les chiffres   *Numbers 1–10*

| | |
|---|---|
| un | one |
| deux | two |
| trois | three |
| quatre | four |
| cinq | five |
| six | six |
| sept (the **p** is not pronounced) | seven |
| huit | eight |
| neuf | nine |
| dix | ten |

# Dialogue

Jane is in **une alimentation** (*grocer's shop*). What does she want to buy? Does she get what she wants? Listen to the tape first.

| | |
|---|---|
| Jane | Vous⁔avez de la bière? |
| Vendeuse | Ah non, je regrette je n'en⁔ai pas. |
| Jane | Et du vin? |
| Vendeuse | Euh oui. **Quel vin?** |
| Jane | Une bouteille de Muscadet. |
| Vendeuse | Oui, **voilà,** et avec ça? |
| Jane | Deux bouteilles d'eau minérale. |
| Vendeuse | Oui **très bien.** C'est tout? |
| Jane | Oui, oui **merci bien.** C'est combien? |
| Vendeuse | Pour le Muscadet, c'est dix francs et pour l'eau minérale quatre francs la bouteille. |

| | |
|---|---|
| **une alimentation** | a grocer's shop |
| **la vendeuse** | the shop assistant (female) |
| **quel vin?** | which wine? |
| **voilà** | there you are |
| **très bien** | very well |
| **merci bien** | thank you |

## ❋ *How to pronounce*

**1** Six et dix

(*a*) when on their own as numbers the **x** is pronounced as **s** and they rhyme with 'peace': **vous_avez des timbres? Oui, six.**

(*b*) when followed by a word starting with a consonant the **x** is not pronounced and they sound like 'dee' and 'see': **dix francs, six bières.** The **c** in **franc** is not pronounced.

(*c*) when followed by a word starting with a vowel or **h** pronounce the **x** and **s** as **z**: **six_aspirines, dix_hôtels, deux_additions, trois_aspirines.**

# Explications

### 1 Un, une *A, an*

The word *a* or *an* is **un** in front of a masculine noun and **une** in front of a feminine noun.

All French nouns belong to one of the two groups: masculine or feminine. Sometimes it is obvious as in **un Français** *a Frenchman*, **une Française** *a Frenchwoman* while other times it is not obvious as in **un café** but **une bière**.

There is no rule to tell you to which group a noun belongs, although the ending of a noun often acts as a guide. For example:

- words ending in **-age, -ment** are often masculine, as in **le village, le moment.**

- words ending in **-lle, -tte, -ion, -ée** are often feminine as in **une bouteille, une cigarette, une alimentation, une année.**

### 2 Le, la, l', les *The*

There are four different ways of saying *the*:

|  |  |
|---|---|
| **le** with masculine nouns | **le** timbre |
| **la** with feminine nouns | **la** gare |

| l' with nouns starting with a vowel or an **h** | **l'**hôtel (m) **l'**eau (f) |
|---|---|
| **les** with plural nouns | **les** toilettes |

✱ Make a habit of learning words together with **le** or **la** before them. If they start with a vowel or **h,** they are followed by (m) or (f) in **Mots-clefs** to indicate if they are masculine or feminine.

## 3 Vous avez ...? *Do you have ...?*

To check if they have what you want, start your request with **vous avez** (*do you have*). To indicate that it is a question raise the voice on the last syllable of the sentence.

| **Vous_avez** une chambre? ↑ | *Do you have a room?* |
|---|---|
| **Vous_avez** de l'eau minérale? ↑ | *Do you have some mineral water?* |

## 4 Du, de la, de l', des *Some, any*

When **de** (*of*) is used in combination with **le, la, l', les** it changes its form and can mean *some, any* according to the context:

| **de + le** | becomes **du.** |
|---|---|
| **de la** | remains unchanged. |
| **de l'** | remains unchanged. |
| **de + les** | becomes **des.** |

Compare the examples below:

| Je voudrais **du** vin | *I would like **some** wine* |
|---|---|
| Je voudrais **le** vin | *I would like **the** wine* |
| Vous avez **de la** bière? | *Do you have **any** beer?* |
| Vous avez **la** bière? | *Do you have **the** beer?* |
| Vous avez **de l'**eau minérale? | *Have you **any** mineral water?* |
| Vous avez **l'**eau minérale? | *Do you have **the** mineral water?* |
| Je voudrais **des** timbres | *I would like **some** stamps* |
| Je voudrais **les** timbres | *I would like **the** stamps* |

✳ In English we often omit the word *some*. In French, **de** + an article is almost always used.

## 5  Un kilo de  *A kilo/one kilo of*

To ask for one of something use **un** with masculine nouns and **une** with feminine nouns.

| | |
|---|---|
| **un** kilo de sucre | one *kilo of sugar or a kilo of sugar* |
| **une** boîte de sardines | one *tin of sardines or a tin of sardines* |

## 6  C'est combien?  *How much is it?*

You need only two words to ask for the price: **C'est combien?** *How much is it?* (lit. it is how much) followed by whatever you want to know the price of.

| | |
|---|---|
| **C'est combien** la carte postale? | *How much is the postcard?* |
| **C'est combien** la baguette? | *How much is the French stick?* |

# ✳ *How to organise your learning*

It may help you to remember the new vocabulary, pronunciation and grammar rules that you learn in the book if you create your own system to organise this information, perhaps using one or more of the following ideas.

1   You could group new words under:
    (*a*) generic categories, e.g. food, furniture.
    (*b*) situations in which they occur, e.g. under restaurant you can put waiter, table, menu, bill.
    (*c*) functions: greeting, parting, thanks, apologising etc.

2   When organising the study of pronunciation you could keep a section of your notebook for pronunciation rules and practise those that trouble you.

3   To organise your study of grammar you may like to write your own grammar glossary and add new information as you go along.

## Activités

1   Look at the objects underneath, and write their names in
    French preceded by **un, une** or **des**.

(a) *un café* (b) *une bière* (c) *un journal*

(d) *des bouteilles* (e) *un franc* (f) *des timbres*

2   You've arrived at a French hotel; you would like three things.
    What are they? You will find them hidden in the string of
    letters below:

> motu̲n̲e̲c̲h̲a̲m̲b̲r̲e̲pozowiu̲n̲c̲a̲f̲é̲moghttu̲n̲j̲o̲u̲r̲n̲a̲l̲dfc

3   Before you leave the hotel you want to buy a few things: how
    would you ask for them in French?

(a) I would like four cards please.
*Je voudrais quatre carte postale*
(b) Do you have four stamps for England?
*Avez vous quatre carte postale* pour l'Angleterre?
(c) And some aspirin please
Et *des aspirines s'il vous plaît*
(d) How much is it?
*C'est combien ?*

**4** The numbers one to ten are listed in this wordsearch except for one. Which one is it? Read horizontally or vertically, either fowards or backwards.

| E | Y | Q | N | I | C |
|---|---|---|---|---|---|
| R | S | E | P | T | R |
| T | M | I | D | I | X |
| A | O | N | E | U | F |
| U | L | U | U | H | I |
| Q | S | H | X | I | S |

**5** Match the words in the left-hand column with the ones in the right.

(a) deux bouteilles     de     (i) chewing gum
(b) un kilo                   (ii) vin
(c) une boîte            (iii) sardines
(d) un paquet         (iv) sucre

**6** Michel, sitting at a café, is ordering some drinks with his friends. He then asks for the bill. Using the words in the box, complete the script then check your version with the cassette and/or the **Réponses**.

| | | |
|---|---|---|
| (a) Garçon | Bonjour .Madame..... | |
| (b) Michel | Je voudrais un .café...... et vous, Marie? | café<br>voudrais<br>addition<br>Messieurs-dames<br>bouteille |
| (c) Marie | Moi, une bouteille de bière. | |
| (d) Sylvie | Je voudrais une limonade | |
| (e) Michel | Et je voudrais aussi l' addition s'il vous plaît. | |

**7** As numbers are very important here's another chance to practise them. Write your answers to the sums below (in words not figures).

(a) deux + trois = *Sept*....    (e) dix  – huit = ~~Deux~~ *euche*

(b) cinq + quatre = *Onze*.  (f) sept – trois = ~~quatre dix~~

(c) neuf + un = ........*Dix*..    (g) trois × trois = ~~six~~ *neuf*

(d) six  + trois = *neuf*..  (h) quatre × deux = ..*huit*

Check your answers in the section **Réponses**, then test yourself on Units 1 and 2 with **Petit test**.

## ☑ *Petit test*

**1** If a French friend said to you **Comment ça va?** what would you answer? *Ca va bien*...............................

**2** You are speaking English to a French speaker. He says **Parlez plus lentement**. What does that mean?

**3** You have a headache. Stop at the chemist's and ask politely for what you need: *Je voudrais de l'asprine*.........
. Thank him and say goodbye. *Merci bien. Au revoir*

**4** What's the word for *station?* *La gare*

# 3

## JE M'APPELLE ... ET VOUS?
### *My name is ... and you?*

### In this unit you will learn

- how to count up to twenty
- how to talk about yourself and your family
- how to say that things are not so
- how to say how old you are

### Avant de commencer

Speaking about yourself and your family in French is fairly easy once you know the vocabulary to describe your home and family and you know how to say what you do or don't have (**j'ai, je n'ai pas**) and what you are or aren't (**je suis, je ne suis pas**).

As we said in the introduction on ➡️**P** 3, to be successful at learning languages try to work towards short-term goals. In this unit concentrate on mastering **avoir** and **être,** the two most useful verbs in French. Keep practising them aloud: in the car, the bus, the bath. Aim at saying them without thinking.

### ✅ Essayez

You've just arrived in France. You stop at **une alimentation** to buy something to drink. How would you ask for two bottles of mineral water and one kilo of oranges? **Je ...**

 ## Mots-clefs

| | |
|---|---|
| **quel est votre nom?** | what is your name? |
| **vous_êtes français?** | are you French? (to a man) |
| **française** | (to a woman) |
| **vous_êtes marié?** | are you married? (to a man) |
| **mariée?** | (to a woman) |
| **vous_avez des_enfants?** | do have any children? |
| **des filles ou des garçons?** | girls (or daughters) or boys? |
| **vous_habitez (à) Londres?** | do you live in London? |
| **vous travaillez?** | do you work? |
| **où ça?** | where about? |
| **je m'appelle ... et vous?** | my name is ... and you? |
| **je suis_anglais** | I'm English (a man) |
| **anglaise** | (a woman) |
| **non, je ne suis pas marié** | no, I'm not married (a man speaking) |
| **je suis célibataire** | I'm single |
| **je n'ai pas d'enfants** | I haven't got any children |
| **oui, j'en_ai trois** | yes, I have got 3 (children) |
| **j'habite en_Angleterre** | I live, I'm living in England |
| **je suis de Vancouver** | I am from Vancouver |
| **avec ma famille** | with my family |
| **je travaille à Paris** | I work in Paris |
| **je suis secrétaire** | I am a secretary |
| **je suis professeur** | I am a teacher (a man or a woman) |
| **la fille** | daughter, girl |
| **le fils** | son |
| **le frère** | brother |
| **la soeur** | sister |
| **je ne comprends pas** | I do not understand |

## Les chiffres 11–20

| | |
|---|---|
| onze | eleven |
| douze | twelve |
| treize | thirteen |
| quatorze | fourteen |
| quinze | fifteen |
| seize | sixteen |
| dix-sept | seventeen |
| dix-huit | eighteen |
| dix-neuf | nineteen |
| vingt (*pronounced vin*) | twenty |

## Dialogue

Jane is sitting on the **terrasse** of a café. She has struck up a conversation with a Frenchwoman. Listen to the tape or read the dialogue below. Does the Frenchwoman work? Has she got any children? Is Jane married?

| | |
|---|---|
| Frenchwoman | Vous_êtes française? |
| Jane | Non, je suis_anglaise. |
| Frenchwoman | Vous_habitez Londres? |
| Jane | Non, Brighton, **dans le sud de l'Angleterre** et vous? |
| Frenchwoman | Moi, je suis **du nord de la France mais** j'habite Paris avec ma famille. |
| Jane | Vous_êtes mariée? |
| Frenchwoman | Oui. J'ai trois_enfants. |
| Jane | Des filles ou des garçons? |
| Frenchwoman | Une fille qui a dix_ans et deux garçons. **Ils_ont huit_ans et six_ans.** |
| Jane | Ah, très bien. |
| Frenchwoman | Et vous, vous_êtes mariée? |
| Jane | Non, je ne suis pas mariée mais j'ai **un petit_ ami.** |
| Frenchwoman | C'est très bien. Et ... vous travaillez? |
| Jane | Oui **bien sûr.** Je suis dentiste et vous? |
| Frenchwoman | Moi, je suis secrétaire. |

| | |
|---|---|
| **dans le sud de l'Angleterre** | in the South of England |
| **du nord de la France** | from the North of France |
| **mais** | but |
| **ils_ont huit_ans et six_ans** | they are 8 and 6 |
| **un petit_ami** | a boyfriend |
| **une petite amie** | a girlfriend |
| **bien sûr** | of course |

## How to pronounce

1 **nom** (*name*) is pronounced like **non** (*no*)

2 **fille** is pronounced fee-ye and **fils** is pronounced fee-sse.

3  Look at the section **Mots-clefs** and try to practise linking the words with a linking mark: e.g. **vous_êtes** (pronounce vou zêtes).

4  To pronounce **secrétaire** French people will tend to pinch their lips for **se,** open the mouth up for **cré** and relax the mouth for **taire.** If you haven't got the cassette check with the **Pronunciation Guide** ➡️ P 5.

 ─────────── **Explications** ───────────

## 1  Regular verbs ending in -ER, eg, parler, *to speak*

In English *to speak* is the infinitive of the verb (this is the form of the verbs you find in the dictionary). In French the equivalent infinitive is **parler.** It follows the same pattern as many other verbs with infinitives ending in **-er.** Here is the present tense of **parler.**

| **parler** *to speak* | | |
|---|---|---|
| je | parle | I speak, I'm speaking |
| tu | parles | you speak, you're speaking |
| il/elle/on | parle | he/she/one speaks, is speaking |
| nous | parlons | we speak, we're speaking |
| vous | parlez | you speak, you're speaking |
| ils/elles | parlent | they speak, they're speaking |

 (*a*) The present tense in French makes no distinction between *I speak* and *I'm speaking*.

(*b*) Before a vowel or **h, je** becomes **j':** **j'habite** *I live*.

(*c*) **On** is commonly used in French when people talk about themselves. In a general sense it is the equivalent of *one, you, we*.

(*d*) **Ils** is used when the group of people is mixed or all males.

(*e*) **Elles** is for an all-female group.

(*f*) Pronunciation: the **je tu il elle on ils elles** forms of the present tense of any regular **-er** verb sound the same. Do not pronounce the 3rd person plural ending **-ent.** If you do, people may not understand you.

**Pratiquez:** can you work out the present tense of **travailler**? Write it down and read it aloud. Remember the pronunciation tips above.

## 2 Two important verbs: avoir *to have*; être *to be*

**Avoir** and **être** are irregular i.e. they do not follow the normal pattern. They are the two most common verbs in French and need to be learnt individually.

| **avoir** *to have* | | **être** *to be* | |
|---|---|---|---|
| **j'ai** | I have | **je suis** | I am |
| **tu as** | you have | **tu es** | you are |
| **il/elle/on a** | he/she/one has | **il/elle/on est** | he/she/one is |
| **nous avons** | we have | **nous sommes** | we are |
| **vous avez** | you have | **vous êtes** | you are |
| **ils/elles ont** | they have | **ils/elles sont** | they are |

**Pratiquez:** practise the verbs **avoir** and **être** in sentences using some of the key words you already know. Remember that for a question, you need to raise the voice on the last syllable. For example:

| | |
|---|---|
| J'ai un enfant. | Je suis marié. |
| Tu as des enfants? | Tu es anglaise? |
| Il a trois frères. | Elle est professeur. |
| Nous avons... | |

## 3 The negative form: ne ... pas

To say something is not so in French, you put **ne ... pas** round the verb: je **ne** comprends **pas** *I don't understand.*

*(a)* **Ne** becomes **n'** if the following verb starts with a vowel or **h**: **j'habite** Paris *but* **je n'habite pas** Paris.
*(b)* After a negative form **du, de la ...** becomes **de**: J'ai **du** vin *but* je n'ai pas **de** vin.

## 4 Adjectives: their agreement

To describe things in detail or talk about yourself you need to add descriptive words (called adjectives) to nouns; an adjective describing a masculine noun has a masculine form, and one describing a feminine noun has a feminine form. As a general rule, feminine adjectives end in **-e** and the plural adjectives take an **-s**.

| | |
|---|---|
| J'ai un_ami américain. | *I have an American friend.* |
| J'ai une amie américaine. | *I have an American friend.* |
| Mes_amis sont_ américains. | *My friends are American.* |

## 5  Capital letters

In French adjectives of nationality and names of languages are not written with a capital letter (unless they start a sentence).

| | |
|---|---|
| Vous parlez français? | *Do you speak French?* |
| Je suis canadien. | *I am Canadian.* |

| but: | un(e) **Anglais(e)** | *an Englishman/woman* |
|---|---|---|
| | un(e) **Américain(e)** | *an American* |
| | un(e) **Français(e)** | *a Frenchman/woman* |

## 6  Quel est votre nom?  *What's your name?*

**Quel,** meaning *what* or *which*, is a useful word to remember; it is always pronounced KEL but it is spelt differently to agree with the noun to which it refers:

| | |
|---|---|
| Quel est votre **nom?** | *What's your name?* |

**Nom** is a masculine noun.

| | |
|---|---|
| Quelle est votre **adresse?** | *What's your address?* |

**Adresse** is a feminine noun.

| | |
|---|---|
| Quels vins? | *Which wines?* |

**Vins** is a masculine plural noun.

| | |
|---|---|
| Quelles **bouteilles?** | *Which bottles?* |

**Bouteilles** is a feminine plural noun.

## 7  Saying how old you are

Start with **j'ai** (not **je suis**), add your age followed by **ans** (*years*):

| | |
|---|---|
| Vous avez quel âge? | *How old are you?* |
| J'ai dix-sept ans. | *I am seventeen.* |

## 8  When to use tu (*you*) and when to use vous (*you*)

The equivalent of *you* in French can be either **tu** or **vous**. French people use **tu** when speaking to children, teenagers, relations and close friends. They use **vous** in work and business situations or when speaking to senior or older people: **vous** is also used to address a group of people to whom one might say **tu** individually. The best advice is to say **vous** until you are addressed as **tu** or asked to use the **tu** form: **on se tutoie?** *shall we call each other tu?*

## ❇ *Be active in your learning*

As all language teachers will assure you, the successful learners are those students who overcome their inhibitions and get into situations where they must speak, write and listen to the foreign language. Here are some useful tips to help you practise French:

1  Rehearse in the foreign language.
(*a*)  Hold a conversation with yourself, using the dialogues of the units as models and the structures you have learnt previously.
(*b*)  After you have conducted a transaction with a salesperson, clerk or waiter in your own language, pretend that you have to do it in French, e.g. buying petrol, groceries, ordering food, drinks and so on.
(*c*)  Look at objects around you and try to name them in French.
(*d*)  Look at people around you and try to describe them in detail.

## ——————— Activités ———————

1  On the tape, you will hear some numbers between 1 and 20. Repeat and write them down in figures.

(*a*) ...........................    (*f*) ...........................

(*b*) ...........................    (*g*) ...........................

(*c*) ...........................    (*h*) ...........................

    (*d*) ............................      (*i*) ............................

    (*e*) ............................      (*j*) ............................

**2**   This time practise these sums aloud and write the answers in words. (+ is **plus** in French and − is **moins**)

    (*a*) $10 + 3 = $ ...............    (*f*) $19 - 8 \ = $ ..............

    (*b*) $\ 7 + 8 = $ ...............    (*g*) $11 - 6 \ = $ ..............

    (*c*) $15 + 5 = $ ...............    (*h*) $16 - 10 = $ ..............

    (*d*) $\ 4 + 9 = $ ...............    (*i*) $12 - 8 \ = $ ..............

    (*e*) $13 + 6 = $ ...............    (*j*) $15 - 3 \ = $ ..............

**3**   Look at the family tree below and fill in the sentences:

Ives    Isabelle

Rosine
25 ans

Anne
32 ans

Marc
34 ans

Didier
10 ans

Solange
12 ans

(*a*) Isabelle ............... mariée avec Yves.

(*b*) Ils ............. deux filles.

(*c*) ............... s'appellent Rosine et Anne.

(*d*) Anne et Marc ont deux .........., une fille et ......... fils.

(*e*) Rosine ............... ............ d'enfants.

(*f*) Elle ................ ............ mariée.

(*g*) Didier a ............... ans.

(*h*) Solange ......... douze ............. .

**4** You are being very negative and answer **non...** to all the following questions using **ne ... pas**:

(a) Vous_avez des timbres?   Non, je n'ai pas des timb..

(b) Elle a du café?   Non, elle .............................

(c) Il est marié?   Non, il n'est pas marié

(d) Elle est secrétaire?   Non, elle n'est pas secr

(e) Vous_avez une chambre?   Non, je n'ai pas

(f) Ils ont quatre enfants?   Non, ils n'ont pas

(g) Brighton est dans le nord de l'Angleterre?
Non, Brighton n'est de pas dans le nord.

(h) Vous parlez français?   Non, je ne parle pas

(i) Il a 18 ans?   Non, il n'a pas 18 ans.

**5** As you listen (or read if you haven't the cassette) the passage on **la famille Guise,** look back at the family tree in **Activité 3** to help you to understand it better.

*La Famille Guise*

Monsieur et Madame Guise sont français. Ils_habitent Chaville, 15 rue de la Gare et travaillent à Paris. Yves est dentiste, Isabelle est_artiste. Ils_ont deux filles, Rosine qui a vingt-cinq ans et qui est célibataire et Anne qui a trente-deux ans. Anne est secrétaire. Elle est mariée avec Marc qui est professeur de Math dans_une école. Ils ont deux_enfants: une fille, Solange et un fils, Didier. Anne et Marc parlent_ anglais.

*Rôle-play*

Now imagine you're Anne and that you've been asked to take part in a survey. What would you reply to the interviewer?

(a) Comment vous_appelez-vous?

(b) Vous_êtes célibataire?

(c) Vous_avez des enfants?

(d) Des filles ou des garçons?

(e) Ils_ont quel_âge?

(f) Où habitez-vous?

(g) Vous travaillez?

Merci beaucoup Madame.

6  This time you are the interviewer, questioning a man. Here are his replies. What were your questions?

(a) _Vous êtes Marie?_
Oui, je suis marié.

(b) _Vous avez des enfants_
Non, je n'ai pas d'enfants.

(c) _Vous etes un professeur?_
Oui, je suis professeur.

(d) _Vous habitez dans Paris_
Oui, j'habite Paris.

(e) _Vous avez des frères i des soeur?_
Oui j'ai deux frères et une soeur.

(f) _Is ont quel âge?_
Ils ont 20 ans, 17 ans et 12 ans.

(g) _Vous êtes francais?_
Non, je suis canadien.

(h) _Vous parlez Anglais?_
Oui, bien sûr (of course) je parle anglais.

7  Match the words in the left-hand column with the ones on the right.

(a) Henri a  iv
(b) ils n'ont pas  iii
(c) ils parlent  i
(d) Marc est  ii
(e) elle est  vii
(f) j'habite  v
(g) je m'appelle  vi

(i)   français
(ii)  professeur
(iii) d'enfants
(iv)  12 ans
(v)   Perth
(vi)  Rosine
(vii) française

Check your answers at the back of the book, then test yourself on Units 1, 2, and 3 with **Petit test**.

## ☑ Petit test

1  How would you ask someone to speak more slowly?

2   **D'accord** means   (*a*) very much
                          (*b*) OK ✓
                          (*c*) sorry
3   What does **je ne comprends pas** mean?
4   How would you ask for a bottle of wine? **Je** *Voudrais* .........
5   You want to know what something costs. What would you say?   *C'est combien?* ...........................................
6   And now say in French:   (*a*) my name is ...
                             (*b*) I am not married.
                             (*c*) I live in Brighton.

You'll find the answers in **Réponses**. If most of the answers are correct you should congratulate yourself for doing so well. Before going on to Unit 4 spend more time revising Units 1, 2, and 3, to consolidate what you've already learnt. You will learn more if you are able to revise regularly.

# 4

## VOUS HABITEZ OU?
### *Where do you live?*

### *In this unit you will learn*

- numbers from twenty to seventy
- simple and useful questions and their likely answers
- how to say that things are yours or someone else's
- how to understand prices

### *Avant de commencer*

In this unit you will meet some simple questions which you will
find useful when coping with everyday situations in France. Some
are formed simply by raising the voice at the end of a statement,
others by including a question word in the statement: **c'est loin,
la gare?** *how far is the station?*, **c'est combien, le billet?** *how
much is the ticket?*

### Essayez

At a party you meet a friend of a friend who does not speak
English. You want to be friendly and try out your French. You

know he/she is married and has a family. Can you think of at least six questions you could ask in French?

## Mots-clefs

| | |
|---|---|
| vous vous_appelez comment? | what's your name? |
| je m'appelle ... | my name is ... |
| vous_habitez où? | where do you live? |
| le magasin est_ouvert? | is the shop open? |
| non, il est fermé | no it's closed |
| c'est loin? | is it far? |
| c'est_au bout de la rue | it is  at the end of the street |
| près d'ici | nearby |
| à 50 mètres d'ici | 50 metres away (lit. 50m from here) |
| à 5 minutes à pied | 5 minutes away on foot |
| c'est_une grande ville | it is a big town |
| c'est_une petite piscine | it is a small swimming pool |
| c'est gratuit, la brochure? | is the brochure free? |
| non, il faut payer | no, you must pay (lit. it's necessary to pay) |
| c'est combien, le billet? | how much is the ticket? |
| c'est où, l'arrêt d'autobus? | where is the bus stop? |
| c'est où, la station de métro? | where is the (tube, subway) station? |
| c'est quand, le départ? | when is the departure? |
| c'est_à quel étage? | what floor is it on? |
| c'est_au premier étage | it's on the first floor |
| c'est cher/bon marché? | it's expensive/cheap? |
| il y a un car pour Caen? | is there a coach for Caen? |
| oui, il y en_a un | yes, there is one |
| il y a un train direct pour Paris? | is there a direct train to Paris? |
| non, il n'y en_a pas | no, there isn't any |
| un restaurant dans l'hôtel | a restaurant in the hotel |
| beaucoup de ... | a lot of ... |

## Les chiffres 20-70

| | | | |
|---|---|---|---|
| vingt | 20 | trente-deux | 32 |
| vingt et un | 21 | quarante | 40 |
| vingt-deux | 22 | quarante et un | 41 |
| vingt-trois | 23 | quarante-deux | 42 |
| vingt-quatre | 24 | cinquante | 50 |
| vingt-cinq | 25 | cinquante et un | 51 |
| vingt-six | 26 | cinquante-deux | 52 |
| vingt-sept | 27 | soixante | 60 |
| vingt-huit | 28 | soixante et un | 61 |
| vingt-neuf | 29 | soixante-deux | 62 |
| trente | 30 | soixante-dix | 70 |
| trente et un | 31 | | |

# Dialogue

Jane has been invited to an office party. She strikes up a conversation with one of her friend's colleagues. Does he work? Does he live near Paris? Is he married? Has he got any children?

| | |
|---|---|
| Jane | Vous vous_appelez comment? |
| Jean Durand | Je m'appelle Jean Durand et vous? |
| Jane | Moi, Jane Wilson. Vous_habitez où? |
| Jean Durand | **Dans la banlieue** de Paris, à Chatou. |
| Jane | Et ... c'est loin Chatou? |
| Jean Durand | C'est_à 45 minutes en train. Il y a un train direct Paris-Chatou. |
| Jane | Et ... vous travaillez? |
| Jean Durand | Oui, je suis_**homme d'affaires** et vous? |
| Jane | Moi, je travaille en Angleterre, à Brighton ... je suis dentiste. |
| Jean Durand | Et vous_êtes_**en vacances?** |
| Jane | Oui, je suis ici **depuis deux semaines. J'aime** beaucoup Paris. Vous_êtes marié? |
| Jean Durand | Oui. |
| Jane | Vous_avez des_enfants? |
| Jean Durand | J'ai trois_enfants: deux garçons et une fille. |
| Jane | Il y a **une école** à Chatou? |
| Jean Durand | Oui. Il y en_a une à dix minutes à pied. |
| Jane | **Votre femme** travaille? |
| Jean Durand | Oui, elle est professeur à l'école de Chatou. |
| Jane | C'est_une grande ville, Chatou? |
| Jean Durand | Oui, c'est grand. Il y a beaucoup de magasins, deux banques, une pharmacie, **un parc** et une piscine. |
| Jane | Il y a un cinéma? |
| Jean Durand | Non, il n'y en_a pas. |

| | |
|---|---|
| **un_homme d'affaires** | a businessman |
| **dans la banlieue** | in the suburbs |
| **depuis deux semaines** | for two weeks |
| **une école** | a school |
| **en vacances** | on holiday |
| **votre femme** | your wife |

| | |
|---|---|
| **un parc** | a park |
| **j'aime** | I like/love |

# Explications

## 1 How to ask simple questions

As you already know, the easiest way to ask a question is to make a statement and raise the voice on the last syllable:

**Vous_êtes marié?** ↑    *Are you married?*

## 2 C'est .....? *Is it.....? Is that .....?*

You can start the question with **c'est** (lit. *it is* .....) and raise the voice at the end of the sentence. To say that *it isn't* use **ce n'est pas**.

**C'est** loin? ↑    *Is it far?*
**Non, ce n'est pas** loin.    *No, it isn't far.*

## 3 Il y a .....? *Is there .....? Are there .....?*

You can also start the question with **il y a** (*there is, there are*) and raise the voice at the end of the sentence. To say *there is no...* or *there are no ...*, use **il n'y a pas de ...**

**Il y a** un restaurant dans l'hôtel? ↑    *Is there a restaurant in the hotel?*
**Non, il n'y a pas de** restaurant ici.    *No, there is no restaurant here.*

## 4 Some likely answers: yes there is, no there isn't

To the question **il y a une banque près d'ici?** *is there a bank nearby?* most people in France would answer **oui, il y en_a une** *yes there is one* or **non, il n'y en_a pas** *no there isn't (one)*; **en** which means *one, some, of it, of them,* can be omitted in English but not in French:

— **40** —

| Il y a une banque à Chatou? | Is there a bank at Chatou? |
|---|---|
| **Oui, il y en_a une.** | Yes there is one. |
| Il y a une cabine téléphonique près d'ici? | Is there a telephone box near here? |
| **Non, il n'y en_a pas.** | No there isn't one. |

## 5 More answers: yes I have, no I haven't

Similarly to the question **vous_avez un/une** ... you will hear the answer **oui, j'en_ai un/une** or **non, je n'en_ai pas.**

| Vous_avez un timbre? | Do you have a stamp? |
|---|---|
| Oui **j'en_ai un.** | Yes I have. |
| Vous_avez une voiture? | Do you have a car? |
| Oui, **j'en_ai une.** | Yes I have. |
| Non, **je n'en_ai pas.** | No I haven't. |

## 6 Other questions

You can form other questions starting with **c'est** or giving a statement and adding the question word afterwards.

| **C'est comment,** le musée? | What is the museum like? |
|---|---|
| **C'est combien,** le billet? | How much is the ticket? |
| **C'est où,** l'arrêt d'autobus? | Where is the bus stop? |
| **C'est quand,** les vacances? | When are the holidays? |
| Les magasins ferment **quand?** | When do the shops shut? |
| Les magasins ouvrent **quand?** | When do the shops open? |

## 7 Mon, ton, son: *My, your, his*

| Thing possessed | *my* | *your* | *his/her/its/ one's* | *our* | *your* | *their* |
|---|---|---|---|---|---|---|
| masc. sing. | **mon** | **ton** | **son** | **notre** | **votre** | **leur** |
| fem. sing. | **ma** | **ta** | **sa** | **notre** | **votre** | **leur** |
| masc. & fem. plur. | **mes** | **tes** | **ses** | **nos** | **vos** | **leurs** |

Like all adjectives in French, these agree with the noun they refer to:

| | |
|---|---|
| **mon mari** | my husband |
| **ma femme** | my wife |
| **mes enfants** | my children |

Take care when using **son** and **sa** to make them agree with the thing being owned, and not the owner:

**le fils de M.Durand** becomes **son fils** (*his son*)
**le fils de Mme Durand** becomes **son fils** (*her son*)
**la fille de M.Durand** becomes **sa fille** (*his daughter*)
**la fille de Mme Durand** becomes **sa fille** (*her daughter*)

## Create every opportunity to speak the language

1  Try to practise your French with other learners or French speakers.
   Find out about French societies, clubs or circles in your area (the library is a good place to find out information). They provide an opportunity to meet other people with whom you can practise your newly acquired language.

2  Listen to some French regularly.
   Not only will it sharpen your comprehension skills but it will help you improve your pronunciation.

3  Read something in French.
   Buy a French magazine and see how many words you can recognise. Try to get the gist of short articles by concentrating on the words you know, getting clues from photographs if there are any and using some guesswork.

## Activités

1  Match the questions in the left-hand column with the answers on the right.

   (a) C'est gratuit?          (i) Non, c'est Monsieur Durand.

   (b) C'est M.Martel?         (ii) Non, c'est bon marché.

   (c) C'est ouvert?           (iii) Non, c'est à 10 minutes à pied.

(*d*) Il y a des timbres?     (*iv*) Oui, c'est tout près.
(*e*) C'est loin?               (*v*) Non, il faut payer.
(*f*) C'est cher?               (*vi*) C'est 50F 40.
(*g*) C'est combien?           (*vii*) Non, c'est fermé.
(*h*) C'est près?              (*viii*) Non, il n'y en a pas.

2 You've just arrived at an hotel. At the reception you find out about the hotel and the amenities in the area. Can you reconstruct the conversation?

(*a*) ................................................................ ?
Non, Monsieur, il n'y a pas de restaurant dans l'hôtel.

(*b*) ................................................................ ?
Oui, il y a une pharmacie au bout de la rue.

(*c*) ................................................................ ?
Oui, il y a beaucoup de magasins près d'ici.

(*d*) ................................................................ ?
Non, Monsieur, la banque est fermée maintenant.

(*e*) ................................................................ ?
Oui, il y a un train direct pour Paris.

(*f*) ................................................................ ?
Non, la gare n'est pas loin. Elle est à 5 minutes à pied.

(*g*) ................................................................ ?
Les toilettes sont au premier étage.

3 That night you have a nightmare; you are in town doing some shopping but it is a very strange town. Using the example as a model describe what you see to your friend?

Exemple: Il y a des cartes postales mais il n'y a pas de timbres.

(*a*) ............une pharmacie ........................aspirine.

(*b*) ............pâtisserie ............................croissants.

(*c*) ............une gare ...............................trains.

(*d*) ...........un arrêt d'autobus ....................bus.

— 43 —

(*e*) ............un bar ....................................bière.

(*f*) ............une cabine téléphonique ...........téléphone.

4  You overhear one side of a conversation in **un café**. These are the answers, but what were the questions?

(*a*)  Oui, je suis en vacances.
(*b*)  Oui, je suis marié.
(*c*)  Non, je n'ai pas d'enfants.
(*d*)  Non, je n'habite pas Londres, j'habite Manchester.
(*e*)  Je travaille comme secrétaire.

5  Fill in the gaps using one of the following question words: **où, quand, comment, combien**.

(*a*) C'est .......... le journal?        C'est 7F50.
(*b*) C'est .......... l'arrêt           C'est au bout de la rue.
d'autobus?
(*c*) C'est .......... les              C'est en Septembre.
vacances?
(*d*) C'est .......... le Sacré-         C'est au nord de Paris.
Coeur?
(*e*) C'est .......... la              C'est près du Louvre.
Pyramide?
(*f*) C'est .......... le film?         C'est super.

6  Listen to how much each item costs and fill in the price tags. Note that price tags are always marked in **francs (F)** and **centimes (c)**. There are 100 centimes to the franc.

Exemple: 7F30, 0F45.

a. □        b. □        c. □        d. □        e. □        f. □

## ☑ *Petit test*

1  Ask someone for his/her name.
2  Find out if he/she works.
3  Find out where he/she lives and say that you live in the suburbs of London.
4  Say how old you are.
5  Say that there is a bank nearby, at the end of the street.

# 5

## QUELLE HEURE EST-IL?
### What time is it?

### In this unit you will learn

- the days of the week
- the months of the year
- some useful expressions of time
- numbers from 70 to 90
- how to say what you want to do
- how to ask what you can or cannot do
- how to ask for help
- the dates
- how to tell the time

### Avant de commencer

For a successful holiday or business trip in France you need to know when things are happening or when shops open. You also need to be able to say what you want to do, find out if it can be done and ask for help. You will be able to achieve all this with the few structures introduced in this unit. You'll also be introduced to quite a lot of vocabulary: days, dates and times.

## ✔ Essayez

1 You are in **l'office du tourisme** (*tourist office*) in Paris. How would you ask for a street map? Ask if there are a bank and a telephone box nearby? Can you think of other questions to ask?

2 Revise the following numbers: say them aloud.

41 – 22 – 68 – 15 – 5 – 55 – 14 – 29 – 31 – 47 – 60 – 11

Check your answers with the numbers ➡ **P.** 212.

## Mots-clefs

| | |
|---|---|
| à quelle heure ... | at what time ... |
| quand ... est-ce que l'avion part? | when ... does the aircraft leave? |
| est-ce que le bus arrive? | does the bus arrive? |
| est-ce qu'on rentre? | do we come back? |
| est-ce qu'on peut prendre le petit déjeuner? | can we have breakfast? |
| est-ce qu'il y a un métro? | is there a (tube, subway) train? |
| finit le concert? | does the concert finish? |
| quelle heure est-il? | what time is it? |
| il est ... | it's ... |
| qu'est-ce que vous faites dans la vie? | what's your job (lit. what do you do in life?) |
| dans 10 minutes | in 10 minutes' time |
| à 10 heures du soir | at ten o'clock in the evening |
| je travaille | I work |
| tous les jours de la semaine | every day of the week |
| sauf le samedi et le dimanche | except Saturdays and Sundays |
| le lundi, le mardi et le mercredi | on Mondays, Tuesdays and Wednesdays |
| le jeudi et le vendredi | on Thursdays and Fridays |
| jusqu'à midi/minuit | until lunch/midnight |
| depuis 10 heures du matin | since 10 in the morning |
| pendant l'après-midi | during the afternoon |
| je regarde la télévision quelquefois | I sometimes watch TV |
| souvent | often |
| toujours | always |
| aujourd'hui | today |
| demain | tomorrow |
| maintenant | now |

| Les mois de l'année | *The months of the year* |
|---|---|
| **janvier** | January |
| **février** | February |
| **mars** | March |
| **avril** | April |
| **mai** | May |
| **juin** | June |
| **juillet** | July |
| **août** | August |
| **septembre** | September |
| **octobre** | October |
| **novembre** | November |
| **décembre** | December |

## Les chiffres 70-90

| | | | |
|---|---|---|---|
| **soixante-dix** | 70 | **quatre-vingts** | 80 |
| **soixante et onze** | 71 | **quatre-vingt-un** | 81 |
| **soixante-douze** | 72 | **quatre-vingt-deux** | 82 |
| **soixante-treize** | 73 | **quatre-vingt-trois** | 83 |
| **soixante-quatorze** | 74 | **quatre-vingt-quatre** | 84 |
| **soixante-quinze** | 75 | **quatre-vingt-cinq** | 85 |
| **soixante-seize** | 76 | **quatre-vingt-six** | 86 |
| **soixante-dix-sept** | 77 | **quatre-vingt-sept** | 87 |
| **soixante-dix-huit** | 78 | **quatre-vingt-huit** | 88 |
| **soixante-dix-neuf** | 79 | **quatre-vingt-neuf** | 89 |
| | | **quatre-vingt-dix** | 90 |

# Dialogue

Jane is asking Mme Durand about her working week. Listen to the tape several times. At what time does Mrs Durand start in the mornings and finish in the evenings? Where does she go for lunch?

| | |
|---|---|
| Jane | Mme Durand, qu'est-ce que vous faites dans la vie? |
| Mme Durand | Je suis professeur de biologie. |
| Jane | Vous travaillez tous les jours? |
| Mme Durand | Oui, je travaille tous les jours sauf le dimanche. |
| Jane | A quelle heure est-ce que vous commencez le matin? |
| Mme Durand | **Ça dépend,** le lundi, le mercredi et le vendredi, je commence à huit heures et demie, mais le mardi et le jeudi je ne travaille pas le matin. |

| | |
|---|---|
| Jane | A quelle heure finissez-vous l'après-midi? |
| Mme Durand | Je finis à cinq heures et demie le lundi, le mardi, le jeudi et le vendredi. Le mercredi après-midi je ne travaille pas **mais je reste** dans mon **bureau**. Le samedi, l'école finit à midi et c'est le week-end jusqu'au lundi matin. |
| Jane | Où est-ce que vous déjeunez_à midi? |
| Mme Durand | Mes_enfants et moi, nous déjeunons_à l'école. Il y a une cafétéria **qui est_ouverte** toute la journée de neuf_heures à cinq_heures. |
| Jane | Et le week-end, qu'est-ce que vous faites? |
| Mme Durand | Ah, le week-end c'est **formidable** mais **il passe trop vite**. Samedi après-midi je regarde souvent le football à la télévision avec mon **mari** et mes enfants. Dimanche **on va** toujours à la piscine de Chatou. |

| | |
|---|---|
| **ça dépend** | it depends |
| **mais je reste** | but I stay |
| **le bureau** | the office |
| **qui est_ouverte** | which is open |
| **formidable** | great |
| **il passe trop vite** | it goes too quickly |
| **mari** | husband |
| **on va** | we go |

# Explications

## 1  Saying what you want/want to do

Instead of saying **je veux** (*I want*), it's more polite to start with **je voudrais** (*I would like*). To say what you want to do, put the infinitive next. (**Je veux** and **je voudrais** are part of the verb **vouloir**, → 94.)

| | |
|---|---|
| **Je voudrais_une chambre pour ce soir.** | *I would like a room for tonight.* |
| **Je voudrais_acheter un timbre pour l'Angleterre.** | *I would like to buy a stamp for England.* |

## 2  Asking what you can do; asking for help

To ask if you can do something use **je peux** or **on peut** followed by the infinitive describing what you want to do. To ask for someone's help use **vous pouvez**. (**Je peux, on peut, vous pouvez,** are part of the verb **pouvoir** →P 94.)

| | |
|---|---|
| **Je peux changer de l'argent?** | *Can I change some money?* |
| **On peut prendre le petit déjeuner à quelle heure?** | *At what time can I/we have breakfast?* |
| **Vous pouvez répéter?** | *Can you repeat that?* |

## 3  Three different ways to ask a question

(*a*)  By giving a questioning tone to what is really a statement:

| | |
|---|---|
| **Tu es française?** | *Are you French?* |

(*b*)  By leaving the verb as it is and using **est-ce que** (pronounced *esker*) which is the equivalent of the English *do, does,* in sentences such as *do you speak English?*:

| | |
|---|---|
| **Est-ce que tu travailles?** | *Do you work?* |
| **Où est-ce que tu habites?** | *Where do you live?* |

(*c*)  By turning the verb round and joining the two parts with a hyphen:

| | |
|---|---|
| **Travailles-tu?** | *Do you work?* |

✳ Out of the three different ways of asking a question, the safest one is (*b*) as there are no situations in which **est-ce que** cannot be used. (*a*) is common in conversation but less so in written French. (*c*) is not usually used with **je**.

## 4  Questions starting with Qu'est-ce que ...?  *What ...?*

Many questions start with **qu'est-ce que ...?**

| | |
|---|---|
| **Qu'est-ce que c'est?** | *What's that?* |
| **Qu'est-ce que vous désirez?** | *What would you like?* (in a shop) |
| **Qu'est-ce que vous faites dans la vie?** | *What's your job?* (lit. what do you do in life?) |

## 5 Verbs ending in -ir and -re

There are three main groups of regular verbs in French:

| | |
|---|---|
| verbs ending in **-er** | e.g. **travailler** |
| verbs ending in **-ir** | e.g. **finir** |
| verbs ending in **-re** | e.g. **attendre** |

To work out the present tense of **-ir** and **-re** verbs, knock the **-ir** and **-re** off the infinitives and then add the following endings:

| **finir** *to finish* | | **attendre** *to wait* | |
|---|---|---|---|
| je | fin**is** | j' | attend**s** |
| tu | fin**is** | tu | attend**s** |
| il/elle/on | fin**it** | il/elle/on | attend |
| nous | fin**issons** | nous | attend**ons** |
| vous | fin**issez** | vous | attend**ez** |
| ils/elles | fin**issent** | ils/elles | attend**ent** |

| | |
|---|---|
| **A quelle heure finissez-vous?** | *At what time do you finish?* |
| **Je finis à 5h.30.** | *I finish at 5.30.* |
| **L'école finit à midi.** | *School finishes at lunchtime.* |
| **J'attends le train de 7h.30.** | *I'm waiting for the 7.30 train.* |
| **Elle attend son petit ami.** | *She's waiting for her boyfriend.* |

✳ Remember not to pronounce the last letters in: finis/finit/finissons/finissent; attends/attend/attendons/attendent.

## 6 Giving the date

The English talk about the 1st, 2nd, 3rd, 4th, etc ... of the month. The French say the 1st (**le premier** or **1er**) but the two, the three, the four, etc ... of the month.

| | |
|---|---|
| **Quelle est la date?** | *What's the date?* |
| **Nous sommes le 1er octobre.** | *It's the 1st October.* |
| **Aujourd'hui c'est le deux avril.** | *Today is the 2nd of April.* |

## 7 Telling the time

(a) The 24-hour clock is used widely in France to distinguish between am and pm.

| | |
|---|---|
| **il est treize_heures** | *it's 1pm* |
| **il est quatorze heures quinze** | *it's 2.15pm* |
| **il est quinze heures trente** | *it's 3.30pm* |
| **il est seize heures quarante-cinq** | *it's 4.45pm* |
| **il est dix-sept heures cinquante** | *it's 5.50pm* |
| **il est dix-huit_heures cinquante-deux** | *it's 6.52pm* |
| **il est dix-neuf_heures cinquante-cinq** | *it's 7.55pm* |

(b) The 12-hour clock. To reply to the question **Quelle heure est-il?** *What time is it?* one is more likely to use the twelve-hour clock.

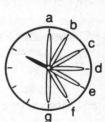

(a)  **il est dix_heures**
(b)  **il est dix_heures cinq**
(c)  **il est dix_heures dix**
(d)  **il est dix_heures et quart**
(*lit. ten hours and quarter*)

(e)  **il est dix_heures vingt**
(f)  **il est dix_heures vingt-cinq**
(g)  **il est dix_heures et demie**
(*lit. ten hours and half*)

(h)  **il est onze_heures moins vingt-cinq**
(*lit. eleven hours minus twenty-five*)

(i)  **il est onze_heures moins vingt**
(j)  **il est onze_heures moins le quart**
(*lit. eleven hours minus the quarter*)

(k)  **il est onze_heures moins dix**
(l)  **il est onze_heures moins cinq**

To distinguish between 9am and 9pm people say:

| | |
|---|---|
| il est neuf heures **du matin** | *it's 9am* |
| il est neuf heures **du soir** | *it's 9pm* |

✳ Pronounce the **f** of **neuf** as a **v** when it is followed by a vowel or an **h**.

Noon and midnight are however distinguished from each other:

| | |
|---|---|
| **il est midi** | *it's 12pm midday* |
| **il est minuit** | *it's 12am midnight* |

## 8 Faire *To do/to make*

**Faire** is an irregular verb as it does not follow the pattern of **attendre** ➡️ 🄿 50. It is used in a number of expressions in French (can you think of a recent one you've seen?). Here is a new one: **faire la cuisine** *to do the cooking*.

| | |
|---|---|
| **je fais** | **nous faisons** |
| **tu fais** | **vous faites** |
| **il/elle/on fait** | **ils/elles font** |

## 9 Prendre *To take*

**Prendre** is also an irregular verb and needs to be learnt on its own. **Apprendre** *to learn* and **comprendre** *to understand* follow the same pattern as **prendre**.

| | |
|---|---|
| **je prends** | **nous prenons** |
| **tu prends** | **vous prenez** |
| **il/elle/on prend** | **ils/elles prennent** |

## ✳ *Experiment while learning*

### Get a feel for the language

Learning a language is like learning any other skill. Take swimming for example: it is only when you go into the water and put into practice what you've read or been told, that real learning starts.

1 Experiment with grammar rules: sit back and reflect on some of the rules you've been learning. See how they compare with your own language or other languages you may already

speak. Try to find out some rules on your own and be ready to spot the exceptions. By doing this you'll remember the rules better and get a feel for the language.

2 Experiment with words: Use the words that you've learnt in new contexts and find out if they are correct. For example you've learnt that **passe** can mean *go* in the context of time e.g. **le dimanche passe trop vite**. Experiment with **passe** in new contexts. **Les vacances passent trop vite; la semaine passe ...** etc. Check the new phrases either in this book, a dictionary or with French speakers.

 ——————————— **Activités** ———————————

1 See how many sentences you can make using the verbs in the boxes below and adding a few words.

| je voudrais<br><br>je peux<br>on peut<br>vous pouvez | + | déjeuner ........................<br>habiter ........................<br>prendre ........................<br>acheter ........................<br>finir ........................<br>commencer ........................<br>apprendre ........................ |
|---|---|---|

2 Put the correct endings to the verbs in brackets

 (*a*) Le matin je (prendre) le train à 7h.30.
 (*b*) Mes_enfants (commencer) l'école à 8h.30.
 (*c*) Le train (arriver) à 8 heures du matin.
 (*d*) Il (apprendre) le français depuis 2 mois.
 (*e*) A midi on (déjeuner) à la cafétéria.
 (*f*) Qu'est-ce que vous (prendre) pour le petit déjeuner?
 (*g*) De huit heures à neuf_heures je (faire) la cuisine
 (*h*) Quelle heure (être) -il?
 (*i*) Le mercredi, la journée (finir) à midi.
 (*j*) Qu'est-ce que vous (faire) dans la vie?
 (*k*) Nous_(attendre) à l'arrêt d'autobus?
 (*l*) Ils (comprendre) l'anglais.

3 Jane is interviewing Mme Durand. Complete the questions she is asking her by selecting the appropriate endings (see overleaf).

| | |
|---|---|
| (*a*) **Comment** | (*i*) **vous faites dans la vie?** |
| (*b*) **Quel âge** | (*ii*) **une banque près d'ici?** |
| (*c*) **C'est_où** | (*iii*) **vous_appelez-vous?** |
| (*d*) **Qu'est-ce que** | (*iv*) **commencez-vous le matin?** |
| (*e*) **Il y a** | (*v*) **la cabine téléphonique?** |
| (*f*) **A quelle heure** | (*vi*) **combien d'enfants?** |
| (*g*) **Vous avez** | (*vii*) **ont-ils?** |

**4** Below is M. Durand's timetable for a typical day. However the lines got muddled up. Can you put them in the right order, starting with the sentence in bold type?

(*a*) Il_arrive au travail à 9_heures.
(*b*) Le soir, il regarde la télévision jusqu'à 22 heures.
(*c*) Il travaille de 9h.15 jusqu'à 13h.
(*d*) Il finit la journée à 17h.30.
(*e*) Il prend le train à 7 heures du matin.
(*f*) **Il prend le petit déjeuner à 6h.30 du matin.**
(*g*) A midi il déjeune au restaurant avec ses collègues.
(*h*) Il rentre à la maison vers 19h.15.

**5** Using the pictures to help you, fill in the missing words.

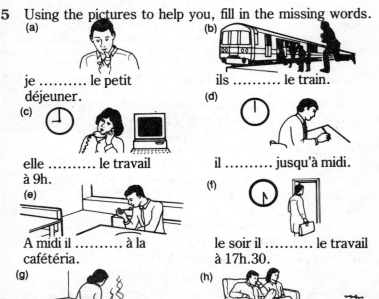

(a) je ………. le petit déjeuner.

(b) ils ………. le train.

(c) elle ………. le travail à 9h.

(d) il ………. jusqu'à midi.

(e) A midi il ………. à la cafétéria.

(f) le soir il ………. le travail à 17h.30.

(g) elle ………. la cuisine.

(h) ils ………. la télévision.

**6** Give the following dates in French:

| | | | |
|---|---|---|---|
| 1st May | 10th June | 3rd February | 13th October |
| 21st March | 30th September | 15th July | 6th August |

**7** Listen to the tape. Michel is talking about what he's going to do this week. Fill in the gaps with the correct day of the week in French (**aller** = *to go*).

(a) ................. **je déjeune au restaurant avec Sophie.**

(b) ................. **je prends le train pour Manchester.**

(c) ................. **je regarde la télévision avec ma famille.**

(d) ................. **je réserve une chambre à l'hôtel Nelson.**

(e) ................. **j'achète trois bouteilles de vin.**

(f) ................. **je voudrais_aller au cinéma avec mes_enfants.**

(g) ................. **je travaille au bureau toute la journée.**

**8** What time is it? Write out your answers in full.

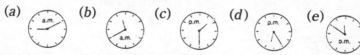

(a)   (b)   (c)   (d)   (e)

**9** Listen to the tape and fill in the clock faces below with times spoken:

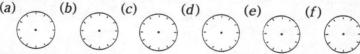

(a)   (b)   (c)   (d)   (e)   (f)

## ✔ *Petit test*

**1** Say the days of the week in reverse order starting with Sunday.

**2** How would you ask 'When does the bank shut?'

**3** Ask the ticket collector in Calais 'Is there a train for Lille?'

**4** How would you ask if you can have breakfast in the hotel?

**5** Give the date and the time.

# 6

## POUR ALLER A ...?
### *The way to ...?*

### *In this unit you will learn*

- how to count from 90 upwards
- how to ask for and understand directions
- useful verbs to describe what you do every day

### *Avant de commencer*

In **Mots-clefs**, Ünit 4, you learnt to say how far somewhere is and how long it takes to go somewhere on foot and by car. Revise these structures as you will need them to understand the dialogue in this unit.

You now know how to ask where things are: **Où est ...?** or **C'est où ...?** Asking the way is also very simple; you start your question with the phrase **pour aller à** and raise the voice at the end of the statement.

Understanding the answer can be more tricky and you'll need to pick out the few essential words such as **tout droit, à gauche, à droite** out of the flow of other words.

As people give you directions, repeat after them, to make sure you have understood. If you do not understand, ask them to repeat or slow down.

### ✍ Essayez

1 Ask someone:
 (*a*) to speak more slowly
 (*b*) to repeat

2 Talk about your typical day. Use the verbs below to make it exciting and busy.

---

je reste ........      je travaille ........

je pars ........      je regarde ........

je commence ........      je finis ........

je rentre ........      je prends le déjeuner ........

---

## Mots-clefs

### To go straight on

| | |
|---|---|
| pour_aller à ... | the way to ... |
| (vous) allez tout droit | (you) go straight on |
| continuez | carry on |
| descendez la rue | go down the street |
| montez l'avenue | go up the avenue |
| passez le magasin | go beyond the shop |
| traversez la place | cross the square |
| prenez la route de ... | take the road to ... |

### To turn

| | |
|---|---|
| (vous) tournez_à gauche | (you) turn left |
| tournez_à droite | turn right |
| vous_allez prendre: | you're going to take: |
| la première rue à droite | the first street on the right |
| la deuxième sur votre gauche | the second on your left |

### Where it is

| | |
|---|---|
| la place du marché est située: | the market place is: |
| au coin de la rue | at the corner of the street |
| à côté du supermarché | next to the supermarket |
| en face de la boulangerie | opposite the baker's |

| au centre ville | in the town centre |
|---|---|
| sur votre gauche | on your left |
| sur, sous | on, under |
| devant, derrière | in front of, behind |
| dans | in, inside |
| entre | between |
| il faut combien de temps? | how long does it take? |
| il faut environ 25 minutes | you need about 25 minutes |

## Les chiffres 90 ...

| | | | |
|---|---|---|---|
| quatre-vingt-dix | 90 | cent | 100 |
| quatre-vingt-onze | 91 | cent un | 101 |
| quatre-vingt-douze | 92 | cent deux | 102 |
| quatre-vingt-treize | 93 | cent vingt-trois | 123 |
| quatre-vingt-quatorze | 94 | cinq cent trente-quatre | 534 |
| quatre-vingt-quinze | 95 | mille | 1000 |
| quatre-vingt-seize | 96 | mille neuf cent quinze | 1915 |
| quatre-vingt-dix-sept | 97 | deux mille | 2000 |
| quatre-vingt-dix-huit | 98 | | |
| quatre-vingt-dix-neuf | 99 | | |

# Dialogue

Jane passe la journée chez les Durand. L'après-midi, elle décide d'aller au centre ville de Chatou.
*Jane is spending the day with the Durands. She decides to go to the town centre in the afternoon.*
While you listen to the cassette, look at the street map (**le plan de ville**) of Chatou on ➡️ 🅿 64. How do you get from M.Durand's house to the park and how long does it take to walk there?

| | |
|---|---|
| Jane | M.Durand, avez-vous un plan de Chatou? Je voudrais aller **d'abord** au parc et puis, **si j'ai le temps,** dans les magasins ... |
| M.Durand | **Voici** le plan. Vous pouvez **le garder** car j'en ai deux. |
| Jane | Merci beaucoup. Où est le parc de Chatou? |
| M.Durand | **Voyons,** nous sommes ici sur le plan. Vous tournez à gauche **en sortant de la maison,** vous allez jusqu'au bout de la rue Vaugirard, vous tournez à droite dans la rue Vincennes et puis c'est sur votre gauche à 200 mètres. |

| | |
|---|---|
| Jane | Bon, alors, à gauche en sortant puis je tourne à droite et c'est sur ma gauche ... C'est loin à pied? |
| M.Durand | Non, pas très loin; il faut_environ 25 minutes. |
| Jane | Oh là là, c'est trop loin pour moi. Euh, on peut_y aller en_autobus? |
| M.Durand | Oui, oui. L'arrêt d'autobus est situé juste au coin de la rue Vaugirard. C'est très pratique et il y a un autobus toutes les dix minutes. |
| Jane | Je voudrais_aussi **faire des_achats** pour moi et acheter quelques souvenirs pour ma famille en Grande-Bretagne et au Canada. |
| M.Durand | Eh bien, vous pouvez_aller au **centre commercial.** Il est sur la place du marché à côté de la gare. Vous_avez un_autobus direct. Il va du parc_au centre commercial. |
| Jane | Bon, je pars tout de suite ... j'ai beaucoup de choses à acheter et ... je voudrais rentrer vers 19 heures. |

| | |
|---|---|
| **d'abord** | firstly |
| **si j'ai le temps** | if I have the time |
| **voici** | here is ... |
| **le garder** | keep it |
| **voyons** | let's see |
| **en sortant** | as you leave |
| **la maison** | the house |
| **faire des_achats** | to do some shopping |
| **le centre commercial** | the shopping centre |

## Explications

### 1 Pour aller à: Asking the way and giving directions

**Pour_aller à** (*to get to*) is a very useful structure to remember. Used in a questioning tone it means *How do I/we get to ...?*

| | |
|---|---|
| **Pardon, Monsieur, pour_aller à Gordes?** | *Excuse me, Sir, how do we get to Gordes?* |
| **Pour_aller à Gordes, prenez la route pour St Saturnin.** | *To get to Gordes, take the road for St Saturnin.* |

### 2 Aller, *to go* Partir, *to leave*

Here are two very useful verbs. Both verbs are irregular, and

**aller** is particularly useful as it is used when speaking about the future (explained in Unit 10).

| aller *to go* | partir *to leave* |
|---|---|
| je vais | je pars |
| tu vas | tu pars |
| il/elle/on va | il/elle/on part |
| nous allons | nous partons |
| vous allez | vous partez |
| ils/elles vont | ils/elles partent |

| | |
|---|---|
| **Vous_allez jusqu'au bout de la rue.** | *You go to the end of the road.* |
| **Je voudrais_aller à la banque.** | *I would like to go to the bank.* |
| **Je pars tout de suite.** | *I'm leaving immediately.* |

## 3 Understanding directions

Understanding directions can be more tricky than asking the way as the directions can sound complicated, so it is important to pick out the essential words:

(*a*) As an answer to your question, you'll probably hear one of the following constructions:

| prenez *take* | descendez *go down* | tournez à *turn* | allez *go* | montez *go up* |
|---|---|---|---|---|

| | |
|---|---|
| **Il faut prendre ...** | *You have to (lit. it's necessary to) take ...* |
| **Il faut descendre ...** | *You have to go down ...* |
| **Il faut tourner ...** | *You have to turn ...* |
| **Il faut_aller ...** | *You have to go ...* |
| **Il faut monter ...** | *You have to go up ...* |

(*b*) The **t** in **droite** *right* is sounded but it is not in **droit** *straight*. **Droit** is usually preceded with **tout: tout droit** *straight on*. **Droite** is preceded with **à** or **sur la: à droite, sur la droite**:

| | |
|---|---|
| **Il faut_aller tout droit.** | *You have to go straight on.* |
| **La gare est sur la droite.** | *The station is on the right.* |

(*c*)  You may be unlucky when asking directions and find that you are asking a tourist! His answer would be **je ne sais pas** (*I don't know*), or **je ne suis pas d'ici** (*I am not from here*).

(*d*)  If you don't understand the information, e.g. the address, the street name, or the number of the building you are given, use the structure **c'est quel(le) ...?** ➡️ 📖 31 to have the information repeated:

| | |
|---|---|
| **C'est quelle rue?** | *Which street is it?* |
| **C'est quel numéro?** | *Which number is it?* |
| **C'est quelle adresse?** | *Which address is it?* |

## 4  When to use 'à';  when to use 'en'

To say that you are in a town or you are going/want to go to a town always use **à** (with an accent to differentiate it from **a** *has*). Study the examples below:

| | |
|---|---|
| **Je suis_à Bordeaux.** | *I'm in Bordeaux.* |
| **Nous_allons_à Bordeaux.** | *We're going to Bordeaux.* |

To say that you are in a country or you're going to a country, use **en** with feminine countries (often finishing with an-**e**) and **au/aux** with the others.

| | |
|---|---|
| **Je suis_en Australie.** | *I am in Australia.* |
| **Je vais_en Angleterre.** | *I'm going to England.* |
| **Vous_allez_au Canada.** | *You're going to Canada.* |

✳️ The country is preceded by its article in sentences such as:

| | |
|---|---|
| **Je connais bien la Suisse.** | *I know Switzerland quite well.* |
| **J'aime beaucoup le Portugal.** | *I like Portugal a lot.* |

## 5  When à (*at, to, in, on*) is followed by le, la, l', les ...

The preposition **à** followed by a definite article **le la l' les** changes its form in the following way:

| | | |
|---|---|---|
| **à + le** | becomes | **au** |
| **à + la** | remains | **à la** |
| **à + l'** | remains | **à l'** |
| **à + les** | becomes | **aux** |

| Pour_aller **au musée** du Louvre, s'il vous plaît? | *Which way to the Louvre Museum please?* |
| Nous_allons_**à l'église** St Paul. | *We are going to St Paul's Church.* |
| Il arrive **à la gare** à 8 heures du matin. | *He arrives at the station at 8 o'clock in the morning.* |
| Il va **aux_Etats_Unis** deux fois par mois. | *He goes to the United States twice a month.* |

## 6  Locating the exact spot

Remember that when **de** is used in a combination with **le, la, l',**
**les** in expressions such as **en face de** *opposite,* **à côté de** *next*
*to,* **au coin de** *at the corner of,* **près de** *near,* you need to
change its form ➡ P. 21:

| au coin **du parc** | *at the corner of the park* |
| près **des grands magasins** | *near the department stores* |
| en face **de la piscine** | *opposite the swimming pool* |
| à côté **de l'office** du tourisme | *near the tourist office* |

## 7  Premier, deuxième, troisième  *1st, 2nd, 3rd*

If you are directed to the 3rd floor, the 2nd street and so on, the
numbers end in **-ième**.

| | | | |
|---|---|---|---|
| **deuxième** | *2nd* | **quatrième** | *4th* |
| **troisième** | *3rd* | | |

But, 1st is **premier** before all masculine nouns, and **première**
before all feminine nouns.

| Vous montez au **premier** étage. | *You go up to the first floor.* |
| C'est la **première** porte. | *It is the first door.* |
| Vous prenez la **deuxième** à gauche. | *You take the second on the left.* |
| C'est le **troisième** bâtiment. | *It's the third building.* |

— **62** —

**Self-evaluation**

1 How well are you doing with speaking French? The revision of the last six dialogues, at the end of this unit, will give you the opportunity to test your overall speaking performance. If you experience some difficulties, look back at the last five units. They give advice on how to organise the study of vocabulary and grammar and how to create opportunities to practise your French.

2 How well are you doing with understanding: are you listening to some French every day? Look at ➡️ 🄿 97 and read about the various ways in which you can improve your understanding. If you have the tape listen to the dialogues again and again pausing and repeating until you feel familiar with the passages. When listening to a passage, pick out the most important key words.

---

✔️ ─────────── **Activités** ───────────

1 You are Jane visiting Chatou for the first time. How would you ask a passer-by the way to:

(a) la piscine

(c) l'église St Paul

(b) la gare

(*d*) le musée

(*e*) l'office du tourisme

**2** Now listen to the passers-by's replies on the tape and work out which letter on the map represents each of these places. If you haven't got the cassette, read the replies overleaf:

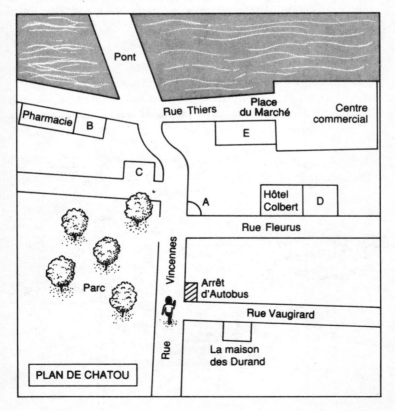

(*a*) C'est très facile. Vous montez la rue Vincennes et vous prenez la première à gauche. La piscine se trouve sur votre droite, en face du parc.

(*b*) Bon, pour la gare, continuez tout droit, toujours tout droit. Juste avant le pont, tournez‿à droite et vous‿êtes dans la rue Thiers. La gare est à côté du centre commercial.

(*c*) L'église St Paul? Eh bien, c'est tout droit, à 100 mètres d'ici, sur votre droite, au coin de la rue Fleurus.

(*d*) Euh ... attendez voir ... Il faut tourner tout de suite à droite puis descendez la rue Fleurus et le musée est‿à 10 minutes à pied sur votre gauche à côté de l'hôtel Colbert.

(*e*) Vous‿allez tout droit jusqu'au pont. Juste avant le pont tournez‿à gauche et l'office du tourisme se trouve à côté d'une pharmacie.

3    Now it's your turn to practise giving directions. Use the text above as a model but you don't have to answer exactly like it; for example instead of **vous montez/descendez la rue** you can say (**vous**) **allez/continuez tout droit.** (The answers are not given in **Réponses**.) Here are the questions:

(*a*) Pardon Monsieur, pour‿aller à la piscine?

(*b*) S'il vous plaît Madame, je voudrais‿aller au musée; pouvez-vous me dire où il se trouve?

(*c*) Pardon Monsieur, savez-vous où est l'office du tourisme?

(*d*) Pardon Mademoiselle, je ne suis pas d'ici ... euh il y a un centre commercial à Chatou?

4    Choose the right answer.

Jane habite à Brighton?
en Brighton?
de Brighton?

Elle et son mari passent leurs vacances    en France
au France
France

mais_ils préfèrent   Allemagne.
                  l'Allemagne.
                  en Allemagne.

Jane est restée une semaine  à Berlin   et trois jours Bonn.
                            Berlin               au Bonn.
                            en Berlin         à Bonn.

L'an prochain (*next year*) elle va  au Danemark  où elle a des
                                Danemark      amis.
                                en Danemark

Son mari va souvent  en Etats-Unis    et  au Japon
                    aux Etats-Unis      en Japon pour
                    les Etats-Unis      Japon

pour ses affaires (*his business*).
Il est homme d'affaires et travaille  en Londres.
                                   à Londres
                                   Londres

5  Can you find the 11 European countries hidden in the wordsearch below? You can read horizontally or vertically and either forwards or backwards.

| N | I | O | M | Y | T | G | S | X | L |
|---|---|---|---|---|---|---|---|---|---|
| S | E | N | G | A | M | E | L | L | A |
| Y | D | O | E | C | N | A | R | F | G |
| U | A | R | N | Z | I | W | E | S | U |
| L | N | V | G | T | T | Í | D | L | T |
| Q | E | E | A | L | A | F | E | Y | R |
| Z | M | G | P | T | L | U | U | Z | O |
| Z | A | E | S | U | I | S | S | E | P |
| E | R | R | E | T | E | L | G | N | A |
| Y | K | E | U | Q | I | G | L | E | B |

**6** Les chiffres   Numbers
Test yourself. Pick a number and say it aloud in French.
Check your answers at the back of the book ➡ **P.** 212 where
all the numbers are listed. Repeat the exercise over a
number of days and see if you can improve your performance.

| 72 | 24 | 80 | 92 | 65 | 43 | 75 | 61 |
|----|----|----|----|----|----|----|----|
| 76 | 68 | 15 | 66 | 17 | 96 | 87 | 70 |
| 19 | 21 | 49 | 55 | 65 | 56 | 13 | 77 |

**7** Look at the **centre commercial de Chatou** and fill in the
blanks using the words from the list overleaf.

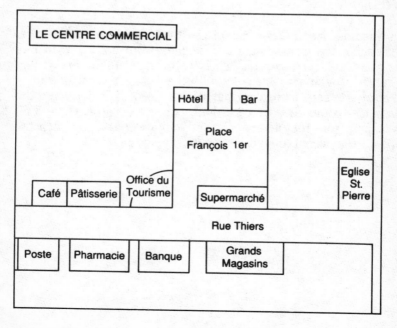

(a) **La poste est .......... café.**

(b) **Le café est .......... pâtisserie.**

(c) **L'office du tourisme est .......... la place François ler.**

(d) **La pharmacie est .......... la poste et la banque.**

(e) **L'église est .......... la rue Thiers.**

(f) **Les .......... sont en face du supermarché.**

(g) **Le .......... est à côté de l'hôtel.**

(h) **La .......... est entre le café et l'office du tourisme.**

(i) **La pharmacie est .......... Thiers.**

(j) **Le supermarché est .......... François ler.**

| |
|---|
| à côté de la |
| en face du |
| dans la rue |
| entre |
| grands magasins |
| pâtisserie |
| sur la place |
| au coin de |
| au bout de |
| bar |

## Test

In this unit, **Petit Test** is replaced by a revision of the last six dialogues: try translating the dialogues from units 1 to 6 into English and then from English retranslate them orally into French. Check your answers with the book. You might like to record yourself, imagining that you're French. If you have the cassette, compare your recording with the original. How different is it from the original? Try in your recording to match the speed, the accent and intonations on the cassette.

# 7

## C'EST COMMENT?
### *What is it like?*

## In this unit you will learn

- how to describe things and people
- how to say precisely what you want
- how to compare people and objects
- colours

## Avant de commencer

In Unit 2 you've already seen how to ask for things using just a few words. Getting precisely what you need may involve giving a few more details. This unit will provide you with some of the keywords you'll need to describe what you are looking for, specifying colours, materials, quantities, prices, etc. There is a lot of new vocabulary in this unit, appearing in the sections **Mots-clefs, Explications** and **Activités.** It will be useful to you when doing Unit 11 which concentrates on the topic of shopping in France.

## Essayez

Fill in the blanks in the sentences below with some of the prepositions you met in the last unit.

1 Les fleurs sont ....... (*in*) le vase.

2 Le croissant est ....... (*on*) l'assiette.

3 Le journal est ....... (*between*) le vase et l'assiette.

4 Le jus d'orange est ....... (*next to the*) journal.

5 La carte postale est ....... (*under*) l'assiette.

6 Les clefs sont ....... (*in front of*) le jus de fruit.

7 Les aspirines sont ....... (*behind*) le vase.

# Mots-clefs

## A dire

| | |
|---|---|
| qu'est ce que vous_avez comme ... souvenirs, cadeaux? | what do you have in the way of ... souvenirs, presents? |
| qu'est-ce que c'est? | what is it? |
| vous_avez autre chose? | do you have anything else? |
| ça fait combien? | how much is it? |
| c'est de quelle couleur? | what colour is it? |
| je cherche quelque chose de/d' grand/moyen/petit | I'm looking for something big/medium/small |
| un peu plus grand | a little bigger |
| un peu moins cher | a little less expensive |
| meilleur marché | cheaper |
| spécial/différent | special/different |
| je cherche quelque chose pour réparer, ouvrir | I'm looking for something to repair, open |
| je vais prendre le plus petit | I'll take the smallest |
| rouge, blanc, vert, marron, bleu jaune | red, white, green, brown, blue yellow |
| qui est-ce? | who is it? |
| c'est_une personne sympathique | he/she is a nice person |
| c'est_un jeune homme français | he's a young French man |
| c'est_une jeune fille anglaise | she's a young English girl |
| c'est quelqu'un de grand/petit/ gros/mince | it's someone tall/small/ big/thin |
| il porte des lunettes de soleil | he wears/is wearing sun glasses |
| il a les cheveux noirs et raides | he has black, straight hair |
| elle porte une chemise unie | she wears/is wearing a plain shirt |
| elle a les yeux marron | she has brown eyes |

## A comprendre

| | |
|---|---|
| je vais vous montrer | I'll show you |
| et avec ceci (ça)? | is that all? (lit. and with this?) |
| on s'occupe de vous? | are you being served? |
| il vaut mieux prendre | you should take (lit. it is better to take) |

# Dialogue

Jane fait des courses dans un grand magasin de Chatou. *Jane is shopping in a department store in Chatou.*
She is looking for something special to bring back to her mother in the UK.

Listen to the tape once or read the dialogue in the book: What does Jane buy? How much is it? Listen a second time: What was the price of the other items? Describe what Jane buys.

Vendeuse     Vous désirez?

Jane     Je cherche un souvenir ... euh quelque chose de spécial pour ma mère en Angleterre.

Vendeuse     Oui, très bien. Je peux vous montrer des **foulards de soie** avec des **scènes typiquement** françaises. (*the shop assistant gets them out*)

Jane     Oh, ils sont très **jolis** et les couleurs sont vraiment superbes. C'est combien?

Vendeuse     Bon, les grands **avec motif** font 350 francs. Les moyens **unis** font 250 francs et les petits **coûtent** 200 francs.

Jane     Je peux voir **ceux qui** sont à 200 francs?

Vendeuse     Mais bien sûr. **Certains** sont jaunes et bleus, **d'autres** représentent les monuments **célèbres** de Paris.

Jane     Je préfère les grands mais ils sont trop chers (*she hesitates.*) Je vais prendre **ce petit** à 200 francs avec les Champs-Elysées. **Je crois que** ma mère **sera** très **contente**. Vous pouvez me **faire un paquet-cadeau**, s'il vous plaît?

Vendeuse     Oui, un instant ... **si vous voulez bien me suivre?** (*after a while ... when the present is wrapped up*) Et maintenant vous **payez à la caisse**.

Jane     Ah bon, merci bien, Madame.

| | |
|---|---|
| **foulard (m)** | scarf |
| **de soie** | made of silk |
| **scène (f)** | scene |
| **typiquement** | typically |
| **joli(e)** | pretty |
| **avec motif** | with pattern |
| **uni (-e)** | plain |
| **coûtent** | cost |
| **ceux qui ...** | the ones which ... |
| **certains ... d'autres** | some ... others |
| **célèbres** | famous |
| **ce petit** | this small one |

| je crois que | I believe that |
| sera contente | will be pleased |
| faire un paquet-cadeau | to gift-wrap |
| si vous voulez bien me suivre | would you come this way? |
| payer à la caisse | pay at the till |

 —————— **Explications** ——————

## 1 Ce, cet, cette, ces *This, that, these, those*

**Ce, cet, cette** all mean *this* or *that*; **ces** means *these* or *those*.
**Ce** comes before masculine singular nouns, **cet** before masculine
singular nouns beginning with a vowel or silent **h**, **cette** before
feminine singular nouns and **ces** before plural nouns.

|  | *masculine* | *masc. (before a vowel or silent* **h***)* | *feminine* |
|---|---|---|---|
| *singular* | ce | cet | cette |
| *plural* | ces | ces | ces |

| **ce foulard** | *this/that scarf* |
| **cet_homme** | *this/that man* |
| **cette femme** | *this/that woman* (**femme** *pronounced 'fam' also means wife*) |
| **ces_enfants** | *these/those children* |

## 2 Saying precisely what you want

You already know how to ask for something ➡ **P** 48: **je voudrais
cette bouteille**. This is the most general way of asking for
things, but you may want to give more information.

(*a*) **How much?** Expressions of quantity are linked with **de**:

| Combien d'enfants? | *How many children?* |
| beaucoup d'enfants | *lots of children* |
| un verre **de** vin | *a glass of wine* |
| un boîte **de** haricots | *a tin of beans* |

(*b*) **Made of what?** You can also use **de** to say what things are
made of:

| une chemise **de** coton | *a cotton shirt* |

une robe **de** soie       *a silk dress*

(*c*) **What kind?** Add adjectives to describe in more detail:

un verre de vin **rouge**       *a glass of red wine*

une boîte de **petits** pois **français**       *a tin of French peas*

un kilo de raisins **noirs**       *a kilo of black grapes*

(*d*) **What's in/on it?** Special features such as patterns, flavours key ingredients are linked with **à:**

un yaourt **à** l'abricot       *an apricot yoghurt*

un sandwich **au** fromage       *a cheese sandwich*

une glace **à la** vanille       *a vanilla ice-cream*

une tarte **aux** pommes       *an apple pie*

�֍ Don't forget to change the **à** to **au** or to **aux** if the following noun is masculine or plural.

(*e*) **With/without.** Put **avec** (*with*) or **sans** (*without*) in front of what you want or don't want:

une chambre **avec** télévision       *a room with (a) television*

un hôtel **sans** parking       *a hotel without car park*

## 3   How adjectives work

As explained in ➡️**P** 30 adjectives change according to what they are describing; they may take masculine, feminine or plural forms.

| | *masculine* | *feminine* |
|---|---|---|
| *singular* | petit | petite |
| *plural* | petits | petites |

ce **petit** foulard       *this little scarf*

c'est une **bonne** école       *it's a good school*

les **petits** pois sont **verts**       *peas are green*

avec des scènes **françaises**       *with French scenes*

(*a*) Adding an **-e** to the masculine (if it has not already got an **-e**) to form the feminine, often changes the pronunciation as in **petit** (m), **petite** (f), but not always e.g. **noir** (m), **noire** (f), **bleu** (m), **bleue** (f). The **-s** in the plural is not sounded.

(*b*) **Brun** is used almost exclusively to refer to the colour of someone's hair or complexion. For most brown objects, use **marron,** which is an invariable form.

(*c*) A few adjectives have two masculine forms: the second one is used in front of nouns beginning with a vowel or silent **h:**

| | |
|---|---|
| le **nouveau** garçon | *the new boy* |
| le **nouvel** élève | *the new pupil* |
| le **vieux** port | *the old harbour* |
| le **vieil** hôtel | *the old hotel* |

(*d*) Here are some common adjectives with irregular endings. You will pick up others as you go along.

| masc. 1 | masc. 2 | fem. | fem. pl. | masc. pl. |
|---|---|---|---|---|
| beau | bel | belle | belles | beaux |
| nouveau | nouvel | nouvelle | nouvelles | nouveaux |
| vieux | vieil | vieille | vieilles | vieux |

(*e*) Adjectives are usually placed after the noun:

| | |
|---|---|
| un café **noir** | *a black coffee* |
| une bière **allemande** | *a German beer* |

except with common ones such as: **petit** (*small*), **bon(ne)** (*good*), **beau** (*beautiful*), **grand** (*tall*), **jeune** (*young*), **vieux** (*old*), **mauvais** (*bad*), **joli** (*beautiful*), **tout** (*all*).

| | |
|---|---|
| un **grand** café | *a large coffee* |
| une **bonne** bière | *a good beer* |

(*f*) If there are two or more adjectives after the noun they are linked with **et:**

| | |
|---|---|
| un homme **grand et mince** | *a tall, slim man* |
| des cheveux **blonds et longs** | *long, blonde hair* |

## 4  Making comparisons

To say that something is *more … than*/or *less … than* use:

**plus … que**        *more … than*
**moins … que**       *less … than*

**La train est plus rapide que la voiture.**
*The train is faster than the car.*

**Il est moins grand que moi.**
*He's less tall than I.*

✳ The **-s** of **plus** is not pronounced except in the following cases:
(a) before a vowel or silent **h**, **-s** is sounded **z: plus_âgé**
(b) whenever the word means *plus* (+), **-s** is sounded **s:**
    **Il y a du beurre plus du lait dans la recette.**
    *There is some butter plus some milk in the recipe.*
(c) when it is followed directly by **que** to produce **plus que** *more than*, (**-s** is sounded **s**):

    **Il travaille plus que moi.**
    *He works more than I.*

To say that something/someone is better, use **meilleur (e)**; to say that you do something better use **mieux:**

**Le film est meilleur que le livre.**
*The film is better than the book.*

**Elle parle français mieux que moi.**
*She speaks French better than I.*

## ✳ *Learning to cope with uncertainty*

1  Don't over-use your dictionary.
   When reading a text in the foreign language, don't be tempted to look up every word you don't know. Underline the words you do not understand and read the passage several times, concentrating on trying to get the gist of the passage. If after the third time there are still words which prevent you getting the general meaning of the passage, look them up in the dictionary.

2  Don't panic if you don't understand.
   If at some point you feel you don't understand what you are

told, don't panic or give up listening. Either try and guess what is being said and keep following the conversation or, if you cannot, isolate the expression or words you haven't understood and have them explained to you. The speaker might paraphrase them and the conversation will carry on.

3   Keep talking.
    The best way to improve your fluency in the foreign language is to talk every time you have the opportunity to do so: keep the conversation flowing and don't worry about the mistakes. If you get stuck for a particular word, don't let the conversation stop; paraphrase or replace the unknown word with one you do know, even if you have to simplify what you want to say. As a last resort use the word from your own language and pronounce it in the foreign accent.

# Activités

1   **A la gare routière:** fill in the blanks with **ce, cet, cette** or **ces.**

Touriste    Pardon Monsieur, ..... autobus va à Quimper?

Homme       Oui, Madame, tous ..... autobus vont à Quimper.

Touriste    Je voudrais partir ..... matin. A quelle heure partent les autobus?

Homme       Bon, ..... deux autobus partent pour Quimper ..... matin. Le premier part à 8h30 et arrive à 12h et le deuxième part à 9h15 et arrive à 13h15 ..... après-midi.

Touriste    Très bien. Je veux rentrer ..... nuit. A quelle heure rentre le dernier autobus de Quimper?

Homme       Alors ..... semaine, le dernier bus quitte Quimper à 20h30.

Touriste    Merci, Monsieur.

2   Using the grid below and M. Durand's description as a model, write down in a few sentences what Mme Durand, and Jane

look like. Make sure that the adjectives agree with the nouns they describe. Check the vocabulary with the drawings below or in the vocabulary list on ➡ **P.** 213. Then write a few sentences describing yourself.

| | M. Durand | Mme Durand | Jane |
|---|---|---|---|
| sexe | homme | femme | femme |
| âge | 40 ans | 35 ans | 23 ans |
| cheveux | noirs/raides | blonds/longs | châtains/courts |
| yeux | marron | verts | bleus |
| taille | 1m78 | 1m70 | 1m62 |
| poids | 79 kg | 65 kg | 55 kg |
| signes particuliers | moustache | lunettes rouges | — |
| vêtements | costume bleu marine, cravate jaune, chaussures noires | ensemble vert uni, chemise blanche, chaussures légères | jean bleu pâle, pullover blanc, bottes blanches |

Monsieur Durand a 40 ans, les cheveux noirs et raides. Il a les yeux marron; il fait 1 mètre 78 et pèse 79 kg. Il a une moustache. Il porte un costume bleu marine, une cravate jaune et des chaussures noires.

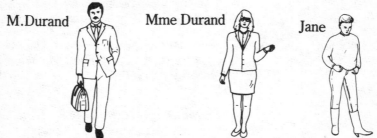

M.Durand          Mme Durand          Jane

Look at **Réponses** at the back of the book and check that what you've written is correct. Using as a model **M.Durand's** description on the cassette, read aloud what you've written.

**3** How would you ask for all the items on the list? The words in the box will help, though they aren't all there!

| | |
|---|---|
| baba (m)      vanille (f)<br>petits   pois (m)<br>vin (m)<br>pommes (f) fromage (m)<br>citron (m)<br>sucre (m)<br>sandwich (m) poulet (m)<br>verre (m)      lait (m)<br>tarte (f)      rhum (m)<br>glace (f)<br>café (m)    sorbet (m)<br>boîte (f)    bouteille (f) | (a)  *a tin of French peas*<br>(b)  *an apple tart*<br>(c)  *a rhum baba*<br>(d)  *a vanilla ice-cream*<br>(e)  *a lemon sorbet*<br>(f)  *a big glass of red wine*<br>(g)  *a white coffee without sugar*<br>(h)  *a chicken at 45.00 francs*<br>(i)  *a small black coffee*<br>(j)  *a cheese sandwich*<br>(k)  *a bottle of milk* |

4  Sally is spending Christmas and New Year in France with a French family. She writes to her friend Isabelle. Can you fill the gaps with the words from the list below? You may have to look up some of the words in the vocabulary on ➡ P. 213.

(a) ........ Isabelle,
Je suis depuis une semaine avec la (b) ....... Guise. Ici (c) ....... le monde est très (d) ....... et je passe de très (e) ....... vacances. La maison est (f) ....... et (g) ....... . Je fais de (h) ....... promenades presque tous les (i) ....... . La cuisine française est (j) ....... que la cuisine (k) ....... et je mange trop. Je parle (l) ....... le français maintenant. Je retourne chez moi la semaine (m) ....... .

Joyeux Noël et Bonne Année
Sally

| | | | | |
|---|---|---|---|---|
| meilleure | longues | tout | jours | confortable |
| prochaine | famille | bonnes | grande | anglaise  mieux |
| chère | sympathique | | | |

5  You are at a **café** with four of your friends. The waiter arrives and you order (**vous commandez**):

| Garçon | Bonjour, Messieurs-Dames. Qu'est-ce que vous désirez? |
|---|---|
| (a) You | *A large black coffee.* |
| Garçon | Un grand café, oui.... |
| (b) You | *Two small beers.* |
| Garçon | Oui. |
| (c) You | *And a small white coffee.* |
| Garçon | Alors un petit crème, deux grandes bières et un petit café noir, c'est ça? |
| (d) You | *No. Two small beers and a large black coffee.* |
| Garçon | Bon très bien. Excusez-moi. |
| (e) You | *Have you got some croissants?* |
| Garçon | Vous_en voulez combien? |
| (f) You | *Say you want four.* |
| Garçon | Très bien, Monsieur. |

## ✔ Petit test

Now test yourself to see how well you remember the information in Units 6 and 7.

1 How would you say:
   (a) at the end of the street
   (b) take the road to Lille
2 **Il faut prendre** means:
   (a) you can take
   (b) you must take
   (c) you take
3 **Vous allez tout droit** means:
   (a) you go straight on
   (b) you turn right
   (c) you take the second on the left
4 How would you say:
   Do you have anything else?
   What colour is it?
   I'll take the smallest.

# 8

## VOUS AIMEZ LE SPORT?
### *Do you like sport?*

### *In this unit you will learn*

- how to ask and talk about likes and dislikes
- how to say what you and others do as a hobby
- how to talk about the weather

### *Avant de commencer*

Once you know a French person well enough you'll find yourself wanting to express your likes and dislikes and talk about your hobbies; here are the structures you'll need:

| | |
|---|---|
| **j'adore** | *I adore, I love* |
| **j'aime beaucoup** | *I like very much* |
| **je n'aime pas** | *I don't like* |
| **je déteste** | *I hate* |
| **je joue** | *I play* |
| **je fais** | *I do* |

Talking about the weather is a particularly important aspect of the British way of life; you may find it useful to enquire about the weather forecast if you are planning some kind of outdoor activity.

### ✔ Essayez

You are in a shop in France looking for a corkscrew. However you don't know the French word for it. How would you say that you're looking for something to open bottles of wine?

*You* ...............................................................................
Shopkeeper  Ah! Vous voulez un tire-bouchon (*a corkscrew*)?

## Mots-clefs

### A dire

| | |
|---|---|
| qu'est-ce que vous faites comme sport? | what sport do you do? |
| qu'est-ce que vous_avez comme loisirs? | what hobbies do you have? |
| vous_aimez faire du sport? | do you like doing sport? |
| quelle est votre cuisine préférée? | which cooking do you prefer? |
| j'adore aller au restaurant | I love going to the restaurant |
| mon sport préféré est la natation | swimming is my favourite sport |
| j'aime (beaucoup) ... | I like (very much) |
|    jouer au squash |    playing squash |
|    la cuisine française |    French cooking |
|    écouter des disques |    playing records |
|    regarder la télévision |    watching television |
| je n'aime pas ... | I don't like |
|    la planche à voile |    windsurfing |
|    la musique classique |    classical music |
|    me promener à pied |    going for a walk |
| je déteste faire la cuisine | I hate cooking |
| je joue au tennis | I play tennis |
| je joue du piano | I play the piano |
| je préfère l'équitation | I prefer riding |

### A comprendre

| | |
|---|---|
| moi, ce que j'aime c'est | what I really like is |
|    sortir avec mes_amis |    going out with my friends |
| moi, ce que je déteste c'est | what I really dislike is |
|    la viande saignante |    rare meat |

### Le temps  *The weather*

| | |
|---|---|
| quel temps fait-il? | what's the weather like? |
| il fait beau, mauvais | the weather is fine, bad |
| il fait chaud, froid | it is hot, cold |
| le soleil brille | the sun shines |
| il pleut | it's raining |
| il neige | it's snowing |

# Dialogue

Jane parle de sports et de loisirs avec les Durand.
*Jane and the Durands are talking about sport and hobbies.*
Listen to the tape or read the dialogue once and then answer the following questions: What's Mrs Durand's favourite hobby? What sports does Mr Durand do? Listen or read a second time: What does Mrs Durand like to cook?   How many times a week does Mr Durand play squash?

| | |
|---|---|
| Jane | Mme Durand, qu'est-ce que vous_avez comme loisirs? |
| Mme Durand | Moi, j'adore faire la cuisine, **surtout** la cuisine française. |
| Jane | Et dans la cuisine française, quels sont vos **plats favoris?** |
| Mme Durand | Eh bien, j'aime beaucoup faire tous les plats_en sauce, en particulier **le boeuf bourguignon** ou **le coq au vin. Vous savez,** mon mari aime bien manger et bien **boire;** il est très gourmet et **il apprécie** ma cuisine..... alors **ça fait plaisir!** |
| Jane | Et vous, Monsieur Durand, vous_aimez faire la cuisine? |
| M. Durand | Moi, **je laisse la cuisine** à ma femme. Elle la fait très bien. Je préfère le sport. |
| Jane | Quels sports **pratiquez**-vous? |
| M. Durand | Je joue au squash deux fois par semaine après mon travail et **quand j'ai le temps,** je fais de la natation avec les_enfants le samedi, à la piscine de Chatou. |
| Mme Durand | Tu aimes bien aussi faire de la planche à voile **en_été.** |
| M. Durand | Oui, **c'est vrai** j'aime beaucoup la planche à voile surtout quand_il y a du **vent** mais je déteste en faire quand_il fait froid ou quand_il pleut. |
| Mme Durand | Et vous Jane, qu'est-ce que vous faites comme sport? |
| Jane | Oh moi, je pratique un peu tous les sports: le badminton, le tennis et quelquefois l'équitation mais je n'ai pas beaucoup de temps pour faire du sport. |

| | |
|---|---|
| **surtout** | mainly |
| **plats favoris** | favourite dishes |
| **le boeuf bourguignon** | beef stew with wine |
| **le coq au vin** | chicken cooked in wine |
| **vous savez** | you know |
| **boire** | to drink |
| **il apprécie** | he appreciates |
| **ça fait plaisir** | it is a pleasure |
| **je laisse la cuisine** | I leave the cooking |
| **pratiquer** | to do |
| **quand j'ai le temps** | when I have the time |
| **c'est vrai** | it's true |
| **en_été** | in summer |
| **le vent** | the wind |

## Explications

### 1 Asking and saying what you do as a hobby

In French to answer questions such as **qu'est-ce vous faites comme sport?** *what do you do in the way of sport?* or **qu'est-ce que vous_avez comme loisirs?** *what are your hobbies?* use **je fais de** … or **je joue à** if it is a game. If you play a musical instrument use **je joue de.**

> Je fais **de la** natation et **du** surf.
> *I swim and I surf.*
> Je joue **au** tennis et **à la** pétanque.
> *I play tennis and petanque* (kind of bowls played in the South of France).
> Je joue **du** piano et **de la** trompette.
> *I play the piano and the trumpet.*

### 2 Likes and dislikes

To express your tastes and feelings, you can use **aimer** (*to like, to love*) or the two extremes **adorer** and **détester:**

| | |
|---|---|
| **j'adore** | aller au restaurant |
| **j'aime (beaucoup)** | jouer au squash |
| | cuisiner |
| | écouter des disques |
| | regarder la télé |

| je n'aime pas | la planche à voile |
| | la musique classique |
| | me promener à pied |
| je déteste | faire la cuisine |

To say what you like/dislike doing, add the infinitive after **j'aime, j'adore, je déteste, je préfère: je déteste faire de la bicyclette:** *I hate cycling.*

Include the article **le, la, les** when making generalisations.

> J'aime **les** fromages français.   *I like French cheese.*
> L'histoire est plus_intéressante que **la** géographie.
> *History is more interesting than geography.*

When stating likes/dislikes you will often hear French people use the following structures:

> Moi, ce que j'aime c'est sortir avec mes amis.
> Moi, ce que je déteste c'est la viande saignante.

## 3  Pronouns: le, la, les   *it, him, her, them*

The pronouns **le** (*it, him*), **la** (*it, her*), **les** (*them*) are used to avoid unnecessary repetitions of nouns; they are placed before the verb to which they refer.

> Vous connaissez M. Durand? Oui, je **le** connais.
> *Do you know Mr Durand? Yes I know **him**.*
> Vous prenez la carte postale? Oui, je **la** prends.
> *Are you taking the postcard? Yes I'm taking **it**.*
> Vous_achetez ces foulards? Oui, je **les**_achète.
> *Are you buying these scarfs? Yes I'm buying **them**.*
> Vous_aimez le thé? Oui, je **l'**aime.
> *Do you like tea? Yes, I like **it**.*

**L'** replaces **le** or **la** when the next word starts with a vowel or silent **h**. In a negative sentence, **l', le, la, les** come between the **ne** or **n'** and the verb:

> Vous préférez le tennis? Non, **je ne le préfère pas.**
> *Do you prefer tennis? No, I don't prefer it.*

## 4  More negatives

You've already seen ➡️ 📰 30 how to make a statement negative in French, using **ne … pas**:

| | |
|---|---|
| Je **n'**ai pas **d'**enfants. | *I have no children.* |

There are other negatives you can use:

| | |
|---|---|
| **ne … plus** | *no more/no longer* |
| **ne … rien** | *nothing* |
| **ne … jamais** | *never* |
| **ne … que** | *only* |

| | |
|---|---|
| Je **n'**ai **plus** de vin. | *I have no more wine.* |
| Il **ne** veut **rien**. | *He wants nothing.* |
| Il **n'**a **jamais** d'argent. | *He never has any money.* |
| Je **n'**ai **que** 10 francs. | *I've only got 10 francs.* |

## 5 *To know*: when to use 'savoir', when to use 'connaître'

There are two verbs for *knowing*: **savoir** and **connaître**.

(*a*) Use **savoir** (on its own) to say that you *know* or don't *know* a fact.

| | |
|---|---|
| **Je sais à quelle heure part le train.** | *I know when the train leaves.* |
| **Je ne sais pas où est l'arrêt d'autobus.** | *I don't know where the bus stop is.* |

(*b*) Use **savoir** followed by the infinitive to say that you *know how to do* something:

| | |
|---|---|
| **Je sais faire la cuisine.** | *I know how to cook.* |
| **Vous savez faire du ski?** | *Do you know how to ski?* |

(*c*) **Connaître** is used to say that you *know people and places*.

| | |
|---|---|
| **Je connais Paris.** | *I know Paris.* |
| **Depuis combien de temps est-ce que vous le connaissez?** | *How long have you known him?* |

## 6 *What's the weather like?* Quel temps fait-il?

The easiest way to talk about the weather is to start with **il fait**:

| | |
|---|---|
| **il fait beau, mauvais** | *it's fine, the weather is bad* |
| **il fait froid, chaud** | *it's cold, hot* |
| **il fait du vent** | *it's windy* |
| **il fait du brouillard** | *it's foggy* |

| | |
|---|---|
| **il pleut** | *it's raining* |
| **il neige** | *it's snowing* |
| **le soleil brille** | *the sun is shining* |

**Pratiquez:** and now how would you answer the question: Quel temps fait-il aujourd'hui? **Aujourd'hui il …**

## ✳ *Learn from errors*

1 Don't let errors interfere with getting your message across. Making errors is part of any normal learning process but some people get so worried that they won't say anything unless they are sure that what they say is correct. This leads to a vicious circle as the less they say, the less practice they get and the more mistakes they make.

2 Note the seriousness of errors. Many errors are not serious as they do not affect the meaning; for example if you use the wrong article (**le** for **la**) or wrong pronoun (**je l'achète** for **je les achète**) or wrong adjective ending (**blanc** for **blanche**). So concentrate on getting your message across and learn from your mistakes.

## Activités

1 Roger Burru has agreed to take part in a survey and is ready to talk about himself. Can you ask him in French the questions on the right? Then listen to the whole survey on the cassette and check your answers (or check them in **Réponses**).

| | | |
|---|---|---|
| (a) Nom | Roger Burru | What's your name? |
| (b) Age | 35 | How old are you? |
| (c) Marié(e) | oui | Are you married? |
| (d) Enfant(s) | non | Have you any children? |
| (e) Profession | professeur | What's your job? |
| (f) Depuis …. | 10 ans | Since when? |
| (g) Adresse | Lille | Where do you live? |
| (h) Sport | natation | What sports do you do? |
| (i) Loisir | faire la cuisine | What are your hobbies? |

Now it's your turn to take part in a survey. Can you answer in French the same questions? (the answers are not included in **Réponses**).

2 On the tape you will hear Cloé talk about her likes and dislikes. Listen carefully and put a tick in the appropriate box below:

|  | adore | aime beaucoup | n'aime pas | déteste |
|---|---|---|---|---|
| (a) Playing volleyball | ☐ | ☐ | ☐ | ☐ |
| (b) Working on Sundays | ☐ | ☐ | ☐ | ☐ |
| (c) Going out in the evenings | ☐ | ☐ | ☐ | ☐ |
| (d) Watching T.V. | ☐ | ☐ | ☐ | ☐ |
| (e) Listening to music | ☐ | ☐ | ☐ | ☐ |
| (f) Shopping | ☐ | ☐ | ☐ | ☐ |
| (g) Eating out | ☐ | ☐ | ☐ | ☐ |
| (h) Cooking | ☐ | ☐ | ☐ | ☐ |

Now it's your turn to tell Cloé what you like and dislike. Can you think of any more likes/dislikes you could add to the box?

3 Answer the following questions using the example as a model. You may have to revise the verbs ending in **-er** → **P.** 29, **-ir** and **-re** → **P.** 50, **prendre** → **P.** 52 and **faire** → **P.** 52.

(a) Vous achetez les oranges?        Oui nous les achetons.
(b) Vous prenez le train?        Oui, je ...
(c) Je connais M. Tordu?        Oui, vous ...
(d) Elle a les timbres?        Oui, elle ...
(e) Vous avez l'adresse de        Oui, je ...
Claude?
(f) Ils aiment la natation?        Oui, ils ...
(g) Vous faites la cuisine?        Oui, je ...
(h) Vous attendez l'autobus?        Oui, nous ...
(i) Il regarde la télé?        Oui, il ...
(j) Vous écoutez les disques?        Oui, nous ...

4 Find the right ending for each sentence:

(a) Il ne va ...        (i) jamais de sport.
(b) Il n'achète ...        (ii) plus car il est trop gros.

(c) Elle ne veut ...          (iii) pas du piano.
(d) Il ne mange ...           (iv) rien_acheter.
(e) Elle ne boit ...          (v) qu'une fille.
(f) Je ne porte ...           (vi) plus comme secrétaire.
(g) Il ne joue ...            (vii) pas de timbres.
(h) Elle ne travaille ...    (viii) jamais à l'église.
(i) Il n'a ...                (ix) que de l'eau.
(j) Elle ne fait ...          (x) plus de lunettes.

**5** Listen to the weather report while looking at the map; Some of the statements below are true (**vrai**), others are false (**faux**); Put an x in the appropriate boxes.

|  | vrai | faux |
|---|---|---|
| (a) Il fait beau à Newcastle. | ☐ | ☐ |
| (b) A Brighton, il pleut. | ☐ | ☐ |
| (c) Il pleut à Calais. | ☐ | ☐ |
| (d) Le soleil brille à Nice. | ☐ | ☐ |
| (e) Il pleut à Strasbourg. | ☐ | ☐ |
| (f) Il fait froid en Espagne. | ☐ | ☐ |
| (g) Il fait du vent à Malaga. | ☐ | ☐ |
| (h) Il fait très chaud en Italie. | ☐ | ☐ |
| (i) Il fait du vent à Rome. | ☐ | ☐ |
| (j) En Suisse il fait chaud. | ☐ | ☐ |
| (k) Il neige à Ostende. | ☐ | ☐ |
| (l) Le soleil brille à Bruxelles. | ☐ | ☐ |

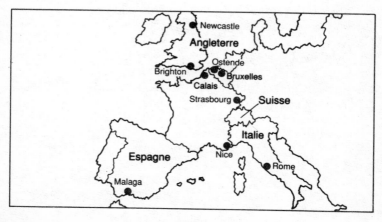

## ✔ Petit test

Check how well you've understood and remembered Units 7 and 8 with this test. How would you say:

1   I play squash better than Fabrice.
2   France is bigger than England.
3   She has glasses and long hair.
4   I'm looking for something to mend my car.
5   I like squash but I prefer playing tennis.
6   I like French cooking very much.

✳ Remember that French people talk about **le** squash, **la** France, l'Angleterre, **la** cuisine française, while the English do not use the article.

# 9

## QU'EST-CE QU'IL FAUT FAIRE?
### What should I do?

### In this unit you will learn

- a few useful linking words
- how to ask for assistance
- how to use **pouvoir** and **vouloir**
- how to give and understand instructions

### Avant de commencer

This unit prepares you to cope with difficulties you may encounter in France. It gives you the few structures you need to let people know that you're having a problem: **je suis perdu, je ne comprends pas, la machine ne marche pas,** and also to ask for help: **vous pouvez me montrer? qu'est-ce qu'il faut faire?** (see **Mots-clefs**).

### ✓ Essayez

1 How would you ask someone politely to:
   (a) repeat
   (b) speak more slowly
2 How would you answer the question:
   Quel temps fait-il aujourd'hui?

# — Mots-clefs —

## A dire

| | |
|---|---|
| pardon Monsieur, Madame ... | excuse me |
| je suis perdu | I'm, lost |
| je ne sais pas ... | I don't know ... |
| je ne comprends pas ... | I don't understand ... |
| vous pouvez m'aider, s'il vous plaît? | can you help me please? |
| qu'est-ce qu'il faut faire? | what must I/we do? |
| la machine ne marche pas | the machine does not work |
| excusez-moi de vous déranger | sorry to disturb you |
| d'abord | firstly |
| et puis | and then |
| après ça | after that |
| finalement | finally |

## A comprendre

| | |
|---|---|
| il faut introduire ... | you must insert ... |
| il faut vérifier le niveau d'huile | you have to check the oil level |
| vous devez composter le billet | you must date-stamp the ticket |
| je vais m'en occuper | I'll attend to it |
| ne pas déranger | do not disturb |
| en dérangement/en panne | out of order (machine, telephone) |
| hors de service | out of order |

# — Dialogues —

Jane est au garage. Elle demande au mécanicien de vérifier le moteur de son auto qui fait un drôle de bruit.
*Jane is at the garage, asking the mechanic to check the engine of her car which is making a strange noise.*

Jane      Ah, bonjour Monsieur. Voilà ... Depuis ce matin il y a un drôle de bruit dans le moteur de ma voiture. Je ne sais pas ce que c'est. Je ne comprends pas, la voiture marche bien mais ...

Mécanicien      Oui, bien sûr! Avez-vous vérifié le niveau d'huile? Le niveau d'eau? Il fait très chaud aujourd'hui et peut-être que **le moteur chauffe trop.**

— 92 —

| Jane | Euh... non. Je ne sais pas ce qu'il faut faire. Vous pouvez vérifier tout ça pour moi, s'il vous plaît? |
| Mécanicien | Bon, allez ... d'accord, **repassez** dans trois heures, je m'en_occupe. |

| le moteur chauffe trop | the engine is heating up too much |
| repassez | come back |

 Jane est sur le quai de la gare. Elle essaie de composter son billet pour le valider mais sans succès. Elle arrête un passant.
*Jane is on the platform at the station. She is trying to date-stamp her ticket but she is having difficulties. She stops a passer-by:*

| Jane | Pardon, Madame, je ne sais pas comment marche cette machine. Vous pouvez m'aider, s'il vous plaît? |
| Passante | Mais oui, Mademoiselle, c'est très facile; il faut introduire votre billet sous **la flèche verte.** |
| Jane | Mais **c'est ce que j'ai fait** et ça ne marche pas. |
| Passante | Alors il faut peut-être tourner le billet **dans l'autre sens?** |
| Jane | (*she hears the click*) Ah, bien, mon billet est composté. Merci, Madame et excusez-moi de vous avoir dérangée. |
| Passante | **De rien,** Mademoiselle. |

| la flèche verte | the green arrow |
| c'est ce que j'ai fait | that's what I've done |
| dans l'autre sens | the other way round |
| de rien | don't mention it (lit. for nothing) |

 —————————— **Explications** ——————————

## 1 Asking for assistance

There are several ways of asking a favour, depending on how polite you want to be and how well you know the person.

The easiest but perhaps least polite way of asking is to use the

verb in the 2nd person plural (i.e. **vous** person) deleting the
**vous**.

> Faites le plein, s'il vous plaît.    *Fill the car up with petrol,*
> *please (lit. make the full,*
> *please).*

A more polite way of asking is to start with **vous pouvez** (*can*
*you*):

> **Vous pouvez** me montrer,    *Can you show me, please?*
> s'il vous plaît?

✳ Some likely answers:

| | |
|---|---|
| Oui, avec plaisir | *Yes, with pleasure* |
| Certainement | *Certainly* |
| D'accord | *OK* |
| Bien sûr | *Of course* |

Like the verbs **aimer, détester, adorer** ➡️P.84, **vous pouvez**
is followed by a verb in the infinitive:

> **Vous pouvez vérifier** le    *Can you check the oil level,*
> niveau d'huile, s'il vous      *please?*
> plaît?

## 2 Two very useful verbs: pouvoir *to be able to,* vouloir *to want*

**Pouvoir** and **vouloir** are two verbs used very frequently in
French:

| **pouvoir** *to be able to, can* | **vouloir** *to want* |
|---|---|
| **je peux** | **je veux** |
| **tu peux** | **tu veux** |
| **il/elle/on peut** | **il/elle/on veut** |
| **nous pouvons** | **nous voulons** |
| **vous pouvez** | **vous voulez** |
| **ils/elles peuvent** | **ils/elles veulent** |

## 3 Giving and understanding instructions

(*a*) The simplest and most commonly used way to give instructions is to use the **vous** or **tu** forms of the present tense:

> Pour téléphoner en Angleterre, **vous composez** le 19, **vous**

**attendez** la tonalité, **vous faites** le 44 puis l'indicatif de la ville.

*To phone England, dial 19, wait for the dialling tone, dial 44 then the local code.*

(*b*) In written instructions a verb is often in the infinitive:

**Introduire** votre billet sous la flèche verte, le **glisser** vers la gauche jusqu'au déclic; si la mention 'tournez votre billet' apparaît, **présenter** l'autre extrémité.

*Insert your ticket under the green arrow and slide it to the left until there is a click; if the sign 'turn your ticket' appears, insert the other end.*

(*c*) **Qu'est-ce qu'il faut..?** To find out what needs to be done use **qu'est-ce qu'il faut** followed by the appropriate verb in the infinitive:

**Qu'est-ce qu'il faut faire** pour composter son billet?
*What do you have to do to date-stamp your ticket?*

(*d*) **Il faut + a verb.** Followed by a verb in the infinitive **il faut** (which is only used in the 3rd person) means any of the following, depending on the context: *it is necessary, I/we/you have to, must, one has to, must*:

| | |
|---|---|
| **Il faut** décrocher l'appareil. | *You must lift the receiver.* |
| **Il faut** attendre la tonalité. | *One must wait for the dialling tone.* |
| **Il faut** composter le billet. | *You must date-stamp your ticket.* |

(*e*) **Il faut + a noun.** Followed by a noun, **il faut** means *you need/one needs/I need*.

| | |
|---|---|
| **Il faut** des pièces de 1 franc pour téléphoner. | *You need 1 franc coins to phone.* |
| **Il me faut** un passeport pour aller en France. | *I need a passport to go to France.* |

## Activités

1 Using the words in the box (see next page) on the right say what is needed in each case.
Practise the questions and answers aloud:

Qu'est-ce qu'il faut
(a) pour ouvrir une bouteille?
(b) pour prendre le train?
(c) pour envoyer une lettre?
(d) pour faire une omelette?
(e) pour jouer au tennis?
(f) pour jouer de la musique?
(g) pour apprendre le français?
(h) pour aller en France?
(i) pour acheter de l'essence?

(i) une station-service
(ii) le livre TY Beginner's French
(iii) une raquette et des balles
(iv) un passeport
(v) un tire-bouchon
(vi) des_oeufs
(vii) un billet
(viii) un_instrument
(ix) un timbre

2 Below is a list of things you need to do to keep fit **pour être en pleine forme.** Match them up with the appropriate verbs on the left. You may need to look up some of the words in the vocabulary list on → P. 213.

Pour être en pleine forme **il faut**
(a) boire            (i) un sport
(b) manger           (ii) les sucreries et le sel
(c) pratiquer        (iii) son travail
(d) dormir           (iv) peu d'alcool
(e) diminuer         (v) beaucoup de légumes et fruits
(f) aimer            (vi) 8 heures par jour

3 Here is a recipe from a children's cookery book. Match the instructions with the corresponding drawings below then answer the questions:

Omelette (pour 4 personnes)
(a) D'abord tu bats 7 oeufs dans un grand bol.
(b) Puis tu poivres et tu sales.
(c) Ensuite tu fais fondre dans la poêle 30 grammes de beurre.
(d) Quand le beurre est chaud, tu verses les oeufs.
(e) Après 3 ou 4 minutes, tu mélanges avec une fourchette.

(*f*) Finalement, quand l'omelette est cuite, tu sers immédiatement.

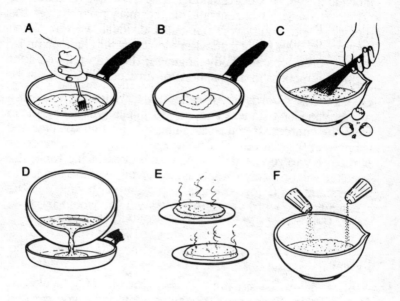

(i)   How many eggs are needed?
(ii)  What do you do after beating the eggs?
(iii) What do you melt in the frying pan?
(iv) When is the egg mixture poured into the bowl?
(v)  What do you use to mix the mixture?

## ✳ *Learn to guess the meaning*

Here are three tips to help your general listening and reading comprehension:

1  Imagine the situation. When listening to the tape try to imagine where the scene is taking place and who the main characters are. Let your experience of the world help you guess the meaning of the conversation e.g. if a dialogue takes place in a snack bar you can predict the kind of vocabulary that is being used.

2 Concentrate on the main part. When watching a foreign film you usually get the meaning of the whole story from a few individual shots. Understanding a foreign conversation or article is similar. Concentrate on the main parts to get the message and don't worry about individual words. When conversing with French speakers look out for clues given by facial expressions and body language; they can tell you a lot about the mood and atmosphere of the conversation.

3 Guess the key words; if you cannot, ask. When there are key words you don't understand, try to guess what they mean from the context. If you're listening to a French speaker and cannot get the gist of a whole passage because of one word or phrase, try to repeat that word with a questioning tone; the speaker will probably paraphrase it, giving you the chance to understand it. If for example you wanted to find out the meaning of the word **voyager** (*to travel*) you would ask **Que veut dire voyager?**

## ✔ Pratiquez

The notice below is situated in the grounds of a sculpture museum in Paris. There are strict rules about what you can and cannot do! What are they? (Check your answers with the translation in **Réponses**.)

---

IL EST EXPRESSEMENT DEFENDU:

– de photographier avec pied ou flash
– de dégrader les sculptures, vases
– de cueillir des fleurs ou des fruits
– d'escalader les sculptures
– de marcher sur le gazon et de monter sur les bancs
– de déjeuner hors de la zone réservée à la cafétéria
– d'introduire des animaux
– de circuler à bicyclette
– de jouer avec des balles et ballons
– de déposer ou de jeter des ordures ailleurs que dans
  des corbeilles à papier.

---

# ✔️ *Grand test*

This test will enable you to check whether you have fully understood and remembered the points covered in Units 1–5. Choose the appropriate word or group of words to complete each sentence or decide which pair of phrases makes sense together. You'll find the answers in **Réponses** at the back of the book.

1 (a) Comment ça va?          Très bien, merci.
  (b) Vous parlez_anglais?
  (c) Parlez plus lentement.

2 Vous_avez
  (a) une pharmacie       s'il vous plaît?
  (b) un timbre
  (c) Messieurs-dames

3 Vous travaillez?
  (a) Oui, j'ai 3 enfants.
  (b) Oui, je suis professeur.
  (c) Non, je ne suis pas marié.

4 (a) Elle habite Londres.       (d) Robert
  (b) Vous_avez des_enfants?     (e) français
  (c) Je m'appelle Jean et vous?    (f) A Londres.

5 (a) Vous_êtes célibataire?      (d) J'habite Brighton
  (b) Ils_ont des_enfants?       (e) Oui, ils_en_ont trois
  (c) Je suis marié?            (f) Oui, j'en_ai deux.

6 Vous_avez quel âge?       (a) Elle est 20 ans
                         (b) J'ai 20 ans
                         (c) J'ai 20.

7 Brighton est au nord de l'Angleterre?
  (a) Oui, en Angleterre.
  (b) Non, au sud de l'Angleterre.
  (c) Non, en France.

8 (a) Je voudrais     une banque près d'ici?
  (b) Il y a
  (c) Nous sommes

(d) au 1er étage
(e) en voiture
(f) à 5 minutes à pied

Oui, il y en_a une

9 C'est
  (a) combien le billet?
  (b) gratuit la brochure?
  (c) fermé?

(d) 30 kilos d'oranges
(e) 30 francs
(f) Dans 30 minutes

10 Il y a un restaurant dans l'hôtel?
  (a) Non, il faut payer.
  (b) Tout près.
  (c) Non, il n'y en_a pas.

11 (a) Les magasins sont ouverts?
  (b) Le magasin est ouvert?
  (c) Les magasins ouvrent quand?

(d) Oui, ils sont ouverts.
(e) Oui, ils sont fermés.
(f) Au bout de la rue.

12 (a) Quand est-ce que tu travailles?
  (b) Est-ce que tu travailles?
  (c) Où est-ce que tu travailles?

Oui je suis (d) dentiste.
         (e) français.
         (f) un dentiste.

13 (a) J'achète     la télévision
  (b) Je préfère
  (c) Je regarde

(d) toutes les 10 minutes
(e) sauf le samedi
(f) tous les jours

14 (a) Est-ce qu'il y a     un métro? (d) Toujours.
  (b) Quand est-ce qu'il y a     (e) Dans 10 minutes.
  (c) Où est     (f) Depuis 1 heure.

15 Vous pouvez répéter s'il vous plaît?
  (a) Oui, bien sûr.
  (b) Non, je suis français.
  (c) Oui, demain.

# 10

## A L'AVENIR

### *In the future*

### *In this unit you will learn*

- how to say what you usually do
- how to say what you need
- how to talk about your future plans
- how to use the pronoun **y**
- two useful verbs **sortir** and **venir**

### *Avant de commencer*

Talking about the future is very easy in French. All you need to do is to use **je vais** followed by the infinitive form of whatever you're going to do. For example to say that you intend to play tennis tomorrow you would say: **demain je vais jouer au tennis.** In this unit you'll learn useful words and expressions to describe your typical day and say what you intend to do in the future.

### Essayez

1  If you see on a telephone box a notice saying **En dérangement** what does it mean?

2  You want to phone to England from a post office in France. How would you ask: *What must I do to phone to England?*

# Mots-clefs

| | |
|---|---|
| demain | tomorrow |
| à l'avenir | in the future |
| qu'est-ce que vous_allez faire? | what are you going to do? |
| je vais ... | I'm going to |
| visiter les monuments_historiques | visit old buildings |
| rendre visite à mes_amis | visit my friends |
| voyager | to travel |
| passer quelques jours ... | spend a few days |
| partir pour_une semaine... | go for a week ... |
| au bord de la mer | to the seaside |
| à la campagne | to the countryside |
| à la montagne | to the mountains |
| en_été, en_automne, en_hiver | in summer, in autumn, in winter |
| au printemps | in spring |
| l'année prochaine | next year |
| en mars | in March |
| pendant le mois d'août | during the month of August |
| j'ai besoin de ... | I need ... |
| j'ai chaud, froid | I'm hot, cold |
| j'ai soif, faim | I'm thirsty, hungry |
| comment passez-vous votre journée? | how do you spend your day? |
| | |
| généralement | generally |
| je me lève | I get up |
| je m'habille | I get dressed |
| je me lave | I wash |
| je prends le petit déjeuner | I have breakfast |
| je pars de la maison | I leave the house |
| j'emmène les_enfants à l'école | I take the children to school |
| je vais chez mes_amis | I go to my friends' house |
| je fais des courses | I do some shopping |
| je prépare le déjeuner | I prepare lunch |
| je vais chercher Jean à la gare | I go and fetch John from the station |
| le soir, je vais_au cinéma | in the evening I go to the cinema |
| je me couche/je vais_au lit | I go to bed |
| quelquefois | sometimes |
| jamais | never |
| toujours | always |
| souvent | often |
| louer | to rent |
| se baigner | to go for a swim |
| surtout | mainly |
| se reposer | to rest |
| lire | to read |
| faire du tourisme | to do some sightseeing |
| à la maison | at home |

——————— **Dialogue** ———————

Les Durand parlent de leurs projets pour les vacances d'été.
*The Durands talk about their summer holiday plans.*

Listen or read at least twice. How long are they going on holiday
for? Where are they going? Note down at least three things M.
and Mme Durand intend to do.

| | |
|---|---|
| Jane | Monsieur et Madame Durand, qu'est-ce que vous_allez faire pour vos vacances cet été? |
| M. Durand | Nous_allons prendre quatre semaines de vacances: une semaine au bord de la mer au mois de juillet et trois semaines **à la montagne** en_août. |
| Jane | Vous_allez rester à l'hôtel ou vous_allez **louer** une maison? |
| Mme Durand | Nous_allons d'abord **passer quelques jours** chez nos amis au bord de la mer. Ils_habitent à 50 km de Nice. Après ça nous_allons dans notre maison de campagne dans le petit village de Puy St Pierre près de Briançon. |
| Jane | Et comment allez-vous passer vos vacances? |
| Mme Durand | Au bord de la mer je vais **me baigner** tous les jours. A Puy St Pierre, je voudrais jouer au tennis, faire de longues promenades et visiter les monuments historiques de la région. |
| M. Durand | Moi, je vais **surtout me reposer, lire** et faire un peu de sport comme le tennis ou jouer à la pétanque avec les_enfants. Le soir, j'espère sortir quelquefois pour voir un bon film ou même aller au restaurant. |
| Rosine | Moi, cette année je ne veux pas **faire de tourisme**. Je préfère rester **à la maison** ou sortir avec mes_amis. |

🔘 —————————— **Explications** ——————————

## 1 Saying what you usually do using some reflexive verbs

When describing your typical day you can't avoid using reflexive verbs i.e. verbs describing things you do to or for yourself such as **se lever** (*to get oneself up*), **s'habiller** (*to get dressed*). While in English the *myself, yourself, himself*, etc... is often dropped, in French the **me, te, se**, etc ... must be kept. Here is the pattern followed by all reflexive verbs in the present.

---

**se laver**  *to wash (oneself)*

| | |
|---|---|
| **je me lave** | *I wash (myself)* |
| **tu te laves** | *you wash (yourself)* |
| **il/elle/on se lave** | *he/she/it/one washes (himself etc...)* |
| **nous nous lavons** | *we wash (ourselves)* |
| **vous vous lavez** | *you wash (yourself/selves)* |
| **ils/elles se lavent** | *they wash (themselves)* |

---

✳️ Perhaps the most useful reflexive verb is **s'appeler** (lit. to call oneself).

> Comment vous_appelez-vous? Je m'appelle ...
> Comment t'appelles-tu? (friendly form) Je m'appelle ...
> Comment s'appellent_ils? Ils s'appellent ...

☑️ **Pratiquez**

To check that you understand reflexive verbs: try to write out **s'habiller** (*to get dressed*). The **me, te, se**, will be shortened to **m', t', s'** as **habiller** starts with an **h**.

## 2 Saying what you need: j'ai besoin de ...

To say what item you need, use **j'ai besoin de (d')** followed by a noun:

> **J'ai besoin d'un passeport pour la France.**
> *I need a passport for France.*

> **Il a besoin d'un timbre de 2F50 pour envoyer
> sa lettre.**
> *He needs a 2F50 stamp to send his letter.*

To say what you need to do, use **j'ai besoin de (d')** followed by a verb in the infinitive:

> J'ai chaud; **j'ai besoin de boire un verre d'eau.**
> *I'm hot; I need to drink a glass of water.*

> Elle n'a plus d'argent. **Elle a besoin d'aller à la banque.**
> *She has no money left. She needs to go the bank.*

✳ **J'ai chaud/froid/faim/soif** use **avoir** (not **être**!).

**Pour** is used before verbs in the infinitive to translate the idea of *in order to*: **Pour** envoyer sa lettre il a besoin d'un timbre.

## 3 Stating your intentions

Just as you use **je voudrais** to say what you would like to do, use **je vais** to say what you are going to do followed by the verb in the infinitive.

| | |
|---|---|
| **Je vais** | **me lever** à 8 heures. |
| *I'm going* | *to get up at 8 o'clock.* |
| **Tu vas** | **prendre** le petit déjeuner à 9 heures. |
| *You're going* | *to have breakfast at 9 o'clock.* |
| **Il/elle va** | **partir** de la maison. |
| *He/she is going* | *to leave the house.* |
| **Nous_allons** | **faire** des courses à midi. |
| *We're going* | *to do some shopping at lunchtime.* |
| **Vous_allez** | **chercher** Jean à la gare. |
| *You're going* | *to fetch John from the station.* |
| **Ils/elles vont** | **se coucher** vers 11 heures. |
| *They're going* | *to go to bed around 11 o'clock.* |

## 4 The pronoun 'y'

To replace an expression of place preceded by **à,** use the pronoun y (*there*):

> Vous_allez **à Paris?** Oui, j'y vais.
> *Are you going to Paris? Yes, I'm going there.*

> Il va travailler **à la pharmacie?** Oui, il va y travailler.
> *Is he going to work at the chemist's? Yes he's going to work there.*

✳ Like other pronouns, e.g. **en, le, la, les**, etc. ➡️ **P** 85 **y** is placed just before the verb to which it refers, e.g. **il faut y aller** we must go there.

## 5 Sortir *to go out*, Venir *to come*

Here are two useful verbs to describe daily activities.

| **sortir** *to go out* | **venir** *to come* |
|---|---|
| **je sors** | **je viens** |
| **tu sors** | **tu viens** |
| **il/elle/on sort** | **il/elle/on vient** |
| **nous sortons** | **nous venons** |
| **vous sortez** | **vous venez** |
| **ils/elles sortent** | **ils/elles viennent** |

## 6 Using capital letters

The months, seasons and days of the week do not take a capital letter in French unless they begin a sentence ➡️ **P** 31: **en juillet, en été, le mardi**.

## 7 When to use visiter (*to visit*) in French

French people talk about visiting museums, old buildings or interesting places but they do not visit the cinema or their relations! They **go** to the cinema or the pub and they **pay a visit** or **see** their relations or friends:

Je vais_aller **visiter** le Louvre l'été prochain.
*I'm going to visit the Louvre next summer.*

Ce week-end je vais **rendre visite** à ma grand-mère.
*This week-end I'm going to visit my grandmother.*

Ils vont **voir** leurs_amis dans le sud de la France.
*They are going to visit their friends in the south of France.*

# ❋Assess yourself and keep up with grammar

Having reached the end of the section **Explications** it may be useful to find out how well you're doing with grammar, ways to practise it and, in Units 11–20 of the book, how to build on what you already know.

1  How well are you doing with grammar? Look at the index with grammar terms on page 233 and decide which functions you feel are particularly important. Test yourself on two or three of these at a time using the **Activités** of Units 1–10. If you find the exercises difficult, revise the **Explications** carefully studying the examples.

2  Test yourself in a practice activity. Once you've completed successfully all the activities in Units 1–10 of TY Beginner's French you may feel that you need to test yourself on another book of grammar exercises with the answers at the back. To test yourself you can read the explanations first and do the exercises or try the questions first, check the answers and work out the rule.

3  Build up a 'pattern bank'. Using the material from Units 11–20 of the book and any other French material, collect examples that can be listed under the structures you've already met. Seeing the structures in various contexts will help you assimilate them.

☑ ─────────────── **Activités** ───────────────

1  Imagine you're the man or woman whose typical day is illustrated on page 108. Write underneath the pictures what you do during the day but first have a go at saying it aloud.

2  Repeat exercise 1. This time pretend that you are describing your friend's, brother's or sister's typical day. Start the sentences with **il...** or **elle...** .

(*a*) D'abord je …　　(*b*) puis je …　　(*c*) ensuite …

(*d*) A 8h.30 j'…　　(*e*) ensuite …　　(*f*) à midi …

(*g*) L'après-midi …　　(*h*) ou je …　　(*i*) ou je …

(*j*) Le soir je …　　(*k*) ou j' …　　(*l*) et finalement …

3 Your friends Robert and Jeanine have just planned their holidays for this summer. You ask them about it:
  (a) What does Robert say?
  (b) What does Jeanine tell you?

| | Robert | Jeanine |
|---|---|---|
| **Tu vas partir quand?** | • in August | • on 21st June |
| **Tu vas partir pour combien de temps?** | • 3 weeks | • 10 days |
| **Où vas-tu aller?** | • to Oxford in England | • to Anglet near Biarritz in the South of France |
| **Comment vas-tu passer tes vacances?** | • learn English<br>• visit old buildings<br>• see some friends<br>• go out in the evening<br>• play tennis | • go swimming<br>• read a lot<br>• watch a bit (**un peu**) of TV<br>• go for long walks<br>• go to bed early (**tôt**) |

Practise the exercise several times and try memorising the questions.

4 What questions would you ask Robert and Jeanine if you said **vous** to them?

5 Jane has received a letter from a French friend who is about to visit her in Brighton. Fill in the gaps using each of the words below:

Chère Jane,

Merci (a)..... pour ta gentille lettre.
Oui, mon (b)....., mon fils et moi allons bientôt te rendre visite en (c)..... Marc (d)..... l'école le 27 juin donc nous pensons quitter Paris le (e)..... 30 juin à midi pour arriver à Gatwick à 2 heures de l' (f).....
Nous pensons (g)..... avec toi quelques (h)....., puis nous

voulons faire un peu de tourisme à Londres pour (*i*)..... les monuments historiques. Ensuite nous voulons aller à Oxford où (*j*)..... nos amis Green. Tu n'as pas (*k*)..... d'aller nous chercher à Gatwick. Nous pouvons très bien (*l*)..... le train jusqu'à Brighton et puis un taxi jusqu'à chez toi. A très bientôt. Amicalement

| | | | |
|---|---|---|---|
| prendre | jours | mari | Grande-Bretagne |
| finit | habitent | samedi | rester   visiter |
| beaucoup | | besoin | après-midi |

 **6** Michel has a lot of things planned for tomorrow. Listen to the tape and try to find out what he's going to do. He has a list of nine things. If you haven't got the cassette, look at the answers in **Réponses** to find out about Michel's plans for tomorrow.

## Grand test

Check your confidence with the material in Units 6 to 10 by doing this test.

Choose the appropriate word or group of words for each sentence. You'll find the answers included in **Réponses** at the back of the book.

**1** Pour (*a*) être  à la gare, s'il vous plait? Vous allez (*d*) tout droit.
    (*b*) aller                                     (*e*) vers Lille.
    (*c*) voir                                        (*f*) à 5 mn à pied

**2** J'habite    (*a*) en Allemagne     et je travaille    (*d*) au Berlin.
              (*b*) Allemagne                                   (*e*) Berlin.
              (*c*) à Allemagne                               (*f*) à Berlin.

**3** Vous allez trouver   (*a*) le train                (*d*) entre le magasin.
                      (*b*) la cabine téléphonique  (*e*) dans le magazin.
                      (*c*) la mer                   (*f*) près du magazin.

**4** A quelle heure   (*a*) pars-tu?     Je pars   (*d*) à 3 heures.
                  (*b*) voulez-vous?                     (*e*) pour Paris.
                  (*c*) faisons-nous?                  (*f*) avec ma fille.

**5** La banque est  (a) finie   entre l'hôtel et la poste, en face  (d) au café.
             (b) faite                                                   (e) le café.
             (c) située                                              (f) du café.

**6**   (a) Quel   jeune homme a les cheveux      (d) noirs.
    (b) Sa                                     (e) en soie.
    (c) Ce                                     (f) petits.

**7** Combien   (a) de   yaourts voulez-vous?   (d) Je voudrais 4 oranges.
             (b) …   yaourts                  (e) J'en voudrais 4.
             (c) les   yaourts                (f) J'en voudrais.

**8** Mon amie Jane   (a) parle     le français    (d) mieux     que moi.
                 (b) regarde                 (e) bien       que moi.
                 (c) pense                    (f) meilleur  que moi.

**9** J'aime (a) trop   faire la cuisine mais je préfère jouer  (d) de  football.
          (b) rien                                      (e) au  football.
          (c) beaucoup                            (f) le  football.

**10** Il ne peut
    (a) personne   jouer au tennis car il a    (d) quelquefois trop de travail.
    (b) jamais                               (e) demain trop de travail.
    (c) rien                                 (f) toujours trop de travail

**11** Vous pouvez (a) m'aider     s'il vous plaît? Je suis   (d) marié.
               (b) me donner                         (e) perdu.
               (c) acheter                            (f) dentiste.

**12** Il  (a) a besoin   introduire une pièce de  (d) jouer à la pétanque.
      (b) faut        1 franc pour              (e) prendre le train.
      (c) fait                                (f) téléphoner.

**13** Nous
    (a) voulons   manger un sandwich car nous   (d) prenons le métro.
    (b) sommes                           (e) avons soif.
    (c) pouvons                          (f) avons faim.

**14** Comment  (a) vous appelez-vous?  Je  (d) s'appelle   Mary.
                (b) ça va?                   (e) m'appelle   Mary.
                (c) s'appeler?             (f) appelle     Mary.

# 11

## LES COURSES
### *Shopping*

### *In this unit you will*

- find out about shops in France
- practise buying groceries
- practise buying something to wear

### *Avant de commencer on révise*

- numbers ➡️ **P.** 19, ➡️ **P.** 27,
➡️ **P.** 38, ➡️ **P.** 47, ➡️ **P.** 58
- asking what's available ➡️ **P.** 40
- 'some' and 'any' ➡️ **P.** 21
- asking the price ➡️ **P.** 22

- saying precisely what you
want ➡️ **P.** 48, ➡️ **P.** 73
- 'less ...', 'more ...' ➡️ **P.** 76
- colours **Mots-clefs**
➡️ **P.** 71

## Les magasins en France
### *Shops in France*

To find out about French shops read the passage below. Answering the questions in **Activité 1** will help you to understand it.

Les magasins, en France, restent ouverts en général jusqu'à 19 heures ou 20 heures. Beaucoup ferment entre 12 heures et 14 heures. Le lundi ils sont souvent fermés.

La boulangerie ouvre très tôt, vers 7 heures du matin et ferme tard car beaucoup de Français achètent leur pain deux fois par jour. Le dimanche matin, beaucoup de magasins comme les pâtisseries et les charcuteries restent ouverts.

Dans toutes les grandes villes il y a un marché presque tous les jours et souvent le dimanche. Dans les petites villes ou villages il y a un marché une fois par semaine: le jour du marché. Au marché, on peut acheter des légumes, des fruits, du poisson, de la viande et même des vêtements.

| les légumes | vegetables | la viande | meat |
|---|---|---|---|
| le poisson | fish | les vêtements | clothes |

### ✔ Activité 1

(a) Until what time do shops generally stay open during the week?
(b) Are they usually open or shut at lunchtime?
(c) What day of the week do they often shut?
(d) Which shops are often open on Sunday morning?

### ✔ Activité 2

Now read the passage several times and then, without looking at it, try to say aloud in French what you know about French shops. Check back with the passage.

❋ 1   The -s at the end of plural nouns is not pronounced.

2   The -nt at the end of verbs such as **ferment, restent** is not pronounced so **ferment** sounds like 'fairm' and **restent** like 'rest'.

## Mots-clefs

With the key words underneath you should be able to cope with most buying situations. A good way to test yourself once you've learnt the **Mots-clefs** is to hide the left side of the page, look at the English and say aloud the French.

| | |
|---|---|
| où est la boulangerie la plus proche s'il vous plaît? | where is the nearest bakery please? |
| où est le supermarché le plus proche? | where is the nearest supermarket? |
| où est-ce que je peux acheter/ trouver un/une/des ... | where can I buy/find a/some ... |
| je voudrais/il me faut | I would like/I need |
| un/une/des ... | a/some ... |
| un paquet de ... | a pack of ... |
| une tranche de ... | a slice of ... |
| un morceau de ... | a piece of ... |
| vous avez autre chose? | do you have anything else? |
| c'est trop grand/petit/cher | it's too big/small/expensive |
| je cherche quelque chose de diffé- rent | I'm looking for something different |
| vous avez quelque chose de plus grand/petit/moins cher? | have you got anything bigger/smaller/cheaper? |
| je vais prendre une tranche/un kilo/ une livre de plus/500 grammes de moins | I'll take a slice/a kilo/a pound more/ 500 grammes less |
| un demi-kilo | half a kilo |
| c'est combien? | how much is it? |
| c'est tout, merci | that's all, thank you |

# Acheter des provisions
## *Food shopping*

### A la boucherie (butcher's), on achète

| | |
|---|---|
| du veau | veal |
| du boeuf | beef |
| du porc | pork |
| des saucisses | sausages |
| un poulet | chicken |

### A la charcuterie (delicatessen), on achète

| | |
|---|---|
| du jambon | ham |
| du saucisson | salami-type sausage |

### A la boulangerie/pâtisserie (baker's), on achète

| | |
|---|---|
| une baguette | French 'stick' |
| un pain complet | wholemeal loaf |
| des petits pains | soft bread rolls |
| une tarte aux fraises | strawberry tart |
| des croissants | croissants |

## A l'épicerie (grocer's), au libre-service (self-service), à l'alimentation (foodstore), on achète:

| | |
|---|---|
| du thé | tea |
| du café | coffee |
| du beurre | butter |
| du lait | milk |
| des oeufs (rhyming with deux) | eggs |
| du fromage | cheese |
| de la lessive | washing powder |
| des pommes | apples |
| des pommes de terre | potatoes |
| une laitue | lettuce |
| des yaourts à la fraise | strawberry yoghurts |
| des boissons (jus de fruit, vins, etc) | drinks (fruit juice, wine, etc) |

### ✔ Activité 3

There is no supermarket around; say in French which shops sell:

(a) chicken
(b) bread rolls
(c) pork
(d) washing powder
(e) milk
(f) salami
(g) wine

### ✔ Activité 4

Below is a dialogue between a grocer and a client. See if you can put the lines in their correct order starting with **Bonjour Madame.**

(a) une douzaine (*a dozen*), s'il vous plaît.
(b) voilà, Madame ça fait 45 francs.
(c) **Bonjour Madame**
(d) non, il me faut aussi du jus de fruit.
(e) oui ... voilà une douzaine d'oeufs, c'est tout?
(f) bonjour Monsieur, je voudrais des oeufs, s'il vous plaît.
(g) qu'est-ce que je vous donne: jus de pomme, orange ou ananas (*pineapple*)?

(*h*)   vous en voulez combien?
(*i*)   je vais prendre le jus d'orange.

## Dialogue

Un client achète des provisions pour un piquenique. *At the market a customer buys some food for a picnic.* Listen to the cassette (read the dialogue if you haven't got the cassette) then without looking back at the text try **Activité 5**.

Client   Bonjour, Mademoiselle. Je voudrais du beurre, s'il vous plaît?
Vendeuse   Un paquet comme ça?
Client   Non, quelque chose de plus petit. Et qu'est-ce que vous avez comme fromages?
Vendeuse   Brie, fromage de chèvre, gruyère. Qu'est-ce que je vous donne?
Client   Du gruyère.
Vendeuse   Un morceau comme ça?
Client   Ah non... ça c'est un peu trop gros. Vous pouvez m'en donner un peu moins, s'il vous plaît? C'est pour notre piquenique.
Vendeuse   Ah bon, d'accord. Voilà ... 300 grammes. Et avec ça? Qu'est-ce qu'il vous faut? Des fruits, des yaourts, des biscuits?
Client   Euh, je vais prendre aussi des fruits.
Vendeuse   Alors nous avons fraises, bananes, pommes, pêches et melon.
Client   Elles sont bonnes les fraises?
Vendeuse   Délicieuses. Je vous en mets un demi-kilo?
Client   500 grammes! Non c'est un peu trop. Une demi-livre c'est assez. Ah oui, je voudrais aussi 2 grandes bouteilles d'eau minérale ... Voilà, c'est tout, c'est combien?
Vendeuse   Alors, ça vous fait 63F50.
Client   Et pour acheter du pain?
Vendeuse   Vous trouverez une boulangerie à 200 mètres sur votre gauche. Et ... bon piquenique.

## Activité 5

Look at the three columns below. Can you pick out the four items bought by the customer?

| | | | | | |
|---|---|---|---|---|---|
| (a) | du poulet | (e) | des pommes | (i) | du lait |
| (b) | du beurre | (f) | du melon | (j) | du vin |
| (c) | du saucisson | (g) | des fraises | (k) | de la bière |
| (d) | du fromage | (h) | des pêches | (l) | de l'eau minérale |

### ✅ Activité 6

Pretend that you're a customer. Using the dialogue above and the **Mots-clefs** on ➡️ 🅿 115 practise buying a small packet of butter, 300 grammes of cheese and half a pound of strawberries. Don't forget to find out where you can buy some bread. (The answers are not given in **Réponses**.)

## _____ Acheter autre chose _____
### *Shopping for other things*

**A la droguerie   (hardware shop)**

| | |
|---|---|
| une brosse à dent | toothbrush |
| un savon | soap |
| un peigne | comb |
| de l'huile pour bronzer | suntan lotion |
| des kleenex | tissues |
| un ouvre-boîte | tin opener |
| un tire-bouchon | corkscrew |

**Au bureau de tabac   (newsagents)**

| | |
|---|---|
| un carnet de timbres | book of stamps |
| des journaux | newspapers |
| du chewing gum | chewing gum |
| une carte postale | postcard |
| des magazines | magazines |

**Au magasin de confection   (clothes shop)**

| | |
|---|---|
| un pull | pullover |
| un pantalon | trousers |
| une chemise | a shirt |
| une paire de chaussures | shoes |
| un maillot de bain | swimming costume |
| une robe | dress |
| une jupe | skirt |
| un jean/des jeans | jeans |

# Dialogue

To understand this dialogue, you need to understand two new questions:

**1 Quelle taille?** (*What size?*) when you're buying clothes. (42 is the European equivalent to the woman's size 12 in Britain and 10 in America, 44 is equivalent to size 14 in Britain and 12 in America, etc ...). **Quelle pointure?** means *What size shoes?* Size 5 in Britain or 6½ in America = 37, size 6 in Britain and 7½ in America = 38, etc ...

**2 Je peux essayer** (*Can I try?*) when you want to try something on.

| | |
|---|---|
| Cliente | Bonjour, Madame, je cherche une jupe noire. |
| Vendeuse | Noire ... euh oui d'accord. **Vous faites quelle taille?** |
| Cliente | 40 ... 40/42 **ça dépend du modèle.** |
| Vendeuse | J'ai ce modèle-ci en 40 et 42. C'est une jupe en coton. En 42, je n'ai pas de noir; j'ai du rouge, du gris mais pas de noir. |
| Cliente | Elles font combien ces jupes? |
| Vendeuse | 250 francs. |
| Cliente | Vous n'avez pas quelque chose de moins cher? |
| Vendeuse | Euh non, sauf ces jupes **en solde** à 190 francs mais elles sont grises. |
| Cliente | Non, il me faut du noir. Bon, eh bien, je vais essayer la jupe à 250 francs. |
| Vendeuse | (*pointing to a fitting room*) Vous avez **la cabine d'essayage là-bas.** |
| | (*after a while*) |
| Vendeuse | Elle vous va bien? |
| Cliente | Ça va; elle est un peu large mais je crois que je vais la prendre car j'en ai besoin pour ce soir. Vous acceptez les cartes de crédit? |
| Vendeuse | Mais bien sûr, Madame. |

| | |
|---|---|
| **vous faites quelle taille?** | what size are you? |
| **ça dépend du modèle** | it depends on the style |
| **en solde** | in the sale |
| **la cabine d'essayage** | fitting room |
| **là-bas** | over there |

## ✔ Activité 7

Listen to the tape again and try to spot the French version of the following phrases, then write them down:

(a) I'm looking for a black skirt ...........................................

(b) What's your size? ...........................................

(c) something cheaper ...........................................

(d) I shall try ...........................................

(e) the skirt at 250 francs ...........................................

(f) How does it fit? ...........................................

## ✔ Activité 8

You're at the **bureau de tabac** (the **c** in **tabac** is not sounded) and wish to buy a newspaper, stamps, cards and a magazine for your wife.

Vendeur  Bonjour, Monsieur, vous désirez?

(a) You  *Say you would like a newspaper. Ask him what English newspapers he's got.*

Vendeur  Comme journaux anglais? Nous avons le Times, le Guardian et le Daily Telegraph.

(b) You  *Say that you will take the Times and these three postcards. Ask how much a stamp for England is.*

Vendeur  Un timbre pour l'Angleterre? C'est le même prix que pour la France 2F50.

(c) You  *Say that you will take eight stamps.*

Vendeur  Voilà, Monsieur; huit timbres à 2F50. C'est tout?

(d) You  *Say that you'll also buy the magazine 'Elle' for your wife.*

Vendeur  Très bien, Monsieur. Ça vous fait 46F50.

## ✔ Activité 9

On the cassette you will hear Michel shopping. Listen to the conversation several times and then answer the questions below, in English.

(a) What does he want to buy?

(b) What colours does he ask for?

(c) What's wrong with the first garment?
(d) What's wrong with the second garment?
(e) How much is the one he buys?

## ✔ *Petit test*

How do you say in French:

1 I need some tissues.
2 I would like something bigger please.
3 Do you have anything else?
4 That's all.
5 Do you accept credit cards?

# 12

## SE REPOSER, DORMIR
### *Resting, sleeping*

### *In this unit you will*

- find out about accommodation in France
- find out how to ask for information at the tourist office
- practise booking at a hotel and at a campsite
- complain about things missing/not working
- learn to spell your name
- write a letter to book accommodation

### *Avant de commencer on révise*

- saying what you want **→ P.** 48
- asking what you can do **→ P.** 49
- different ways to ask a question **→ P.** 49
- asking the price **→ P.** 22
- recognising 1st, 2nd, 3rd etc **→ P.** 62
- saying that there isn't any **→ P.** 40
- dates **→ P.** 50

## Choisir un hôtel
### *Choosing a hotel*

Vous pouvez trouver la liste des hôtels et des restaurants en France dans le guide rouge Michelin. **A l'étranger** vous pouvez aussi vous renseigner **auprès** des offices du tourisme français à l'étranger ou de la Société Nationale des Chemins de Fer Français.

En France, les offices du tourisme (appelés également Syndicat d'Initiative) donnent gratuitement des brochures avec la liste des hôtels et des restaurants de la région. Ils peuvent aussi faire une réservation dans l'hôtel de votre choix. A Paris, l'office du tourisme est situé au 127, avenue des Champs Elysées, 75008.

Les hôtels sont **homologués** par le gouvernement: d'**une étoile** (★) à 4 étoiles (★★★★L). Vous pouvez choisir entre **pension complète** et **demi-pension.** Il faut demander si le petit déjeuner est **compris** dans le prix de la chambre. Il est souvent **en supplément.**

| | |
|---|---|
| **à l'étranger** | abroad |
| **auprès de** | next to, at |
| **homologué** | classified |
| **une étoile** | star |
| **la pension complète** | full board |
| **la demi-pension** | half board |
| **compris** | included |
| **en supplément** | extra |

## ☑ Activité 1

(*a*)  Which French guide book has a list of hotels?
(*b*)  Are **offices du tourisme** the same as **syndicats d'initiative?**
(*c*)  Do you have to pay for tourist brochures?
(*d*)  What are the **offices du tourisme** prepared to do for you?
(*e*)  Is breakfast usually included in the price list of a hotel?

## ✳ *How to pronounce*

Practise reading aloud the French key words in the diagram on page 123:

- **baignoire** and **WC** are pronounced as 'bé-noir' and 'vais-c'est'.
- pronounce the words: **radio, télévision** and **bar** the French way. Check their pronunciation on ➡ 🄿 5.
- **ascenseur** is pronounced as 'as-cent-soeur'.

**CHOISIR SON HÔTEL**

| Le confort dépend du nombre d'étoiles | ★ | ★★ | ★★★ | ★★★★ | ★★★★L |
|---|---|---|---|---|---|
| l'eau courante chaude et froide au lavabo | ★ | ★ | ★ | ★ | ★ |
| une douche | ☆ | ★ | ★ | ★ | ★ |
| un bidet | ⊘ | ☆ | ★ | ★ | ★ |
| une baignoire | ⊘ | ☆ | ★ | ★ | ★ |
| un W.C. dans la chambre | ⊘ | ☆ | ☆ | ★ | ★ |
| le téléphone intérieur | ⊘ | ☆ | ★ | ★ | ★ |
| le téléphone extérieur | ⊘ | ⊘ | ⊘ | ☆ | ★ |
| la radio | ⊘ | ⊘ | ⊘ | ☆ | ★ |
| la télévision | ⊘ | ⊘ | ⊘ | ★ | ★ |
| un bar privé | ⊘ | ⊘ | ⊘ | ☆ | ★ |
| l'ascenseur | ☆ | ★ | ★ | ★ | ★ |

★ = oui toujours
☆ = oui le plus souvent
⊘ = non

## Activité 2

Can you name in English:

(a) four things you will not find in a one star hotel?
(b) four things that you will probably find in a two-star hotel?
(c) four things that you always find in a four-star hotel?

## Mots-clefs

| | |
|---|---|
| **est-ce que vous avez ...?** | have you ...? |
| **je cherche** | I'm looking for |
| **un emplacement** | a site |
| **pour une tente** | for a tent |
| **pour une caravane** | for a caravan |
| **une chambre simple/double** | a room single/double |
| **à 2 lits** | with 2 single beds |
| **avec un grand lit** | with a double bed |
| **avec douche** | with shower |
| **avec WC** | with WC |
| **avec salle de bains** | with bathroom |
| **avec cabinet de toilette** | with basin and bidet partitioned off |
| **avec demi-pension** | with half board |
| **avec pension complète** | with full board |
| **pour ..... personnes** | for ..... persons |
| **pour ..... nuits** | for ..... nights |
| **le petit déjeuner est compris?** | is breakfast included? |
| **non, c'est en supplément/en plus** | no, it's extra |
| **c'est à quel nom?** | in who's name? |
| **c'est complet** | it's full up |
| **TTC (toutes taxes comprises)** | tax included |

# Dialogue

A l'office du tourisme une touriste accompagnée de son mari se renseigne sur les hôtels à Paris.
*At the tourist office, a tourist accompanied by her husband inquires about hotels in Paris.*

Touriste     Bonjour Madame. Je viens d'arriver à Paris et je cherche une chambre. Vous avez une liste d'hôtels, s'il vous plaît?

Hôtesse     Oui Madame, voilà.
*(the tourists look at the brochure)*

Touriste     Pouvez-vous me réserver une chambre, s'il vous plaît?

Hôtesse     Oui, bien sûr. Vous choisissez quel hôtel?

Touriste     Un hôtel à deux étoiles, l'hôtel Victor Hugo, dans le 16ème arrondissement.

Hôtesse     C'est pour combien de personnes?

Touriste     Euh, pour mon mari et moi ...

Hôtesse     Et pour combien de nuits?

Touriste     Pour deux nuits.

Hôtesse     Bien. Une chambre à deux lits ou un grand lit?

Touriste     Un grand lit. Nous voulons une douche également.

Hôtesse     Bon, alors une chambre pour deux nuits, pour deux personnes avec un grand lit et douche. Très bien, je vais téléphoner et je vous réserve ça tout de suite.

Touriste     J'espère que l'hôtel ne sera pas complet!

Hôtesse     Je crois qu'en cette saison, il y aura de la place.

## ✔ Activité 3

Listen to the dialogue as often as you need and spot the French version of the following phrases:

(a)   Do you have a list of hotels? .....................................
(b)   Can you book me a room? .......................................
(c)   Which hotel are you choosing? .................................
(d)   In the 16th district .................................................
(e)   I hope the hotel is not full ......................................
(f)   There will be some room ........................................

# Dialogue

A la réception: les Wilson arrivent à leur hôtel.
*At reception: the Wilsons arrive at their hotel.*

| | |
|---|---|
| Touriste | Bonjour, Monsieur. Nous avons une réservation au nom de Wilson. |
| Réceptionniste | Ah oui, vous êtes les Anglais qui ont téléphoné cet après-midi! |
| Touriste | Oui, c'est ça. |
| Réceptionniste | Bon, vous avez la chambre 43 au deuxième étage. C'est une chambre très agréable avec grand lit, douche et WC. |
| Touriste | Le petit déjeuner est compris dans le prix de la chambre? |
| Réceptionniste | Ah non, Madame c'est en plus: 27 francs par personne. |
| Touriste | Et à quelle heure servez-vous le petit déjeuner? |
| Réceptionniste | A partir de 8 heures jusqu'à 9h.30. |
| Touriste | Vous servez le petit déjeuner dans la chambre? |
| Réceptionniste | Mais oui, Madame, bien sûr. |
| Touriste | Très bien. Pouvez-vous nous apporter le petit déjeuner à 8h30, s'il vous plaît? |
| Receptionniste | C'est entendu, Madame. |
| Touriste | Et est-ce qu'il y a un ascenseur dans l'hôtel? Nos valises sont très lourdes. |
| Réceptionniste | Oui, au fond du couloir à droite. |
| Touriste | On peut prendre un repas dans l'hôtel? |
| Réceptionniste | Non, je regrette mais nous ne servons que le petit déjeuner. Il y a beaucoup de bons petits restaurants tout près d'ici sur la place, où l'on peut très bien manger. |

## Activité 4

Respond with **vrai** or **faux** to the following statements:

|  | vrai | faux |
|---|---|---|
| (a) Room 43 is on the 3rd floor. | ☐ | ☐ |
| (b) Breakfast is included in the price. | ☐ | ☐ |
| (c) Breakfast is served from 8 o'clock. | ☐ | ☐ |

| | | |
|---|---|---|
| (d) | Their suitcases are heavy. | □ □ |
| (e) | The lift is at the end of the corridor on the left. | □ □ |
| (f) | They serve only breakfast. | □ □ |
| (g) | There are a lot of restaurants nearby. | □ □ |

### ☑ Activité 5

Take part in this conversation at the hotel.

| | |
|---|---|
| Vous | *Say good evening and ask if they have a room.* |
| Réceptionniste | Oui, qu'est-ce que vous voulez comme chambre? Une chambre pour une personne? |
| Vous | *Say no, a double room with two beds and a bathroom.* |
| Réceptionniste | C'est pour combien de nuits? |
| Vous | *It's for three nights.* |
| Réceptionniste | Oui, j'ai une chambre avec salle de bains. |
| Vous | *How much is it?* |
| Réceptionniste | 350F |
| Vous | *Ask if breakfast is included.* |
| Réceptionniste | Oui, le petit déjeuner est compris. |
| Vous | *Ask what time breakfast is served.* |
| Réceptionniste | Entre 8 heures et 10 heures. |
| Vous | *Ask if you can have a meal in the hotel.* |
| Réceptionniste | Mais oui bien sûr. Le restaurant est au premier étage. |

## —— Se plaindre *Complaining* ——

Things aren't always as they ought to be and you may have to complain about things not working ... **ne marche(ent) pas** or things that are missing **il n'y a pas de ...** . If the situation is really bad you can always ask to speak to the **directeur** (*manager*).

### ☑ Activité 6

How would you explain to the **directeur** that some objects in your room are not working (those in the square boxes) and some are missing (those in the circular boxes)?

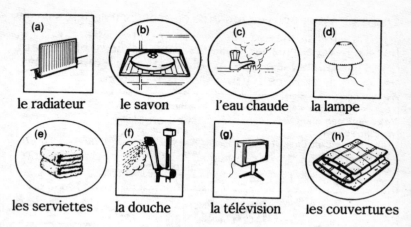

(a) le radiateur    (b) le savon    (c) l'eau chaude    (d) la lampe

(e) les serviettes    (f) la douche    (g) la télévision    (h) les couvertures

## —— Au camping   *At the campsite* ——

Les offices du tourisme ont la liste des campings; ils peuvent vous aider à réserver un emplacement pour votre tente ou votre caravane. Si vous n'avez pas de carnet de camping international (*international camping card*) on vous demandera peut-être de payer à l'arrivée ou de laisser votre passeport au bureau (*you'll be asked to pay when you arrive or to leave your passport at the office*).

## —————— Dialogue ——————

| | |
|---|---|
| Touriste | Bonjour Madame. **Est-ce qu'il reste encore** un emplacement pour une tente? |
| Femme | C'est pour combien de jours? |
| Touriste | Je ne sais pas exactement ... Peut-être une semaine. |
| Femme | Bon, une semaine, ça va. Vous avez le carnet de camping international? |
| Touriste | Ah non, je ne l'ai pas. |
| Femme | Bon ... votre nom, sil vous plaît. |
| Touriste | Bradford. |
| Femme | **Ça s'écrit comment?** |
| Touriste | B-R-A-D-F-O-R-D |
| Femme | Est-ce que vous avez **une pièce d'identité?** |
| Touriste | Oui, voici mon passeport. |
| Femme | Bien. Alors vous payez quand vous partez. |

| Touriste | **Vous pouvez me dire** où sont les toilettes, s'il vous plaît? |
|---|---|
| Femme | Vous avez des toilettes dans les deux **blocs sanitaires**. Le plus proche est **celui qui** est juste derrière **ce bâtiment** de la réception. |

| | |
|---|---|
| **est-ce qu'il reste encore ...** | is there any ... left? |
| **ça s'écrit comment?** | how do you write it? |
| **la pièce d'identité** | identification |
| **vous pouvez me dire ...?** | can you tell me ...? |
| **le bloc sanitaire** | washing facilities |
| **celui qui** | the one which |
| **ce bâtiment** | this building |

## L'alphabet français
### *The French Alphabet*

When booking accommodation or tickets you may be asked to give your name: **votre nom?** or **(c'est) à quel nom?** and to spell it: **ça s'écrit comment?** or **vous pouvez épeler?**

 **Activité 7**

Read the alphabet below several times and practise spelling your name and your address.

| A | B | C | D | E | F | G |
|---|---|---|---|---|---|---|
| ah | bé | cé | dé | eux | eff | j'ai |
| **H** | **I** | **J** | **K** | **L** | **M** | **N** |
| ahsh | ee | j'y | kah | elle | emm | enne |
| **O** | **P** | **Q** | **R** | **S** | **T** | **U** |
| oh | pé | ku | erre | ess | té | u* |
| **V** | **W** | **X** | **Y** | **Z** | | |
| vé | doubl'vé | eeks | ee grec | zed | | |

*as in **du**

- To spell double consonants the French will say **deux ...**: For example to spell **mallet** they'll say: emm - ah - *deux elle* - eux - té; and to spell **poussin**: pé - oh - u - *deux ess* - ee - enne
- Be particularly careful when spelling the French letters **e, i, g** and **j** as they can be confusing for English speakers.

## ✔ Activité 8

Michael Rice has just received confirmation for his booking in the French campsite La Mignardière; look at the confirmation form and say which of the following are **vrai** or **faux**:

|  |  | vrai | faux |
|---|---|---|---|
| (a) | il a réservé un emplacement pour une tente | ☐ | ☐ |
| (b) | il va au camping avec une autre famille | ☐ | ☐ |
| (c) | il va passer huit jours au camping | ☐ | ☐ |
| (d) | il habite dans le nord de l'Angleterre | ☐ | ☐ |
| (e) | il a réservé un emplacement 'Grand Confort' | ☐ | ☐ |
| (f) | il a payé 70F pour la réservation de l'emplacement | ☐ | ☐ |

CAMPING · CARAVANING
★ ★ ★ ★ NN
**LA MIGNARDIÈRE**
BALLAN-MIRÉ
37510 JOUÉ-LÈS-TOURS
Tél. 47 53 26 49

Fiche de Réservation

(minimum **3** nuits)

Nom **RICE**

Prénom **Michael**

Adresse **54 Wanderdown Road**
**Oving dean**
**BRIGHTON** **East Sussex**
**BN 2? BT**

reçu 70F
le 13/5/91
pour l'famille.

SOUHAITE RÉSERVER UN EMPLACEMENT POUR LA PÉRIODE **(Angleterre)**

- du : **29/7/91** (à partir de 12 h)
- au : **10/8/91** (jusqu'à 12 h)

soit      nuits     (avec la famille Ashworth)

POUR : UNE CARAVANE ☒
UNE TENTE ☐
UNE CARAVANE PLIANTE ☐
AUTRES ☐

AVEC : ÉLECTRICITÉ      OUI ☐ NON ☒
EMPL. SIMPLE ☒      EMPL. GRAND CONFORT ☐

| TARIFS : | | PL Saison | Hors Saison |
|---|---|---|---|
| – Emplacement + voiture | | 28 | 23 |
| – Adulte | | 20 | 18 |
| – Enfant (– 7 ans) | | 12 | 10 |
| – Branchement électricité | | 17 | 17 |
| – Chien | | 10 | 10 |
| – Emplacement Grand Confort | Forfait : | 140 | 130 |
| (FORFAIT 4 PERSONNES .SUP ADU 20 . ENF 12 ) | | | |
| – FRAIS DE RÉSERVATION NON RÉCUPÉRABLES | (lrecupérables) | | 70 |

Votre emplacement est réservé.

Prière de renvoyer ces deux fiches avec les frais de réservation

Merci de votre confiance avec le plaisir de vous recevoir bientôt

Salutations distinguées

# Ecrire des lettres
## *Writing letters*

## Réserver une chambre   *Booking accommodation*

Si vouz avez l'intention de faire du camping ou de réserver un hôtel en France il vaut mieux (*it's better*) réserver longtemps à l'avance surtout pendant les périodes de vacances. Si vous réservez par téléphone, le directeur de l'hôtel vous demandera de confirmer par écrit (*confirm by writing*) et de verser des arrhes ou un acompte (*and ask you for an advance*).

Monsieur,

Je voudrais réserver une chambre à 2 lits avec douche pour les nuits du 28 juin au 4 juillet.

Je vous serais reconnaissant(e) de bien vouloir m'indiquer vos prix.

En vous remerciant d'avance, je vous prie de croire, Monsieur, à l'expression de mes sentiments distingués.

*Dear Sir,*

*I would like to book a twin-bedded room with shower for the nights of 28 June to 4 July.*

*I would be grateful if you would be kind enough to let me know your charges.*

*Thanking you in anticipation,*
*Yours faithfully ...*

# Confirmation écrite  *Written confirmation*

Hôtel du Lac
Avenue des Pins
64 682 Anglet

Anglet, le 15 mai

Madame,

Je vous remercie de votre lettre du 5 mai. Je confirme votre réservation pour une chambre à 2 lits et avec douche pour deux personnes du 28 juin au 4 juillet.

La chambre, qui se trouve au premier étage, a vue sur le lac. Le tarif de la chambre avec douche et TTC est de 350F par nuit. Le petit déjeuner est en supplément et coûte 30F par personne.

Je vous prie, Madame, d'agréer mes salutations distinguées.

R. Michel, Directeur

*15th May*

*Dear Madam,*

*Thank you for your letter of 5th May. I confirm your reservation for a double-bedded room with shower for 2 persons from 28 June to 4 July.*

*The room is on the 1st floor and looks on to the lake. The price for the room including shower and tax is 350F per night. Breakfast is extra and costs 30F per person.*

*Yours faithfully ...*

*R. Michel, Director*

## ✔ Petit test

How do you say in French:

1  I'm looking for a two-star hotel.
2  Can you book a room for me?
3  Is breakfast included?
4  There's no telephone in the room.
5  Is there a campsite near here?

# 13

## BIEN MANGER, BIEN BOIRE
### *Eating and drinking well*

### In this unit you will

- find out where to eat
- practise ordering a snack
- choose a menu and order a meal

### Avant de commencer on révise

- saying what you want ➡️ **P.** 48, ➡️ **P.** 73
- the verb **prendre** ➡️ **P.** 52
- some, any ➡️ **P.** 21
- asking questions ➡️ **P.** 40, ➡️ **P.** 49
- likes and dislikes ➡️ **P.** 84

## ——— Bien manger  *Eating well* ———

Pour trouver les grands restaurants, consultez les guides célèbres: le Michelin, le Gault-Millau; ils donnent des étoiles aux meilleurs restaurants. Les offices du tourisme, à Paris comme en province, ont également la liste des restaurants locaux.

On peut très bien manger en France dans des restaurants plus modestes appelés **les petits restaurants du coin**. Au menu ils ont souvent des plats simples mais appétissants comme un pâté maison et **un plat garni**.

Si on est en voiture, on peut toujours s'arrêter dans **un relais routier** pour manger un repas rapide et abondant à un prix raisonnable; les boissons sont souvent comprises dans le prix du menu.

On peut aussi manger dans **une brasserie** et commander un plat unique comme **la choucroute** avec de la bière; ou encore dans **un bistrot** où on choisira entre un bifteck-frites, une excellente spécialité et **le plat du jour**.

On peut également manger pour pas cher dans **des crêperies**, des bars et des cafés.

Souvent dans les restaurants on peut choisir entre plusieurs **menus**: du plus cher, le menu gastronomique, au plus modeste, le menu touristique et **la carte**.

| | |
|---|---|
| **le petit restaurant du coin** | local restaurant offering good but cheap food |
| **le plat garni** | dish with meat and vegetable or salad |
| **le relais routier** | roadside restaurant for motorists |
| **la brasserie** | cross between a café and a restaurant |
| **la choucroute** | cabbage, bacon, sausages, potatoes |
| **le bistrot** | cheap restaurant |
| **le plat du jour** | today's special |
| **la crêperie** | pancake house |
| **le menu** | list of dishes served at a fixed price for the whole meal |
| **la carte** | list of dishes individually priced |

 **Activité 1**

Without looking at the passage above, answer the following questions then check your answers with **Réponses** at the end of the book.

(a) **Les petits restaurants du coin** are usually cheap/expensive.

(b) **Un plat garni** is a dish with meat only/meat with vegetable or noodles.

(c) **Les relais routiers** are situated in towns/outside towns.

(d) **Boisson comprise** means drink is extra/drink is included in the price.

(*e*) In a **brasserie** one can eat pancakes/a limited range of dishes.

(*f*) **Le plat du jour** is 'today's special'/a dish with cold food.

(*g*) If you want a pancake you go to a **crêperie/bar**.

(*h*) If you want the cheapest menu you choose **le menu gastronomique/le menu touristique**.

 ———————— **Mots-clefs** ————————

| | |
|---|---|
| **vous désirez?** | what will you have? |
| **vous avez choisi?** | have you made a choice? |
| **qu'est-ce que vous avez** | what do you have |
|   **à manger?** |   to eat? |
|   **à boire?** |   to drink? |
| **qu'est-ce que vous avez comme** | what do you have in the way of |
|   **boissons?** |   drinks? |
|   **snacks?** |   snacks? |
| **des sandwiches au jambon** | ham sandwiches |
|          **au fromage** | cheese sandwiches |
| **une glace à la vanille** | vanilla ice-cream |
| **de la bière en bouteille** | bottled beer |
| **de la pression** | draught beer |
| **un café** | a black coffee |
| **un café crème** | a white coffee (with milk not cream) |
| **un thé au citron** | lemon tea |
|   **nature** | tea (without milk, etc...) |
|   **avec du lait froid** | tea with cold milk |
| **une orange pressée** | freshly-squeezed orange |
| **un jus de fruit** | fruit juice |
| **un jus de pomme** | apple juice |
|     **d'ananas** | pineapple juice |
|     **de pamplemousse** | grapefruit juice |
| | |
| **qu'est-ce que c'est le/la/les?** | what's the ...? |
| **je vais en prendre un (une)** | I'll take one |
| **pour commencer ...** | to start with ... |
| **ensuite ...** | then ... |
| **comme dessert ...** | for desert ... |
| **le plat** | dish, course |
| **plats à emporter** | takeaway food |
| **saignant/bleu** | rare (lit. bleeding/blue) |
| **à point** | medium |
| **bien cuit** | well done |
| **l'addition (f)** | the bill |

**Dialogue**

## Commander un snack

A la terrasse d'un café deux touristes sont prêts à commander. *Two tourists sitting outside a café are ready to order.* The man asks the waiter what a **croque-monsieur** is. Listen to or read the waiter's explanations: how would you explain to someone English what a **croque-monsieur** is? What is the woman ordering? What drinks are they having?

| | |
|---|---|
| Garçon | Bonjour, Messieurs-dames. Qu'est-ce que vous désirez? |
| Homme | Qu'est-ce que vous avez à manger? |
| Garçon | A manger, nous avons des sandwiches au jambon blanc, **rillettes,** pâté de campagne, saucisson sec, hot-dogs, omelettes, croque-monsieur … |
| Homme | Qu'est-ce que c'est, un croque-monsieur? |
| Garçon | Un croque-monsieur? C'est **deux tranches de pain grillé** avec jambon et fromage **au milieu.** |
| Homme | **Ça a l'air** délicieux … je vais en prendre un. |
| Garçon | Et pour vous Madame? |
| Femme | Moi, je crois que je vais prendre une omelette … qu'est-ce que vous avez comme omelette? |
| Garçon | Omelette au fromage, aux **champignons,** aux herbes … |
| Femme | Une omelette aux champignons. |
| Garçon | Et comme boisson, Messieurs-dames? |
| Homme | Vous avez de la bière? |
| Garçon | Oui … nous avons de la bière pression et de la Kronenbourg en bouteille. |
| Homme | Bon, une pression s'il vous plaît. |
| Garçon | Une petite, une grande? |
| Homme | Une petite. |
| Femme | Moi je vais prendre un café crème. |
| Garçon | Bon, alors une pression, un café crème, une omelette aux champignons et un croque-monsieur. |
| Homme | Merci bien, Monsieur. |

| | |
|---|---|
| **rillettes** | type of potted meat, usually pork, similar to pâté |
| **tranche de pain grillé** | slice of toasted bread |
| **au milieu** | in the middle |
| **ça a l'air** | it seems |
| **les champignons** | mushrooms |

## ✔Activité 2

See if you can unscramble the dialogue below, starting with the sentence in bold:

(a) Je vais prendre une pression.
(b) A manger nous avons des sandwiches, des croque-monsieur, des pizzas ...
(c) **Bonjour Monsieur, qu'est-ce que vous désirez?**
(d) De la pression et de la Kronenbourg en bouteille.
(e) Qu'est-ce que vous avez à manger?
(f) Je vais prendre une pizza; et comme bière, qu'est-ce que vous avez?

## ✔Activité 3

You're hungry and decide to go to a café for a snack. Here comes the waiter ... be prepared to order:

| | |
|---|---|
| Garçon | Qu'est-ce que vous désirez? |
| (a) Vous | *Say that you would like a croque-monsieur.* |
| Garçon | Je suis désolé, Monsieur mais nous n'en avons plus. |
| (b) Vous | *Ask him if he has any omelettes?* |
| Garçon | Oui, nous avons omelette nature, jambon et Parmentier. |
| (c) Vous | *Ask what parmentier is.* |
| Garçon | Omelette parmentier? C'est une omelette avec des pommes de terre. |
| (d) Vous | *Say that you'll take the potato omelette.* |
| Garçon | Bien, alors une omelette parmentier; et à boire, Monsieur qu'est-ce que je vous sers? |
| (e) Vous | *Ask him what he has in the way of fruit juice (the **s** of **jus** is not pronounced).* |
| Garçon | Comme jus de fruit nous avons du jus d'orange, du jus d'ananas, du jus de pamplemousse ... |

(f) **Vous** *Say that you would like a pineapple juice and the bill please.*

---

## Salades composées

**SALADE MIXTE**.........................40
Tomates, salade, oeuf.

**SALADE VEGETARIENNE** ......43
Tomates, poivron, maïs, carotte
concombre, salade.

**CHEF SALADE**.........................50
Tomates, pommes à l'huile, jambon, gruyère
salade, oeuf dur

**SALADE NICOISE**....................52
Tomates, oeuf, thon, poivrons,
concombre, olives, salade, anchois

## Buffet chaud

CROQUE MONSIEUR...............................30
CROQUE MADAME..................................35
CROQUE NICOIS.....................................37
Croque monsieur avec tomate et anchois

## Buffet froid

POULET FROID MAYONNAISE ......48
ASSIETTE CHARCUTIERE ............52
ASSIETTE ANGLAISE ....................52
ASSIETTE DE VIANDE FROIDE .....52

## Les oeufs

OMELETTE NATURE (3 pièces)......30
OMELETTE JAMBON ......................37
OMELETTE FROMAGE ...................37
OMELETTE SAVOYARDE................39
OMELETTE PARMENTIER..............37

## Sandwiches

JAMBON DE PARIS.........................25
PATE OU RILLETTES......................23
CAMEMBERT OU GRUYERE ........23
SAUCISSON SEC OU A L'AIL........23

## Boissons

CAFE EXPRESS.........................7F50
THE AU CITRON...............................12
JUS DE FRUIT ..................................16
BIÈRE PRESSION.....................12F50
BIÈRE BOUTEILLE ..........................18
EAU MINERALE................................12
SODA .................................................15
APERITIF ANISE...............................15

---

✔️**Activité 4**

Using the menu and dialogue above as a guide, act out similar situations varying the dishes and drinks. (The answers are not given in **Réponses**.)

# Dialogue: Au 'Petit Zinc'

## Au restaurant

Listen carefully to the tape. What menu does the customer choose? How does he want his meat? What does he want for dessert?

| | |
|---|---|
| Customer | Vous avez **une table** pour une personne? |
| Garçon | Oui, Monsieur. Il y a une place là-bas, près de **la fenêtre.** |
| Garçon | (*later*) Alors Monsieur, qu'est-ce que vous prenez? (*pause*) Nous avons un excellent plat du jour. C'est une blanquette de veau. |
| Customer | Qu'est-ce que c'est, une blanquette de veau? |
| Garçon | C'est du veau en sauce blanche ... C'est très bon. |
| Customer | Ah non, je n'aime pas les viandes en sauce. |
| Garçon | Si vous préférez les **grillades, je vous conseille** le menu à 105F; pour commencer **hors d'oeuvres** et charcuterie **à volonté,** puis ensuite, **au choix,** steak au poivre ou **truite meunière.** |
| Customer | Très bien. Le menu à 105F avec steak. |
| Garçon | Vous le voulez comment votre steak, saignant, à point ou bien cuit? |
| Customer | Bien cuit, s'il vous plaît. |
| Garçon | Et comme légumes nous avons **des petits pois, des haricots verts** et puis des frites bien sûr. |
| Customer | Des frites ... |
| Garçon | Et comme boisson? Qu'est-ce que je vous sers? **Un pichet** de vin rouge? |
| Customer | Oui, un demi-litre de vin rouge et de l'eau minérale? |
| Garçon | Très bien. (*later*) **C'était bon?** |
| Customer | Très bon, merci. Qu'est-ce que vous avez comme dessert? |
| Garçon | Fromage, glace vanille, tarte aux abricots, crème au caramel. |
| Customer | Je vais prendre une glace à la vanille et un express. (*later*) Monsieur, l'addition, s'il vous plaît. |

| | |
|---|---|
| **une table** | a table |
| **la fenêtre** | window |
| **la grillade** | grilled meat |
| **je vous conseille** | I advise you, I recommend to you |
| **hors-d'oeuvres** | starters |
| **à volonté** | at will, of your choice |
| **au choix** | as you wish |
| **truite meunière** | trout fried in butter |
| **petits pois** | peas |
| **haricots verts** | green beans |
| **le pichet** | jug |
| **c'était bon** | it was good |

## ✅ Activité 5

After looking at the dialogue how would you say:

(a) What's a **blanquette de veau?**
(b) I don't like meat in sauce.
(c) I prefer grilled meats.
(d) I would like my steak well cooked.
(e) In the way of vegetables, I'll have some green beans.
(f) Half a litre of red wine.
(g) For dessert, I'll have a cream caramel.

## ✅ Activité 6

Now it's your turn to order a meal. When you check your answers in **Réponses,** remember that there are variations to the answers given.

| Serveuse | Bonjour, Monsieur, vous avez choisi? |
|---|---|
| (a) You | *Say that to start with you'll have a* **filet de hareng.** |
| Serveuse | Je regrette, il n'y a plus de filet de hareng. |
| (b) You | *Say thay you'll have an* **avocat cocktail.** |
| Serveuse | Bien, un avocat cocktail, et ensuite … |
| (c) You | *Ask what is* **cassoulet.** |
| Serveuse | C'est une spécialité française avec de la viande de porc et haricots blancs. |
| (d) You | *Say that you don't like beans. Say you'll have one* **Grillade du jour** *with* **frites.** |
| Serveuse | Vous la voulez comment, votre viande? |

| (e) You | *Say medium and say that you would also like a bottle of Sauvignon.* |
| Serveuse | (*After the first course*) Voilà, Monsieur. Une grillade avec frites. |
| (f) You | *Ask for bread.* |
| Serveuse | Encore du pain (*more bread*), oui Monsieur, tout de suite. |

## Activité 7

Below is an extract from a restaurant/hotel guide. See if you can understand it well enough to answer the following questions in English (**fermeture hebdomadaire** = *weekly closure*; **mi août** = *mid August*):

(a) Pendant la semaine le restaurant est fermé quel jour?
(b) En été, le restaurant est fermé pendant quelle période?
(c) Pour manger, il est meilleur marché de choisir les menus ou la carte?
(d) Est-ce qu'il y a une réduction pour les enfants?
(e) On peut manger dans le jardin?
(f) Ils acceptent les cartes de crédit?

## ✅ Petit test

You can now test yourself on Units 11, 12 and 13.

1 How would you say:
   (a) Where is the nearest restaurant?
   (b) I'm looking for something cheaper.
   (c) Do you have anything else?
2 You are asked to spell your name. Choose the French equivalent:
   (a) Ça s'écrit comment?
   (b) C'est à quel nom?
   (c) Est-ce qu'il reste encore des chambres?
3 How would you say:
   (a) There are no more cheese sandwiches.
   (b) For dessert I'll have a vanilla ice-cream.
   (c) Which drinks do you have?

# 14

## LES TRANSPORTS PUBLICS

*Public transport*

### In this unit you will

- find out about public transport in France
- learn key expressions to make travelling by bus, taxi, train and underground easier
- find out how to ask for information

### Avant de commencer on révise

- finding out what's available →P. 40
- asking for and understanding directions →P. 59, →P. 60, →P. 62
- expressions of time, days of the week **Mots-clefs** →P. 46
- numbers →P. 212

# Mots-clefs

| | |
|---|---|
| où est-ce que je peux ...? | where can I? |
| où est-ce qu'il faut ...? | where do you have to ...? |
| il faut descendre | you have to get off |
|     monter | get on |
|     changer | change |
|     voyager | travel |
|     composter le billet | date-stamp the ticket |
|     réserver une place | book a seat |
|         une couchette | a sleeper |
| le billet/ticket | ticket |
| le carnet (de tickets) | set of 10 tickets |
| c'est quelle direction? | which line is it? |
| c'est direct? | is it direct? |
| le voyage | travel, journey |
| de jour, de nuit | in the daytime, overnight |
| le trajet | journey |
| le métro | the underground |
| le RER (réseau express régional) | fast extension of the métro to the suburbs of Paris |
| la banlieue | the suburbs |
| la station de métro | tube station |
| la correspondance | connection |
| la sortie | exit |
| le taxi | taxi |
| la station de taxis | taxi rank |
| le pourboire | tip |
| l'autobus (m.) (bus) | town bus |
| l'autocar (m.) (car) | coach/long distance bus |
| la gare routière | bus station |
| l'arrêt (m.) d'autobus | bus stop |
| c'est quelle ligne? | what number (bus) is it? |
| la SNCF (Société Nationale des Chemins de Fer) | French railways |
| la gare | station (train) |
| le guichet | ticket office |
| une place | a seat (also square, as in **place du Marché**) |
| un aller (simple) | single ticket |
| un aller-retour | return ticket |
| le bureau de renseignements | information office |
| la consigne | left luggage (**consigne automatique** means left luggage lockers) |
| un horaire | timetable |
| le prochain/dernier train | the next/last train |
| en première/seconde | first/second class |
| le quai | platform |
| la voie | track (often used for 'platform' instead of **quai**) |

# Le Métro parisien
## *The Paris underground*

Le métro parisien est très pratique et économique. Avec un seul ticket vous pouvez aller n'importe où dans Paris (*anywhere in Paris*). Si vous achetez les tickets par carnet ils coûtent moins cher. Pour faire un nombre illimité de voyages pendant 2, 4 ou 7 jours, achetez une Carte Touristique.

Le métro a 15 lignes. Chaque ligne est connue sous les noms des 2 stations terminus. Pour changer d'une ligne à l'autre, suivez les panneaux oranges Correspondance et le nom de la ligne que vous désirez prendre. Du métro vous pouvez passer facilement au RER. C'est un métro ultra-rapide qui va aussi dans les banlieues de Paris. Il faut quelquefois payer un supplément si vous prenez le RER.

### ✔ Activité 1

Answer the following assertions with **vrai** or **faux**:

|  | vrai | faux |
|---|---|---|
| (a) There is a flat rate in central Paris. | ☐ | ☐ |
| (b) A set of 10 tickets is more expensive than 10 single tickets. | ☐ | ☐ |
| (c) One can buy a tourist pass for 10 days. | ☐ | ☐ |
| (d) Each line is known under one name. | ☐ | ☐ |
| (e) **Correspondance** is the sign to look for to change line. | ☐ | ☐ |
| (f) To go on the RER you may pay more. | ☐ | ☐ |

### ✔ Activité 2

Look at the diagram on page 145 then complete the dialogue filling the the spaces with the words in the box: the tourist is standing at the Champs-Elysées station.

Touriste      Pardon Monsieur, c'est quelle (a).......... pour la gare du Nord?

Homme       La gare du Nord? Vous (b).......... direction Vincennes.

Touriste      C'est direct?

| Homme | Non, il faut (c).......... à Châtelet. |
|---|---|
| Touriste | Bon je change à Châtelet et puis? |
| Homme | Puis vous prenez direction (d).......... et voilà vous (e).......... à la septième station. |

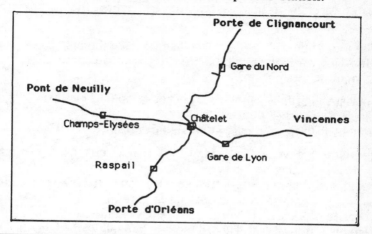

| Porte de Clignancourt | | descendez |
|---|---|---|
| | changer | |
| prenez | | direction |

###  Activité 3

An Englishman cannot understand the directions he's given to get from **gare de Lyon** to **Raspail**. Listen to the cassette (if you haven't got it look at the diagram above) and tell him in English what to do.

## —— Prendre un taxi  *Taking a taxi* ——

If you need a taxi look for the blue and white sign **station de taxis;** the taxis have a white light on the roofs. There is a slight supplement to pay for having the luggage put in the boot of the taxi and another charge if you book a **radio taxi** by phone, known as **la prise en charge.** Taxi drivers expect a 12-15% tip – **le pourboire.**

# Dialogue 1

## La station de taxis

Listen carefully to the cassette, or read below, then answer the following questions:

The tourist doesn't get any information from the first passer-by: why? How far is the taxi rank? At the crossroads does he have to go right or straight on?

Touriste    Pardon, Monsieur, où est la station de taxis la plus proche?

Homme      Je ne sais pas, je ne suis pas d'ici …

Touriste    S'il vous plaît, Madame, savez-vous où il y a une station de taxis?

Femme      Mais oui, c'est très simple, vous en avez une, à cinq cents mètres, à côté de la gare du Nord.

Touriste    La gare du Nord, c'est où exactement?

Femme      Bon, il faut d'abord monter le boulevard Magenta. Au carrefour, vous allez continuer tout droit et prendre le boulevard Denain et à droite de la gare du Nord vous allez trouver la station de taxis.

## Activité 4

Would you be able to find the taxi rank? Choose the correct meaning:

(a) **Il faut monter** means

   (i)   turn …
   (ii)  go up …
   (iii) cross

(b) **Un carrefour** is
   (i)   crossroads
   (ii)  traffic light
   (iii) sign post

(c) **Vous continuez tout droit** means
   (i)   turn left
   (ii)  turn right
   (iii) carry straight on

# Voyager en autobus
## *Travelling by bus*

In Paris the underground tickets are also valid for buses. You buy them in advance at **une station de métro, une gare routière,** or **un bureau de tabac.** Depending on the journey (**le trajet**) you'll need to insert one or two tickets in the machine situated at the front of the bus. Each bus stop has a diagram showing the route of the bus and indicating how many tickets are needed for any particular trip on that route.

# Dialogue 2

## A la gare routière

| | |
|---|---|
| Touriste | Pardon, Monsieur, c'est quelle ligne pour aller au musée d'Orsay? |
| Homme | La ligne 49 … |
| Touriste | C'est direct? |
| Homme | Non, il faut changer; vous descendez aux Invalides puis vous pouvez prendre la ligne 63 ou bien vous y allez à pied. |
| Touriste | C'est loin à pied? |
| Homme | Des Invalides? Non, **il vous faudra** une quinzaine de minutes. |
| Touriste | Le bus part à quelle heure? |
| Homme | Dans 10 minutes. |
| Touriste | Et … où est-ce que je peux acheter un ticket? |
| Homme | Au guichet là-bas … |
| Touriste | (*later*) Je voudrais acheter un ticket aller-retour pour les Invalides. |
| Femme | Il n'y a pas de tickets aller-retour. Achetez 2 tickets ou bien alors un carnet, c'est plus pratique et moins cher. |
| Touriste | Un carnet, qu'est-ce que c'est? |
| Femme | C'est dix tickets pour le prix de 7. |
| Touriste | Très bien. Je vais prendre un carnet. |

(**il vous faudra** … = it will take you …)

# Dialogue 3

## Etre dans le bon autobus

| Touriste | Ce bus va bien aux Invalides? |
|---|---|
| Chauffeur | Oui, c'est bien ça. |
| Touriste | Vous pouvez me dire où il faut descendre? |
| Chauffeur | Oui, bien sûr mais c'est très facile, c'est l'arrêt où il y a un grand monument avec un dôme. |
| Touriste | Euh ... oui mais je ne connais pas Paris. |

## Activité 5

How would you say:

(a) What bus number goes to the **musée d'Orsay?**

(b) Is it direct?

(c) Is it far on foot?

(d) At what time does the bus leave?

(e) Where can I buy a ticket?

(f) I would like to buy a return-ticket to les **Invalides.**

(g) I'll take a set of tickets.

## Activité 6

Match the questions on the left with the correct answers on the right.

(a) C'est quelle ligne pour Le Louvre?

(b) C'est combien le carnet?

(c) C'est direct?

(d) C'est loin en bus?

(e) Où est la gare du Nord?

(f) Où faut-il descendre?

(g) A quelle heure part le car?

(i) A l'arrêt Hôtel de Ville.

(ii) C'est à une trentaine de minutes.

(iii) Il part dans 10 minutes.

(iv) Non, il faut changer.

(v) C'est 34F50.

(vi) Je ne sais pas, je ne suis pas d'ici.

(vii) La ligne 42.

# — La SNCF (Société Nationale des — Chemins de Fer) *French railways*

To make the most of travel bargains (**tarifs réduits**) giving up to a 50% reduction to young people, couples and families, go to the French Railways office in London or British Rail. In France go to any **bureau de renseignements** for travel information. You can travel on an express (**un rapide**), an air-conditioned inter-city train (**un Corail**) or a high speed train (**TGV - train à grande vitesse**). To book your seat (**une place assise**) you'll need to go to the **bureau des réservations**.

If a train ticket is bought in France it must be date-stamped (**composté**) in one of the orange **composteurs** (machine in which you have to insert your ticket) in the station before you board the train. If you travel on the TGV you'll have to reserve your seat and pay a supplement when travelling during peak hours (**heures de pointe**).

 ——————— **Dialogue 4** ———————

## Au bureau de renseignements

Listen to the cassette and/or read the dialogue and try to answer the following questions:   Where does the man want to go? How many trains are there in the morning? With whom will he be travelling? Is there a restaurant on board the train?

| Homme | Bonjour Madame, je voudrais partir à Paris avec ma femme et mes deux enfants et je voudrais voyager le matin si possible. |
| Hôtesse | Oui, alors vous avez un Corail qui part de Bordeaux à 9h33 et qui arrive à Paris à 14h55. |
| Homme | Très bien. Il met un peu plus de cinq heures jusqu'à Paris. |
| Hôtesse | Oui, c'est ça et vous avez aussi un TGV qui part à 10 heures et qui arrive à 12h58 à Paris-Montparnasse. |

| Homme | Bon je vais prendre le TGV; c'est beaucoup plus rapide. Est-ce que vous pouvez me donner le prix du billet, s'il vous plaît, pour ma famille? |
|---|---|
| Hôtesse | Le prix pour l'aller-retour? |
| Homme | Oui, c'est ça. |
| Hôtesse | Vous voyagez en première ou en seconde classe? |
| Homme | En seconde classe. |
| Hôtesse | En seconde classe, bien ... et vous avez une réduction? |
| Homme | Oui, une Carte de Famille. |
| Hôtesse | Avec une Carte de Famille, le prix du billet aller-retour pour quatre est de 1990 francs. Et il y a aussi un supplément à payer de 100F par personne. |
| Homme | Merci bien; est-ce qu'il y a un restaurant dans ce train? |
| Hôtesse | Non, il n'y a pas de voiture-restaurant mais vous avez un bar qui sert des sandwiches, des plats chauds et froids et des boissons. |
| Homme | Et il faut réserver les places? |
| Hôtesse | Ah oui, c'est obligatoire dans le TGV. Pour la réservation des places il faut aller au bureau des réservations. |

## Activité 7

Take the part of the traveller in this conversation:

| (a) Vous | *Say you want to go to Grenoble. Ask for one return ticket.* |
|---|---|
| Employé | Oui, un aller-retour. Il y a deux trains: un le matin et l'autre l'après-midi. |
| (b) Vous | *Say you would like to travel in the morning.* |
| Employé | Alors, vous avez un train qui part à 10h42 et qui arrive à Grenoble à 12h25. Vous voyagez en première ou deuxième classe? |
| (c) Vous | *Say first.* |
| Employé | Vous avez des réductions? |
| (d) Vous | *Say no. Ask if you have to change?* |
| Employé | Non, c'est direct. |
| (e) Vous | *Find out if there is a restaurant car.* |
| Employé | Non, mais il y a un bar ouvert pendant tout le voyage. |

## ✅ *Petit test*

Test yourself to find out how much you can remember from Units 13 and 14.

How would you say:

1　I would like a cheese sandwich?
2　What do you have to drink?
3　I would like a set of 10 tickets?
4　At what time does the next train to Paris leave?

# 15

## FAIRE DU TOURISME
### *Sightseeing*

### *In this unit you will*

- learn how to ask for a town map
- find out about visiting interesting places
- practise buying admission tickets
- find out about museums in France
- book an excursion

### *Avant de commencer on révise*

- saying what you want ➔ **P.** 48
- asking and understanding directions ➔ **P.** 59, ➔ **P.** 60, ➔ **P.** 62
- asking what you can do ➔ **P.** 49
- expressions of time, days of the week **Mots-clefs** ➔ **P.** 46

## ━━━━━ Mots-clefs ━━━━━

| | |
|---|---|
| **le plan de la ville** | town map |
| **les environs** | surroundings |
| **qu'est-ce qu'il y a à faire?** | what is there to do? |
| **qu'est-ce qu'il y a à voir?** | what is there to see? |

| | |
|---|---|
| une visite guidée | guided tour |
| les jours fériés/les jours de fête | public holidays |
| l'entrée | way in, admission charge |
| en pleine saison | in high season |
| hors saison | out of season |
| le musée | museum |
| faire une excursion | to go on an excursion |
| piqueniquer | to picnic |
| une agence de voyages | travel agency |
| une agence de location | booking office |

# _ Se renseigner sur les choses à voir _
## *Getting information on things to see*

Avant de visiter une ville ou une région, allez à l'office du tourisme ou au syndicat d'initiative pour demander un plan de la ville et des brochures sur la ville et ses environs. Les offices du tourisme proposent souvent des visites guidées des villes; renseignez-vous.

 —————————— **Dialogue** ——————————

Touriste   Bonjour Madame, je voudrais un plan de la ville s'il vous plaît.

Hôtesse   Oui, voilà.

Touriste   Nous ne sommes pas d'ici. Qu'est-ce qu'il y a à voir à Orléans?

Hôtesse   Il y a beaucoup de monuments historiques, surtout dans la vieille ville, comme la maison de Jeanne d'Arc, au numéro 52 sur le plan, à côté de la cathédrale Sainte-Croix; et puis il y a une belle promenade à faire le long de la Loire. Du pont George V, vous avez une vue magnifique sur la Loire.

Touriste   Et qu'est-ce qu'il y a à faire pour les enfants?

Hôtesse   Près d'ici, il y a une piscine couverte ou même le musée des Sciences Naturelles qui se trouve rue Emile Zola. Un peu plus loin, vous avez le Parc Floral.

Touriste   Et pour aller au Parc Floral … il y a un bus?

Hôtesse   Oui, vous avez un autobus toutes les 30 minutes. Il part du centre ville, place du Martroi.

—— **153** ——

## ✔ Activité 1

(a) How would you ask for a town map?
(b) Ask what there is to see.
(c) Ask what there is to do for the children.
(d) Ask if there is an indoor swimming pool.
(e) Ask if there is a bus to go to the Parc Floral.

## ✔ Activité 2

You are visiting the Parc Floral with your son, aged seven, in August. See if you understand the information on the Parc Floral, by answering the questions.

---

**EN SAISON: du 1er AVRIL au 11 NOVEMBRE 1988**
HEURES D'OUVERTURE: accès du public tous les jours de 9h à 18h - GRATUIT: pour enfants de moins de 12 ans accompagnés.
TARIF NORMAL adultes: 14F - DEMI TARIF: 7F (étudiants, militaires en tenue, sociétés horticoles)
GROUPES: 15 à 99 personnes: 11F - 100 personnes et plus: 7F - GRATUITE: chauffeur et accompagnateur.
PETIT TRAIN: de mai au 15 spetembre: tous les après-midi sauf vendredi - avril/15 septembre au 11 novembre: après-midi des mercredis, samedis, dimanches et fêtes - TARIF NORMAL adultes: 6F - GRATUIT pour enfants de moins de 4 ans accompagnés - Enfants de 4 à 11 ans et groupes scolaires: 4F - GROUPES 15 personnes et plus : 5F - GRATUIT pour l'accompagnateur. Pour bénéficier de TARIF GROUPE, les billets doivent être pris par le RESPONSABLE. AUCUNE RESERVATION ne sera faite. Pour INFORMATION, nous préciser par téléphone ou par courrier promenade en petit train. Durée du parcours: 20 minutes - Nombre de places: 100.
Les BILLETS sont delivrés à l'arrivée, réglés en espèces ou par chèques.
VISITES NON GUIDEES: prévoir environ 1h 30.
INFORMATION JARDINAGE: renseignements horticoles, montage audio-visuel.
MINI-GOLF: avril à septembre tous les après-midi - octobre à mars tous les week-ends.
RESTAURANT SERRE: écrire Restaurant Serre, Plarc Floral 45072 Orléans Cedex 02 - Tél. 38.63.20.51.
AMIS DU PARC FLORAL: cartes permanentes au secrétariat.
SALLE DE REUNION: pour 20 à 40 personnes - écrire au secrétariat.
RENSEIGNEMENTS: **PARC FLORAL** - 45072 Orléans Cedex 02 - Tél. 38.63.33.17.
**HORS SAISON: du 12 Novembre 1988 à FIN MARS 1989**
Parc Floral ouvert tous les jours de 14h à 17h - Tarif unique: 7F.

---

(a) What are the opening hours?
(b) What is the entrance fee for yourself and your child (you have no reduction).
(c) You want to have a ride on the **petit train**. Will you have to pay extra?
(d) If so, how much?
(e) How long does the ride take?
(f) Does it say how long the tour of the Parc will take?
(g) Can you play mini-golf in the morning?
(h) How much is the admission fee in the low season?

## On visite *Visiting*

──────────────── **Dialogue** ────────────────

Au Parc Floral: un touriste achète des tickets pour l'entrée au Parc Floral.

*A tourist is buying some tickets for admission to the Parc Floral. Read the dialogue twice and answer the following questions: How many tickets is he buying? How old are the children?*

| | |
|---|---|
| Touriste | Je voudrais quatre billets, s'il vous plaît. |
| Employée | Quel âge ont les enfants? |
| Touriste | Onze ans et treize ans. |
| Employée | Bon, le plus jeune ne paye pas et pour l'autre c'est demi-tarif. Alors deux adultes et un enfant, ça fait 35F. |
| Touriste | Il y a des visites guidées? |
| Employée | Oui, toutes les heures vous avez une visite qui commence au pavillon 'Information Jardinage'. |
| Touriste | Et ... on peut faire un piquenique dans le parc? |
| Employée | Oui, bien sûr, il y a une aire de piquenique près des stands souvenirs. |
| Touriste | Et ... la visite dure combien de temps? |
| Employée | Ça dépend ... mais en principe en 1h.30 vous pouvez tout voir. |
| Touriste | Merci bien, Mademoiselle. |

### Activité 3

Now it's your turn to buy some tickets. You are accompanied by your son who is nine.

| | |
|---|---|
| (a) You | *Ask how much the admission charge is.* |
| Employé | L'entrée coûte 14 francs par personne. Quel âge a l'enfant? |
| (b) You | *Say his age.* |
| Employé | Neuf ans. Alors c'est gratuit pour lui. Voilà, ça fait 14F. |
| (c) You | *Ask if you need to pay for the mini-golf.* |
| Employé | Non, il ne faut pas payer mais c'est fermé le matin. |
| (d) You | *Ask if you can have a picnic.* |

| Employé | Bien sûr; l'aire de piquenique est derrière le restaurant. |
|---|---|
| (e) You | *Ask what time the park closes.* |
| Employé | Nous fermons à 18 heures. |

# —— Les musées  *Museums* ——

Les musées sont généralement ouverts tous les jours sauf le lundi ou le mardi. Quelquefois l'entrée est gratuite un jour par semaine. Avec une carte d'étudiant vous avez droit à une réduction. Renseignez-vous sur les jours et heures d'ouverture; certains musées sont fermés entre midi et 2 heures et pendant les fêtes et jours fériés.

## ☑ Activité 4

Look at the information below – this is the kind of information you may find about places of interest – then answer the questions.

**Arc de Triomphe**
*Place Charles-de-Gaulle - 75008*
*Tél. 43.80.31.31*  Ⓜ Charles-de-Gaulle - Etoile
Ouvert du 1er octobre au 31 mars de 10 h à 17 h, du 1er avril au 30 septembre de 10 h à 18 h. Fermé les jours fériés.
Admirable perspective sur tout Paris et le Bois de Boulogne et, au premier plan, sur les douze avenues rayonnant en étoile. C'est le point culminant de la Voie Triomphale, à mi-chemin entre le jardin des Tuileries et la Défense.

**Musée Picasso**
*5, rue de Thorigny - 75003 - Tél. 42.71.25.21.*  Ⓜ Chemin-Vert
Tous les jours, sauf mardi, de 10 h à 17 h 15. Le mercredi jusqu'à 22 h.

**Le Louvre**
*Palais du Louvre - 75041 Paris Cedex 01 - Tél. 42.60.39.26*  Ⓜ Louvre
Tous les jours de 9 h 45 à 18 h 30, sauf mardi et jours fériés.
Entrée gratuite le dimanche.
Les prestigieuses collections sont actuellement réparties en sept départements : Peintures - Dessins - Antiquités égyptiennes - Antiquités orientales - Antiquités grecques et romaines - Sculptures - Objets d'Art.

**Le Panthéon**
*Place du Panthéon - 75005 - Tél. 43.54.34.51*  RER Luxembourg
Ouvert tous les jours de 10 h à 12 h et de 14 h à 17 h.
En 1791, la Constituante décide que cette ancienne église sera destinée, sous le nom de Panthéon, à recevoir les cendres des "grands hommes de l'époque de la liberté française" : parmi eux, Mirabeau, Voltaire, Rousseau, puis, Victor Hugo, Emile Zola et plus près de nous, un des héros de la Résistance : Jean Moulin.

(a) If you were in Paris on a Tuesday, which buildings could you visit?

(b) If you didn't have much money, which day would you choose to visit Le Louvre?

(c) What could you visit late in the evening?

(d) If you were interested in visiting the building which contains the tombs of famous French men where would you go?

(e) Could you visit it on a Sunday between 12.00 and 14.00?

# Faire une excursion
## *Going on an excursion*

### ✔ Activité 5

You're interested in French wines so you've decided to go with your partner on a coach excursion following **la route des vins de Bourgogne.** Look at the information and answer the questions below:

---

## LA ROUTE DES VINS DE BOURGOGNE

**1 JOUR**

13 mai
3/17 juin
22 juillet
9 sept
20 oct
11 nov

Aller/retour . . . . . . . . . . . . . . . . . . . . **200 F**

**Rendez-vous 7h15.
Départ 7h30.**

Arrivée à Vezelay vers 10h.
Arrêt d'une heure pour visiter la basilique Sainte-Madeleine.
Continuation vers Beaune. Arrêt pour déjeu-

ner et temps libre pour visiter les Hospices et le Musée du vin. Visite d'une cave avec dégustation.

Départ à 16h par la route de vins.
(Nuits-Saint-Georges, Gevrey-Chambertin).

Retour à Paris vers 23h.

---

(a) At what time should you be at the bus stop in the morning?
(b) How long do you stop for at Vezelay?
(c) Name at least 2 things you could do from lunch time until 4pm.
(d) How much is the excursion for 2 people?

### ✔ Activité 6

You and your friend decide to book the trip to Beaune. Speak for both of you.

| | |
|---|---|
| (a) You | *Say you'd like to go on the excursion of **la route des vins de Bourgogne.*** |
| Employé | Vous voulez réserver des places pour quel jour? |
| (b) You | *Say you'd like 2 places for the 22nd July.* |
| Employé | Le 22 juillet? Bon ... ça va, il y a de la place ... ça fait 400F. |

*(c)* You      *Ask if the coach leaves from here.*

Employé    Non, le car part de la place Denfert-Rochereau, devant le café de Belfort.

*(d)* You      *Ask him to repeat.*

Employé    Oui, place Denfert-Rochereau devant le café de Belfort; mais je vais vous donner tous ces renseignements par écrit.

*(e)* You      *Thank him; ask what time the coach leaves.*

Employé    Le car part à 7h30 mais il faut être là à 7h15.

*(f)* You      *Ask if you can buy some wine in the wine cellar.*

Employé    Oui, vous pouvez déguster et acheter des vins de Bourgogne à un prix spécial.

## ✔️ Activité 7

Listen to Michel discussing with his friend Rosine the possibility of going on a coach excursion to Mont St-Michel (if you haven't got the cassette, look at the transcription below). Then fill in the grid on the next page.

Michel    Dis, Rosine, tu veux venir avec moi au Mont Saint-Michel?

Rosine    Au Mont Saint-Michel! Quelle bonne idée; j'aime tellement la Bretagne.

Michel    Il y a une excursion, en car, organisée par le Club Alliance le 23 septembre, c'est un samedi; ça te va comme date?

Rosine    Le 23 septembre? Oui, c'est très bien. Et à quelle heure part-on de Paris?

Michel    Oh, il faut se lever très tôt. On part à 7h30 de Paris pour arriver au Mont Saint-Michel pour le déjeuner.

Rosine    Qu'est-ce qu'il y a à voir exactement au Mont Saint-Michel?

Michel    Eh bien il y a beaucoup de monuments historiques à visiter; tu as d'abord l'abbaye puis il y a un très beau cloître et il faut aussi voir les remparts bien sûr.

Rosine    Mais il nous faut beaucoup de temps pour visiter tout ça! A quelle heure repart-on pour Paris?

Michel    On quitte le Mont Saint-Michel à 18 heures et on arrive à Paris vers 23 heures.

## Mont St-Michel

(a) Jour du départ _____.
(b) Heure du départ de Paris _____.
(c) Arrivée au Mont St-Michel _____.
(d) Monuments à visiter _____.
(e) Arrivée à Paris _____.

## ✅ Petit test

How would you ask:

1 for a town map?
2 if the museum closes between 12.00 and 14.00?
3 if there is a guided tour?

# 16

## SORTIR
### *Going out*

---

### *In this unit you will*

- practise finding out what's on
- book seats for a concert
- find out where you can play tennis and other sports

### *Avant de commencer on révise*

- finding out what's on and where ➡️ **P** 153
- saying what you want ➡️ **P** 48
- asking what you can do ➡️ **P** 49
- talking about your likes and dislikes ➡️ **P** 84
- expressions of time, days of the week **Mots-clefs** ➡️ **P** 46

---

## Mots-clefs

---

| | |
|---|---|
| **qu'est-ce qu'il y a comme ...?** | what sort of ... is/are there? |
| **qu'est-ce qu'on peut faire?** | what can I/we/one do? |
| **un spectacle** | a show |
| **une soirée** | evening entertainment, party |
| **un dîner-dansant** | dinner and dance |
| **l'ambiance (f.)** | atmosphere |
| **la salle** | room, hall, auditorium |
| **une boîte (de nuit)** | nightclub |

— 160 —

| | |
|---|---|
| un piano-bar | all night restaurant with small band |
| louer | to book, to hire |
| la location | hiring |
| le prêt | lending |
| le bureau de location | booking office |
| la place | a seat |
| une séance | performance, film showing |
| tarif (m.) réduit | reduced rate |
| entrée (f.) libre | free admission |
| il/elle doit payer? | he/she must pay? |
| c'est combien l'heure? | how much is it an hour? |
| c'est combien la journée? | how much is it a day? |
| une carte d'abonnement | season ticket |
| un court de tennis | tennis court |
| un cours particulier | private lesson |
| l'inscription (f.) | enrolment |
| faire une promenade | to go for a walk |
| faire une randonnée | to go for a walk/hike |
| faire du vélo | to go cycling |
| le jeu de société | board game |

# ───── Où aller? *Where to go?* ─────

Pour connaître le programme et les horaires des spectacles, demandez à l'office du tourisme la brochure La France en Fête. Si vous êtes à Paris, achetez dans un kiosque à journaux un journal spécialisé comme **Pariscope** ou **l'Officiel des Spectacles**.

Vous pouvez louer (réserver) votre place au théatre ou au concert dans une agence le location.

Pour pratiquer votre sport préféré, renseignez-vous à l'office du tourisme.

## ✔ Activité 1

Fill in the blanks with words from the passage above.

Before going to a show you need to know the (a) ............

and the (b) ............

The brochure 'La France en Fête' (equivalent of 'what's on') is available from the (c) ............

You will also find out what's on in Paris if you buy (d) ............

and (e) ............

You can book your seat at an (f) ............

## Sortir le soir *Going out at night*

—————————— **Dialogue 1** ——————————

| | |
|---|---|
| Touriste | Je passe quelques jours dans la région. Qu'est-ce qu'on peut faire ici le soir? |
| Hôtesse | Il y a beaucoup de choses à faire mais ça dépend, qu'est-ce que vous aimez? Le jazz? La danse? |
| Touriste | Oui, nous aimons danser mais surtout ... bien manger. |
| Hôtesse | Eh bien pourquoi n'allez-vous pas à un dîner-dansant ou dans un restaurant piano-bar? |
| Touriste | Un restaurant piano-bar, qu'est-ce que c'est? |
| Hôtesse | C'est un restaurant où il y a de la musique avec orchestre. En général, il y a une très bonne ambiance et ça reste ouvert toute la nuit. Mais ... (*pause*) si vous aimez danser vous avez le restaurant 'Raspoutine' tout près d'ici qui organise des soirées dansantes avec repas et orchestre tzigane. |
| Touriste | C'est combien pour la soirée dansante? |
| Hôtesse | C'est 350F par personne, tout compris, avec spectacle. |
| Touriste | Je peux acheter les billets ici? |
| Hôtesse | Non, il faut aller au bureau de location qui se trouve au bout du boulevard Victor Hugo; mais ... attendez un instant, je vais vous chercher le programme des spectacles de la semaine avec la liste des restaurants et des bars. |

## ✔ Activité 2

Without looking back at the text say if the following assertions are **vrai** or **faux**:

|  | vrai | faux |
|---|---|---|
| (a) The tourist wants to know what's on in the day-time. | ☐ | ☐ |
| (b) She likes going to concerts. | ☐ | ☐ |

(c)  A piano-bar is a place that is open only at lunchtime.  □ □

(d)  At 'Raspoutine' you can eat and dance.  □ □

(e)  The price for everything including the meal is 350F per person.  □ □

(f)  The hostess gives the tourist the programme of the week.  □ □

## ✔ Activité 3

Here is the kind of night attraction described in 'l'Officiel des Spectacles et Loisirs'. Work out what is on at each night-spot and say who would enjoy which one most.

(i)  **Vos Soirées**

**AIX-EN-PROVENCE**

**OSMOSE**
Ne restez plus seul(e) le week-end OSMOSE organise des soirées dansantes avec repas et animation
Téléphonez vite pour réserver:
AIX-EN-PROVENCE – 42 26 96 69

(ii)

**ARLES**

37'2 COCKTAIL BAR GLACIER, 19, place Honoré-Clerc, près de la place du Forum à ARLES. Tél. 90 96 11 44.
Ouvert tous les jours à partir de 17 heures.
Après le spectacle et dans une ambiance Jazz le nouveau rendez-vous d'Arles.

(iii)

**CHATEAUNEUF-LES-MARTIGUES**

**CLUB 1805**

Discothèque
Deux salles climatisées
Attractions. Soirées à thèmes
Ouvert du Mercredi au Dimanche
Plage du Jaï
13220 Châteauneuf-les-Martigues
Tél. 42 43 11 42

(iv)  **SAINT-CYR-SUR-MER**

**DINER SPECTACLES**

LES ENFANTS TERRIBLES

● LES ENFANTS TERRIBLES, Rte de Port-d'Alon, 83270 ST-CYR/MER.

Tél. 94 26 15 62. Ouvert tous les soirs en saison ainsi que le restaurant à midi. Menus tout compris avec spectacle 180F. Terrasse. Parking assuré. (v) est prudent de réserver.

**SALON-DE-PROVENCE**

**Au Grenier d'Abondance**
LE RENDEZ-VOUS CHIC DE LA NUIT

RESTAURANT ● PIANO ● BAR ouvert tous les soirs à partir de 19 heures
Fermé le Mardi

38, rue Auguste-Moutin - Face à la Maine
SALON-DE-PROVENCE – Tél. 90 56 34 99

(a)  Two tourists who decide to go out on a Tuesday night. They want to eat out and see a show at the same time.

(b)  Someone who enjoys listening to the piano and staying up late at night.

(c)  Two people who love dancing.

(d)  A single person looking for a night out during the week-end.

(e)  A group of students who decide to go for a drink, after a show, in a jazzy night spot.

## Activité 4

Listen to Michel booking by phone a table at the 'Fiesta' restaurant. Can you answer the following questions? You will need to listen to the cassette to be able to answer all the questions (**dîner aux chandelles** = *dinner by candlelight*).

### CHATELET – LES HALLES

**FIESTA**, 49, rue de l'Arbre-sec, 42 61 26 19. F. dim. gastronomie Franco-Espagnole. Déj. dîner spectacles aux chandelles avec amb. musicale. Chants et guitare. Jusq. 2h du matin. Consommation sans dîner 70 F.

**PETIT CASINO**, 17, rue Chapon. Rés. 42 78 36 50. *(Voir rubrique « Cafés-Théatres ».)*

(a)  Which day does the restaurant close?
(b)  Michel books a table for how many people?
(c)  At what time does the show start?
(d)  What does Michel particularly like?
(e)  What type of cooking is served?
(f)  At what time does the show finish?
(g)  How much is it per person?

## ———— Dialogue 2 ————

| | |
|---|---|
| Jeune fille | Pardon Monsieur, je voudrais des places pour le récital de guitare, samedi prochain. |
| Employé | Je regrette, samedi c'est complet mais il reste encore des places pour jeudi et vendredi. |
| Jeune fille | Bon, eh bien je vais prendre deux places pour jeudi. Ça finit à quelle heure le concert? |
| Employé | Le concert commence à 17h45 donc je pense qu'il finira vers 22h30. |
| Jeune fille | Bon, ça va, ce n'est pas trop tard. C'est combien la place, j'ai une carte étudiante? |
| Employé | Alors avec une carte étudiante, c'est tarif réduit à 75F. |
| Jeune fille | Ma soeur a 15 ans. Elle doit payer? |
| Employé | C'est entrée libre jusqu'à 16 ans. |

## ✔ Activité 5

How do you say:

(a)  I would like some seats for next Saturday.
(b)  At what time does the concert finish?
(c)  How much is it for a ticket?
(d)  It is reduced rate.
(e)  Does my sister have to pay?

## ✔ Activité 6

Below is an extract from the film section in 'l'Officiel des Spectacles': can you understand it well enough to answer the questions? To understand the abbreviations, look at the box:

| | |
|---|---|
| **Pathe Imperial,** 29 bd des Italiens, 47 42 72 52, Mᵒ Opéra. CB. Pl. 38F. TR. 30F : lun + étud., FN aux 3 premières séances. Séances: 13h35, 16h15, 18h55, 21h35. Film 25 mn après: **Le Cercle des Poètes Disparus** | bd  boulevard<br>Mᵒ  métro<br>CB  carte bleue<br>Pl.  place<br>TR  tarif réduit<br>lun.  lundi<br>étud.  étudiant<br>FN  famille nombreuse |

(a)  What's the nearest underground station?
(b)  Which credit card is accepted?
(c)  How much is a ticket without reduction?
(d)  Which day is cheaper for students?
(e)  For which shows are large families given reductions?

## ━━━━ Dialogue 3 ━━━━

Une touriste veut jouer au tennis. Elle se renseigne à l'office du tourisme.
*A tourist wants to play tennis. She inquires at the tourist office.*
She asks five questions; try to note at least three of them.

Touriste    Où est-ce qu'on peut jouer au tennis?
Hôtesse     Vous avez à Anglet le Club de Chiberta avec 15 courts.

Touriste  Ah très bien et où est-ce qu'on réserve le court?
Hôtesse  Vous réservez les courts au Club.
Touriste  C'est combien l'heure?
Hôtesse  Je ne sais pas. Il faut vous renseigner là-bas mais si vous jouez souvent, vous pouvez certainement prendre une carte d'abonnement.
Touriste  Je n'ai pas ma raquette de tennis avec moi. On peut louer une raquette au Club?
Hôtesse  Je pense que oui.
Touriste  Vous pouvez me donner l'adresse du Club, s'il vous plaît?
Hôtesse  Mais oui, la voilà.

## ☑ Activité 7

How would you ask:

(a) Where can I play tennis?
(b) Where do I book the court?
(c) How much is it for one hour?
(d) Can one hire a racket?
(e) Can you give me the address of the Club?

## ☑ Activité 8

You are working at the office du tourisme in Vittel. An English family comes in. The members are all very eager to join in the various activities organised by the town (see below). Can you answer their questions?

---

● **ACTIVITES SPORTIVES ET DE LOISIRS avec JEAN-LOUIS et ANNE**

**Jogging:** dans le parc en petites foulées sur un rythme progressif.
**Gymnastique:** en salle, assouplissement et tonification musculaire.
**Tir à l'arc:** initiation et perfectionnement de la maîtrise du tir.
**Promenades et randonnées (pédestre, vélo):** parcourir la campagne et les bois environnants.
**Self défense:** initiation, découverte des gestes d'auto-défense.
**Volley et sports collectifs,** ✎
**Gym, danse et stretching.**
**Promenade VTT:** initiation. ✎ ✳

● **ACTIVITES TENNIS et GOLF avec BRUNO**

Usage des cours et du practice, du putting green.
Initiation golf et tennis en groupe. ✎
Cours particuliers. ✎ ✳

● **L'OFFICE DU TOURISME EST A VOTRE DISPOSITION POUR**

Ses locations ou prêts de vélos, matériels de golf, ● de tennis de table, jeux de société;

Son coin lecture (journaux, hebdomadaires).

✳ Activité avec participation financière,
✎ Activité avec inscription,

---

(a) The woman is very keen on playing tennis:
    (i)  Can she have private classes?
    (ii)  Can she hire a tennis racket?

(b) The husband would like to go for a bicycle ride:
    (i)  Can he hire a bicycle?
    (ii)  Does he need to enrol if he goes on an organised trip?

(c) Her youngest son would like to try out mountain biking (**VTT – vélo tous terrains**).
    (i)  Is it free?
    (ii)  Does he need to enrol?

(d) Her daughter is very keen on doing archery. They have been told that the town runs archery classes:
    (i)  Is it true?
    (ii)  Does she have to pay?

(e) If it rains what can they do indoors?
    (i)  .................................................................................
    (ii)  .................................................................................

## ☑ *Petit test* on Units 14, 15 and 16

1   If you saw the following signs in a French station, would you know what they meant?
    (a)  composter
    (b)  sortie
    (c)  correspondance
    (d)  consigne
    (e)  quai
    (f)  guichet

2   Can you ask for:
    (a)  a book of 10 tickets
    (b)  a return ticket
    (c)  a time-table
    (d)  the bus stop
    (e)  the information office
    (f)  a single ticket?

Complete the three following sentences by choosing the ending (a) (b) or (c).

**3** Si vous voulez faire un piquenique vous cherchez le panneau (*sign*)

(*a*) sortie.

(*b*) restaurant.

(*c*) aire de piquenique.

**4** Pour faire une excursion vous allez

(*a*) au musée.

(*b*) à la piscine couverte.

(*c*) à l'agence de voyages.

**5** L'entrée dans les parcs et les monuments historiques est souvent plus chère

(*a*) en pleine saison.

(*b*) hors saison.

(*c*) les jours fériés.

**6** Fill in the blanks:

(*a*) (au cinéma) Je voudrais une p..... pour la séance de 17h30.

(*b*) Le lundi, c'est t..... réduit pour les étudiants.

(*c*) J'adore danser; je voudrais aller dans une b..... d..... n.....

(*d*) Il y a une très bonne a..... dans ce piano-bar.

(*e*) Demandez le programme des s..... à l'office du tourisme.

# 17

# BONNE ROUTE
*Safe journey*

## In this unit you will

- learn useful information for travelling on French roads
- learn some French road signs
- practise asking directions
- buy some petrol and get your tyre pressures checked
- find out what to do in case of breakdown
- learn some essential words describing what's wrong with your car

## Avant de commencer on révise

- asking the way and understanding directions **➡ P.** 59, **➡ P.** 60
- asking for assistance **➡ P.** 93
- understanding what you need to do **➡ P.** 94
- numbers **➡ P.** 212

## Les routes françaises
### French roads

En France, il y a plus de 5000 kilomètres d'autoroutes, beaucoup sont à péage. On y trouve des aires de repos et des stations service tous les 10 à 15km, et un poste téléphonique tous les 2km.

La vitesse est limitée à:

- 130 km/h sur les autoroutes (indiquées sur les cartes par A).
- 110 km/h sur les routes à 4 voies.
- 90 km/h sur les autres routes, comme les routes nationales (N) et les départementales (D).
- 60 km/h en ville et en agglomération.

Evitez de voyager le lundi de Pâques et le lundi de Pentecôte, le dernier week-end de juin, les premiers week-ends de juillet, août et septembre, le 14 juillet, le 15 août et généralement tous les jours fériés car il y a beaucoup de circulation sur les routes.

Pour éviter les bouchons (longues files de voitures bloquées) téléphonez avant votre départ aux services de renseignements, et suivez les informations données par **Bison Futé\*** et les **itinéraires bis\*** indiqués par des panneaux verts.

\* These **itinéraires bis** (secondary routes) are shown on maps issued free by the French Ministry of Transport. They are available at roadside information kiosks where you see the 'clever Red Indian' character called **Bison Futé**.

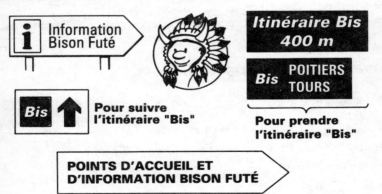

## Activité 1

To see how well you've understood the passage above, try to answer the following questions (See **Mots-Clefs** ➔ 171):

(a) Do you pay on French motorways? ................................
(b) How many km are there between the service areas? ...........
(c) If you wanted to buy a road map, what would you ask for? ....
(d) What does **N** stand for on French road maps? ...................

## ✔ Activité 2

Study the 'Extrait du calendrier Bison Futé 1991' below and answer the questions:

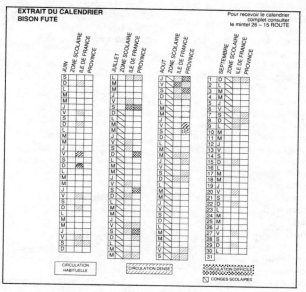

(a) Quel est le mois où la circulation est la moins dense en province (la France sans la région de Paris)?

(b) Quel est le mois où il faut éviter de voyager en province et dans l'île de France? (région de Paris).

(c) Quand est-ce que les vacances scolaires commencent et finissent?

# Mots-clefs

| | |
|---|---|
| **c'est quelle route pour ...?** | which is the way to ...? |
| **pour aller à ...?** | how do I get to ...? |
| **voyager** | to travel |
| **l'autoroute (f.)** | motorway |
| **la route nationale (N)** | similiar to an 'A' road in Britain |
| **à péage** | toll payable |
| **une aire de repos** | service area |
| **suivez le panneau** | follow the sign |

| | |
|---|---|
| c'est indiqué | it is signposted |
| à 5 km | 5 km away |
| le carrefour | the crossroads |
| les feux (m.pl.) rouges | traffic lights (often shortened to **les feux**) |
| une station service | petrol station |
| où peut-on se garer? | where can I park? |
| le parking | car park |
| stationnement interdit | no parking |
| défense de stationner | no parking |
| le parcmètre | parking meter |
| le conducteur/la conductrice | driver |
| vous pouvez m'aider? | can you help me? |
| je suis en panne | I've broken down |
| le service de dépannage | breakdown service |
| le moteur ne marche pas | the engine does not work |
| vérifier la pression des pneus | to check the tyre pressure |
| le gonflage des pneus est gratuit | pumping up the tyres is free |
| faire le plein | filling up the car with petrol |
| je vous en remets? | shall I top it up for you? |
| l'essence (f.) | petrol |
| le super | 4 star (petrol) |
| le sans plomb | lead free (petrol) |
| l'huile (f.) | the oil |
| réparer | to repair |
| la carte | map |
| la route à quatre voies | dual carriageway |
| une agglomération | built-up area |
| la (route) départementale (D) | equivalent to a 'B' road in the UK |
| éviter | to avoid |
| Pâques | Easter |
| Pentecôte | Pentecost |
| le jour férié | bank holiday |
| le bouchon | bottleneck, traffic jam |
| suivre | to follow |
| la plupart de | most of |
| le pompiste | petrol pump attendant |
| le mécanicien | mechanic |

When driving in France, remember that at junctions you normally give way to traffic from the right (**priorité à droite**). But you always have right of way on a priority road marked with a yellow-on-white sign.

# Dialogue 1

You may want to look at the road map on page 174 before listening to the cassette or reading the dialogue to familiarise yourself with the area where Jane is going camping. She has just got through to Mme Michel, the owner of the campsite, and is asking her the directions from Paris.

| | |
|---|---|
| Mme Michel | **Allô,** le camping de la Mignardière, **j'écoute.** |
| Jane | Bonjour, Madame. Nous avons réservé un emplacement dans votre camping pour le 21 juillet. Nous habitons Brighton et nous voulons faire le voyage en voiture. Pouvez-vous me dire quelles routes il faut prendre depuis Paris? |
| Mme Michel | Oui, bien sûr, c'est très simple. De Paris vous prenez l'autoroute A10 puis après Tours, vous prenez sortie Chambray-les-Tours... |
| Jane | Un instant... vous pouvez parler plus lentement, s'il vous plaît? |
| Mme Michel | Oui, l'autoroute A10. Vous sortez à Chambray-les-Tours, vous prenez direction Azay-le-Rideau ... |
| Jane | C'est sur quelle route? |
| Mme Michel | A la sortie Chambray-les-Tours, vous allez d'abord prendre la N143 puis la N10 et enfin la N751. |
| Jane | Oh là là, mais c'est très compliqué! |
| Mme Michel | Non, non **vous ne pouvez pas vous tromper.** Suivez toujours la route pour Azay-le-Rideau. Quand vous êtes sur la N751, après le deuxième carrefour vous allez voir un panneau qui indique le Camping La Mignardière; vous tournez à droite et c'est à 2km sur votre gauche. |
| Jane | Bon, alors après la sortie Chambray-les-Tours je prends la N143, N10 et N751. Après le deuxième carrefour sur la N751 le camping est indiqué, je tourne à droite et après 2km, j'arrive. C'est bien ça? |
| Mme Michel | Oui c'est ça et **si vous vous perdez, passez-moi un coup de fil .... bonne route!** |

| | |
|---|---|
| **allô, j'écoute** | hello, can I help you (lit. I'm listening) |
| **vous ne pouvez pas vous tromper** | you cannot make a mistake |
| **si vous vous perdez** | if you get lost |
| **passez-moi un coup de fil** | give me a ring |
| **bonne route** | have a good journey |

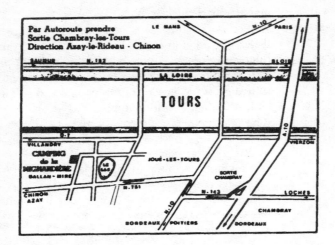

Par Autoroute prendre
Sortie Chambray-les-Tours
Direction Azay-le-Rideau · Chinon

## Activité 3

Have you understood Mme Michel's explanations? As you listen
to the tape a second time, put her directions below in the right
sequence; start with the sentence in bold type:

(a) Vous tournez à droite.
(b) Après Tours, vous prenez sortie Chambray-les-Tours.
(c) Sur la N 751 après le deuxième carrefour il y a un panneau qui
indique le camping la Mignardière.
(d) **De Paris vous prenez l'autoroute A10.**
(e) Après 2km vous arrivez au camping.
(f) A la sortie Chambray-les-Tours vous allez prendre les N143,
N10 et N751.

## Activité 4

Your holiday is now over and it's time to hit the road again.
Here's your conversation with Mme Michel. Fill in your part.

(a) You        *Ask her politely how to get to Paris.*
Mme Michel  Pour Paris vous pouvez prendre l'autoroute A10
            ou la Nationale 10.
(b) You        *Is it expensive (to take) the motorway?*

| Mme Michel | Oui, c'est assez cher car l'autoroute est à péage mais c'est beaucoup plus rapide. |
| (c) You | *Where is the N10?* |
| Mme Michel | Il faut prendre la (route) nationale 751, direction Loches jusqu'aux feux. Aux feux, vous prenez à gauche, direction Paris. |
| (d) You | *Is the N10 signposted?* |
| Mme Michel | Oui, c'est très bien indiqué. |
| (e) You | *Repeat the directions.* |
| Mme Michel | Oui, c'est ça. |

 ## Stationnement *Parking*

Listen to Cloé giving you a quick list of 'do's and don'ts' to remember when parking your car in France. The illustrations below give you the summary of Cloé's advice. Although a lot of the signs need to be recognised, very few words need to be learnt.

## ☑️ Activité 5

Fill in the blanks in the passage below using the signs on the previous page; then listen to Cloé's instructions again to check your version against his.

Si votre voiture est en (*a*) s..... i..... devant le panneau (*b*) d..... d..... s..... ou dans un parking pour cars, vous pouvez avoir une (*c*) a..... ou une contravention.

Si vous garez votre voiture dans une zone (*d*) p..... ou (*e*) d'....., elle peut être enlevée par la (*f*) p..... et mise en fourrière. Il faut alors s'adresser au Commissariat de Police le plus proche.

Pour vous garer, cherchez un (*g*) p..... g..... ou un (*h*) p..... p..... . Si vous ne trouvez pas de parking, cherchez un (*i*) h..... ou un (*j*) p.....

## _____ Le code français de la route _____
### *The French highway code*

## ☑️ Activité 6

See how good a driver you are! Match the signs below with the right definition then check your answers in **Réponses** giving yourself three points for each right answer.

| | |
|---|---|
| (*a*)<br>Cédez le passage à l'intersection.<br>*Give way at intersection* | (i)  |
| (*b*)<br>Indication du caractère prioritaire d'une route à grande circulation.<br>*Priority for all vehicles on this type of road.* | (ii)  |
| (*c*)<br>Perte de priorité. *The road loses its priority, i.e. in a built-up area.* | (iii)  |

| | |
|---|---|
| (d)<br>Stationnement interdit à tous véhicules de façon permanente.<br>*Parking forbidden at all times.* | (iv) |
| (e)<br>Stationnement interdit du 1er au 15 du mois. *Parking forbidden from 1st to 15th of the month.* | (v) |
| (f)<br>Le conducteur est tenu de céder le passage aux véhicules venant de sa droite. *The driver must give way to vehicles on the right.* | (vi) |
| (g)<br>Circulation interdite à tout véhicule dans les deux sens. *No thoroughfare for all vehicles, from both directions.* | (vii) |

Si vous avez 15 points ou plus vous êtes **un bon conducteur/ une bonne conductrice.**
Si vous avez 9 points ou plus il faut réviser le code français.
Si vous avez moins de 9 points vous êtes un conducteur dangereux/une conductrice dangereuse: **un chauffard!** Apprenez le code!

## ˙Faire le plein
## *Filling up with petrol*

When travelling through France you'll probably buy **l'essence** or **le carburant** at a self-service station. If you don't and are faced with an attendant, **pompiste,** ask for **le plein,** to have the tank filled up or buy so many francs' worth, say 150F or 200F. There is usually a choice between **le super** (equivalent to 4-star leaded petrol), **l'octane 95 sans plomb** (lead-free petrol with an octane rating of 95) and **l'octane 98 sans plomb** (super plus lead-free petrol). Look at the leaflet on page 178; can you work out which petrol you should take?

● **Tous les modèles à l'exception des véhicules équipés de pot catalytique**

*AVEC PLOMB* **OCTANE**

---

● **Modèles avec pot catalytique**
● **Quelques modèles récents du parc actuel**
● **Presque la totalité des nouvelles immatriculations (millésime 90)**
**(Consulter la liste en station)**

*SANS PLOMB*
*RON 95/MON 85*

**OCTANE**
**95**

---

● **La plupart des modèles récents (moins de 4/5 ans) soit environ 40% du parc actuel (Consulter la liste en station)**
● **Modèles avec pot catalytique**
● **Totalité des nouvelles immatriculations (millésime 90)**

*SANS PLOMB*
*RON 98/MON 88*

**OCTANE**
**98**

# Dialogue 2

| | |
|---|---|
| Pompiste | Bonjour, Monsieur, qu'est-ce que vous voulez? du super? du sans plomb? |
| Client | Je prends du sans plomb 95. |
| Pompiste | Je vous fais le plein? |
| Client | Non, seulement pour cent cinquante francs ... et vous pouvez vérifier l'huile? |
| Pompiste | Oui, bien sûr ... votre niveau d'huile est un peu bas, je vous en remets un peu? |
| Client | Oui, un litre alors. |
| Pompiste | Et pour la pression des pneus, vous voulez que je regarde? Le gonflage des pneus est gratuit! |
| Client | Bon, d'accord. |
| | *(after a while)* |
| Pompiste | Voilà, ça fait 200F avec l'huile. |

## ✅Activité 7

Most of the dialogue above is based on two key structures:
vous pouvez ...? *can you ...?*     to ask for help
vous voulez ...? *do you want ...?*     to offer something

Read the questions below; can you guess who's asking them?
The client or the pompiste? Put a tick in the correct column.

|  | Client | Pompiste |
|---|---|---|
| (a) **Vous voulez le plein?** | | |
| (b) **Vous pouvez regarder le niveau d'eau?** | | |
| (c) **Vous voulez du super?** | | |
| (d) **Vous pouvez me faire le plein?** | | |
| (e) **Vous pouvez vérifier la pression des pneus?** | | |
| (f) **Vous voulez 1 litre d'huile?** | | |

## ✅Activité 8

Now it's your turn: you need some 4-star petrol and want to have
your oil checked.

(a) You       *Say hello. Ask for 4 star petrol.*
Pompiste   Vous voulez le plein?
(b) You       *Say no. 180F's worth.*
Pompiste   C'est tout?
(c) You       *Ask if he can check the oil.*
Pompiste   Oui, effectivement, vous avez besoin d'huile. Vous
               en voulez combien?
(d) You       *Say one litre.*
Pompiste   Un litre, bon très bien. Vous voulez que je vérifie la
               pression des pneus? Le gonflage est gratuit.
(e) You       *Say no thank you; it's OK (ça va).*
Pompiste   Ça fait 230F. Vous payez à la caisse.

——— **En panne**  *Broken down* ———

In case of accidents and thefts (**accidents et vols**) phone the
police. In case of breakdowns look up in the yellow pages
(**annuaire professions**) under **dépannage** or call the police.

If you break down on the motorway, go to the nearest telephone. All you need to do is press the emergency button, release it and wait for the operator to connect you.

## ━━━━━━━━ Dialogue 3 ━━━━━━━━

Une femme est tombée en panne sur l'autoroute. Elle appelle le service de dépannage.
*A woman has broken down on the motorway. She rings the breakdown service.*
Listen to the cassette or read the dialogue and try to answer the following questions: On which motorway has the woman broken down? Where is she going? How long is it going to take the **garagiste** to get there?

| | |
|---|---|
| Femme | Allô, le service de dépannage? |
| Garagiste | Ici, Dépannage Ultra-rapide, j'écoute. |
| Femme | Voilà, je suis en panne; je ne comprends pas, le moteur ne marche plus. Vous pouvez m'aider? |
| Garagiste | Où êtes-vous, Madame? |
| Femme | Je suis sur l'autoroute A26, entre Reims et St Quentin. |
| Garagiste | Et dans quelle direction allez-vous? |
| Femme | Vers Calais. |
| Garagiste | Elle est comment votre voiture? |
| Femme | C'est une Renault 21 blanche. |
| Garagiste | Bon, j'arrive dans une demi-heure. |

### ✔ Activité 9

Let's hope you won't be so unlucky! But to be prepared for all emergencies practise the following situation: look at the map on page 181; you've just broken down with your English Vauxhall and you've just got through to the breakdown service. Fill in your part:

| | |
|---|---|
| Homme | Allô, service de dépannage. |
| (a) You | *Ask if they can help you – say you've broken down.* |
| Homme | Quel est le problème? |
| (b) You | *Say that you don't know; the engine is not working.* |
| Homme | Où êtes-vous? |

(c) You    *Say you are on the motorway A10 between Orléans and Blois.*

Homme    Où allez-vous?

(d) You    *Give your direction (Tours).*

Homme    Qu'est-ce que vous avez comme voiture?

(e) You    *Say that it's an English car: a blue Vauxhall Astra. Ask him when he's arriving.*

Homme    D'ici une heure (*within an hour*).

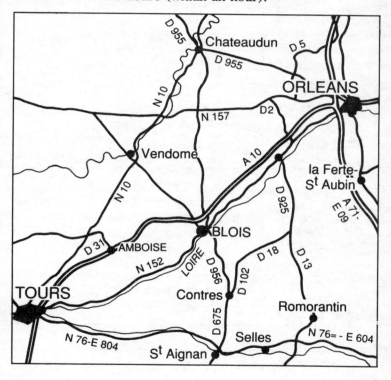

## 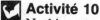 Activité 10

Nothing seems to work in Michel's car. Study the illustrations and explanations below describing what's wrong with his car. Now listen to him explaining his trouble to the mechanic (**mécanicien**). What he says is not in the same order as overleaf. Fill in the boxes with A,B,C,D,E,F,G,H to show the order you hear it. (Check your answers at the back of the book.)

(a)

mon pneu est crevé
*I have a puncture*

(b)

la batterie est à plat
*the battery is flat*

(c)

mon phare avant gauche ne marche pas
*the front light on the off-side does not work*

(d)

mon pare-brise est cassé
*my windscreen is broken*

(e)

l'essuie-glace arrière ne fonctionne pas
*the back wiper does not work*

(f)

ma roue de secours est à plat
*my spare wheel is flat*

(g)

le moteur chauffe et fait un drôle de bruit
*the engine is heating up and makes a strange noise*

(h)

les freins ne marchent pas
*the brakes aren't working any more*

## ☑ Activité 11

Now test yourself. Without looking at the previous, captioned, illustrations, can you explain to the mechanic what's wrong with your car?

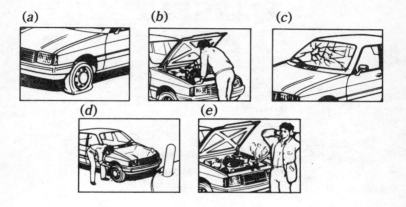

(a)   (b)   (c)

(d)   (e)

There is a lot of new material in Unit 17. Go over it once again before going on to Unit 18. In the next unit you'll be tested on Units 17 and 18

# 18

## L'ARGENT

*Money*

### In this unit you will

- find out how to ask for change
- familiarise yourself with French coins and notes
- practise changing traveller's cheques
- learn to say that there is an error in a bill

### Avant de commencer on révise

- saying what you want ➔ P. 48
- asking for help ➔ P. 49
- expressions of time, days of the week **Mots-clefs** ➔ P. 46
- numbers ➔ P. 212 ˙

# Les banques françaises
## *French banks*

Avant d'aller à une banque, renseignez-vous pour les horaires d'ouverture et de fermeture; certaines banques, à Paris, restent ouvertes plus tard. En général, dans les petites villes, les banques sont ouvertes du mardi au vendredi inclus; elles sont fermées pendant l'heure du déjeuner et après 4h30 de l'après-midi. Comme banques principales il y a le Crédit Lyonnais, la Société Générale, la BNP (Banque Nationale de Paris). Beaucoup de banques ont un distributeur automatique acceptant les cartes bancaires (Visa, etc.).

Vous pouvez également changer de l'argent à la Caisse d'Epargne (*Savings Bank*) et aux bureaux de change; à Paris, les bureaux de change de la gare de l'Est, de la gare Saint-Lazare et de la gare du Nord sont ouverts tous les jours de 7h à 21h30.

 **Activité 1**

How would you ask:

(a) Where is the nearest bank?
(b) At what time does the bank open today?
(c) At what time does the bank close?

 ━━━━━━━━━━ **Mots-clefs** ━━━━━━━━━━

If you have not got the cassette, check the pronunciation of the words preceded by an * in the section below, **Pronunciation tips.**

| | |
|---|---|
| * **une pièce** | coin (there are 5c, 10c, 20c, 50c, 1F, 2F, 5F and 10F coins) |
| * **un billet** | banknote (there are 50F, 100F, 200F and 500F notes) |
| * **un franc** | franc |
| * **la monnaie** | small change |
| * **l'argent** (m.) | money |
| **la livre** (sterling) | (English) pound |
| **le dollar** | dollar |

| | |
|---|---|
| * le cours du change | exchange rate |
| le traveller (*or* chèque de voyage) | traveller's cheque |
| en bas | at the bottom |
| un stylo | a pen |
| une pièce d'identité | means of identification |
| un changeur de monnaie | coin changing machine |
| une télécarte | telephone card |
| une carte bancaire | banker's card |
| la note | hotel bill |
| l'addition (f.) | bill (drinks, snacks) |
| régler | to settle (bill) |
| une erreur | a mistake |
| un distributeur automatique | a cashpoint machine |

## Useful sentences to say:

| | |
|---|---|
| vous pouvez changer ... francs? | can you change ... francs? |
| vous avez de la monnaie svp? | do you have any change please? |
| il me faut des pièces de 1F | I need 1F coins |
| changer de l'argent | change some money |
| la livre est à combien? | what's the rate of exchange for the pound? |
| vous acceptez les cartes de crédit? | do you accept credit cards? |

## Worth knowing:

| | |
|---|---|
| faites (faire) l'appoint | put in the exact money |
| l'appareil ne rend pas l'argent | no change given |

## ✳ Pronunciation tips

You do not need to know many words when changing money but they need to be pronounced correctly; here is an opportunity to practise saying them:

| | |
|---|---|
| **pièce** | pee – esse |
| **billet** | bee – yeah |
| **franc** | remember not to pronounce the **c** |
| **monnaie** | mo – nay |
| **argent** | make sure the **r** is pronounced otherwise it could sound like **agent** (**de police**): *policeman* |
| **cours** | don't pronounce the **s** |
| **traveller** | as in English but with a French **r** |

And now re-read **Mots-clefs**, checking your pronunciation.

# Pièces et billets de banque
## *Coins and banknotes*

**Les pièces**
dix centimes
vingt centimes
cinquante centimes ou 1/2 franc
un franc
deux francs
cinq francs
dix francs

**Les billets**
50F
100F
200F

# Faire de la monnaie
## *Getting small change*

### ✔ Activité 2

Before reading the dialogue try to answer the following:

(a) How would you ask: *Can you change 10F please?*
(b) How would you say: *I need 1F coins?*
(c) What does **la machine ne rend pas l'argent** mean?
(Check your answers in **Réponses**.)

# Dialogue 1

 Une automobiliste a besoin de monnaie pour l'horodateur. Elle arrête une passante.
*A motorist needs some small change for the pay-and-display machine. She stops a passer-by.*

| | |
|---|---|
| Femme | Pardon Madame, vous pouvez changer 10F s'il vous plaît? |
| Passante | Je ne sais pas mais je vais regarder. Qu'est-ce qu'il vous faut? |
| Femme | C'est pour l'horodateur. Il me faut 4 pièces de 1F ou 2 pièces de 2F et moi **je n'ai que** 10F. |
| Passante | La machine ne rend pas l'argent? |
| Femme | Non, je ne crois pas. |
| Passante | Eh bien, **vous avez de la chance!** J'ai 4 pièces de 2F et 2 pièces de 1F. Ça vous va? |
| Femme | Merci beaucoup, Madame. |

| | |
|---|---|
| **je n'ai que** | I've only got → **P.** 85 |
| **vous avez de la chance** | you're lucky, you're in luck |
| **ça vous va?** | is that OK (for you)? |

## Activité 3

You want to make a phonecall but only have a 10F coin with you. Fill in your part of the dialogue.

| | |
|---|---|
| (a) You | *Stop a man in the street. Ask him if he has any small change for the telephone.* |
| Passant | Qu'est-ce qu'il vous faut? |
| (b) You | *Say: I've only got a 10F coin and I need 1F coins.* |
| Passant | Je suis désolé mais je n'ai pas de monnaie. Pourquoi n'achetez-vous pas une télecarte? |
| (c) You | *Ask: what is a 'télécarte'?* |
| Passant | C'est une carte pour téléphoner; c'est très pratique et on n'a pas besoin de monnaie. |
| (d) You | *Ask: where can I buy a phone card?* |
| Passant | Dans tous les bars et à la poste bien sûr! |

## Changer de l'argent *Changing money*

—————————— **Dialogue 2** ——————————

Un étranger change des travellers dans une banque.
*A foreigner is in a bank changing traveller's cheques.*
Listen to the cassette or read below and find out: How many
pounds does he want to change? What does he need before
signing his traveller's cheques?

| | |
|---|---|
| Etranger | Je voudrais changer des travellers, s'il vous plaît. |
| Employée | Oui, très bien. Vous avez une pièce d'identité? |
| Etranger | Oui, voici mon passeport. |
| Employée | Bon, qu'est-ce que vous voulez? |
| Etranger | Je voudrais changer 60 livres sterling en francs. |
| Employée | D'accord, alors vous allez signer en bas. |
| Etranger | Euh... vous avez quelque chose pour écrire s'il vous plaît? |
| Employée | Un instant ... voici un stylo. |
| Etranger | La livre est à combien aujourd'hui? |
| Employée | Aujourd'hui le cours de la livre est à 9F30. |
| Etranger | Il y a une commission à payer? |
| Employée | Non, pas pour les travellers. |

### Activité 4

Without looking at the text above, fill in the missing words.

(a) Je voudrais c...... des travellers.
(b) Vous avez une p.... d'identité?
(c) Vous allez s..... en bas du traveller.
(d) Vous avez quelque chose pour é.....?
(e) La livre est à c......... aujourd'hui?
(f) Il y a une commission à p.....?

### Activité 5

Take part in this conversation in **le bureau de change** at the
**gare du Nord** in Paris.

| | |
|---|---|
| (a) You | *Say that you would like to change some dollars.* |
| Employé | Des dollars américains, canadiens, australiens? |
| (b) You | *Say American dollars.* |
| Employé | Oui; vous voulez changer des billets ou des travellers? |
| (c) You | *Say bank notes.* |
| Employé | Combien voulez-vous changer? |
| (d) You | *Say 100 dollars. Ask the exchange rate.* |
| Employé | Le dollar est à 5F50 aujourd'hui. |
| (e) You | *Ask if they are open on Sundays.* |
| Employé | Oui, tous les jours de 7h à 21h30. ...(*later*) Voici votre argent! |

# Une erreur dans la note
## An error in the bill

### Quelques conseils  *A few tips*

- It's a good idea to ask for the bill in advance in order to check it.
- You ask for **la note** to pay for your hotel bill and for **l'addition** to pay for food and drink.
- Remember to check the price of hotel rooms which, by law, should be displayed at the reception and in each room.
- Extras (telephone, mini-bar, etc.) should be charged separately.
- TTC (toutes taxes comprises) means inclusive of tax.
- TVA (taxe à la valeur ajoutée) means VAT.

## Dialogue 3

| | |
|---|---|
| A la réception | |
| Client | Je voudrais régler ma note, s'il vous plaît. |
| Réceptionniste | Bien, vous partez aujourd'hui? |
| Client | Oui, après le petit déjeuner. |
| Réceptionniste | Bon, c'est pour quelle chambre? |
| Client | Chambre quatorze. Vous acceptez les cartes de crédit? |
| Réceptionniste | Oui, bien sûr. Alors un instant... Voici votre note. |

| Client | Merci. Pardon Madame, il y a une erreur. Qu'est-ce que c'est 'mini-bar soixante-huit francs'? |
| Réceptionniste | Ce sont les boissons mini-bar **que vous avez prises** dans votre chambre. |
| Client | Mais **je n'ai rien pris** du mini-bar. |
| Réceptionniste | Vraiment? Bon, eh bien c'est sans doute une erreur de notre part...! Je m'excuse Monsieur. Donc ça fait cinq cent quatorze francs moins soixante-huit francs... quatre cent quarante-six francs. |
| Client | C'est avec service et taxes? |
| Réceptionniste | Oui, taxes et service sont compris. |

| | |
|---|---|
| **que vous avez prises** | that you've taken |
| **je n'ai rien pris** | I haven't taken anything |

## Activité 6

Have you understood the dialogue well enough to answer the following questions?

(a) When does the client intend to leave the hotel? .................

(b) What was the number of his room? ............................

(c) Was the bill correct? ...................................

(d) What does the amount 68F correspond to? ......................

(e) Is the final total of the bill 226F, 446F or 886F? ...............

(f) Is it inclusive of tax and service? ...........................

## Activité 7

It is essential for you to be confident in using and understanding the numbers as they're needed in most situations. You can revise them on ➡ P 212 where they are all listed.

Here is some extra practice to help you cope with French prices. Listen to Michel and write down the prices you hear. Remember that in hand-written French the 7 (seven) is always crossed and looks like 7.

(a) .......        (f) .......

(b) .......        (g) .......

(c) .......        (h) .......

(d) .......        (i) .......

(e) .......        (j) .......

## ☑ Petit test on Units 17 and 18

How would you ask/say:

1  Is there a car park near here?
2  I need four 1F coins for the parking meter.
3  Can you help me please, I've broken down?
4  I need 1 litre of oil.
5  Have you any small change?
6  Do you accept credit cards?
7  I would like to settle my bill.
8  Can you check the tyre pressure?
9  Can you fill up my car with petrol?
10  I would like to change £50 into francs.

# 19

## LES PROBLEMES
*Coping with problems*

### *In this unit you will*

- find out how to ask for medicine at the chemist
- familiarise yourself with the French health system
- practise making an appointment with the doctor/dentist
- find out about the telephone in France
- learn some key expressions to describe your problems

### *Avant de commencer on révise*

- saying what you want **→ P.** 48
- how to describe things **→ P.** 74
- how to spell in French **→ P.** 128
- how to say my, your, his, etc. ... **→ P.** 41
- expressions of time, days of the week **Mots-clefs** **→ P.** 46
- numbers **→ P.** 212

Sign for a
French chemist's

## *La pharmacie en France*   *Chemists in France*

The French chemist's is easily recognisable, with its green neon cross sign outside. For minor ailments you'll find that the trained pharmacist, **pharmacien (-ne)** is usually happy to give you advice. For more serious problems he/she will recommend a doctor. At the **pharmacie** they sell medicines and medicated beauty products. You will not be able to buy medicines (even aspirin!) anywhere except at the pharmacie. For buying and developing films you have to go to a photographic shop which is usually indicated by the sign **'photo'**. For perfumes and cosmetics you'll need the **parfumerie.**

Look up in the **annuaire professions** under **pharmacies** to find out which pharmacies stay open late. The **drugstores** (a kind of shopping arcade selling medicine among other goods) in Paris stay open until 2am.

 ## Mots-clefs

### A dire

| | |
|---|---|
| la pharmacie | chemist's |
| le pharmacien – la pharmacienne | chemist |
| chez le médecin | at the doctor's |
| chez le dentiste | at the dentist |
| le cabinet médical/dentaire | doctor's/dentist's surgery |
| prendre rendez-vous | to make an appointment |
| souffrir | to suffer, be in pain, feel ill |
| depuis quand | since when |
| je voudrais quelque chose pour ... | I would like something for ... |
| * la piqûre d'insecte | insect bite |
| le mal de gorge | sore throat |
| le mal de dents | toothache |
| le mal à la tête | headache |
| j'ai mal à la gorge | I've got a sore throat |
|        aux dents | toothache |
|        à la tête | a headache |
|        au ventre | stomach ache |
| il a de la fièvre | he's got a temperature |
| le dentifrice | toothpaste |
| le shampooing | shampoo |
| contre | against |
| j'ai perdu (il a perdu) ... | I've lost (he's lost) ... |
| j'ai laissé (il a laissé) ... | I've left (he's left) ... |

| | |
|---|---|
| ... est cassé (e) | ... is broken |
| ... sont cassés (ées) | ... are broken |
| on a volé ... | ... was stolen |
| le sac à main | handbag |
| le portefeuille | wallet |
| le porte-monnaie | purse |
| les lunettes | glasses |

## A comprendre

| | |
|---|---|
| un médicament | medicine |
| une crème | cream |
| une huile | oil |
| une aspirine effervescente | soluble aspirin |
| en comprimés | in tablet form |
| je vous conseille | I advise you, I recommend to you |

\* piqûre is pronounced pic-oore (with a French u)

# Dialogue 1

Listen to the cassette or read below: What's wrong with the customer's husband? Has he got a temperature? Name at least three items the customer buys.

| | |
|---|---|
| Pharmacien | Bonjour Madame. Vous désirez? |
| Cliente | Vous avez quelque chose pour le mal de gorge? |
| Pharmacien | C'est pour vous, Madame? |
| Cliente | Non, c'est pour mon mari. |
| Pharmacien | Il a de la fièvre? |
| Cliente | Non mais il a aussi mal à la tête. |
| Pharmacien | Bon, pour le mal de gorge je vous donne des pastilles. Il en prend une quand il a mal. Pour le mal de tête, je vous donne de l'aspirine effervescente, 2 comprimés toutes les 4 heures. Il n'est pas allergique à l'aspirine? |
| Cliente | Non, non, merci. Je voudrais aussi du dentifrice et quelque chose contre le soleil. |
| Pharmacien | Vous préférez une crème ou une huile? |
| Cliente | Une crème. |
| Pharmacien | Alors voici du dentifrice fluoré et une crème pour le soleil; c'est tout? |
| Cliente | Oui, merci. |
| Pharmacien | Bon eh bien ça fait 250F. |

# ✅ Activité 1

Read the dialogue again and choose the right answers for the patient's medical record card below. (Check your answers in **Réponses**.)

| (a) Patient complains of | | (b) Temperature | |
|---|---|---|---|
| (i) stomach ache | ☐ | | |
| (ii) headache | ☐ | Yes ☐ | |
| (iii) toothache | ☐ | | |
| (iv) sore throat | ☐ | No ☐ | |

| (c) Treatment | | Dosage | To be taken |
|---|---|---|---|
| (i) antibiotics | ☐ | .......................... | .......................... |
| (ii) suppositories | ☐ | .......................... | .......................... |
| (iii) aspirin | ☐ | .......................... | .......................... |
| (iv) pastilles | ☐ | .......................... | .......................... |

# ✅ Activité 2

Now it's your turn to go to the chemist to get some medicine for your daughter who has toothache.

| Pharmacienne | Bonjour Monsieur/Madame. Vous désirez? |
|---|---|
| (a) You | *Say: my daughter has toothache.* |
| Pharmacienne | Elle a de la fièvre? |
| (b) You | *Say: yes, a little.* |
| Pharmacienne | Depuis quand souffre-t-elle? |
| (c) You | *Say: since yesterday.* |
| Pharmacienne | Bon, je vais vous donner de l'aspirine vitaminée et si ça continue dans un jour ou deux il faudra aller chez le dentiste. |
| (d) You | *Thank her. Ask for something for insect bites.* |
| Pharmacienne | Pour les piqûres d'insectes? Certainement. Je vous conseille cette crème anti-démangeaisons ... elle est très bonne ... |
| (e) You | *You didn't get everything she said but you understood that she was recommending the cream. Say: I'll take it and ask to pay.* |

# Prendre rendez-vous
## *Making an appointment*

Before making an appointment to see a doctor or a dentist in France, make sure that they are **conventionnés** (working within the French health insurance scheme), otherwise you may not be able to claim for a refund.

After the treatment, for which you'll have to pay, they'll give you:
- a **feuille de soins** (the signed statement of treatment given)
- an **ordonnance** (the prescription for the medicine to buy).

Once you've bought the medicine, detach the **vignettes** (stamps) which show the name and cost of the medicine from the medicine containers and stick them on the **feuille de soins**.

You can now ask for a refund, sending to the local sickness insurance office the **ordonnance**, the **feuille de soins** signed and dated and the form E111 (keep a photocopy with you) which you get from any post office in the UK. The refund will be sent on to your home address.

### Activité 3

Mrs Jones phones Dr Leroux's surgery to make an appointment. Read the questions below. Then listen to, or read the dialogue on page 198 as many times as you need and try to note down the answers.

(a) Why does Mrs Jones phone?
(b) Who is the patient?
(c) Has the patient got a temperature?
(d) What other symptom?
(e) At what time is the appointment?

# Dialogue 2

 Mrs Jones téléphone au cabinet médical du Dr Leroux pour prendre rendez-vous.
*Mrs Jones phones Dr Leroux's surgery to make an appointment.*

| | |
|---|---|
| Secrétaire | Allô, le cabinet du docteur Leroux, j'écoute. |
| Mrs Jones | Je voudrais prendre rendez-vous, s'il vous plaît. |
| Secrétaire | Bon, c'est pour une consultation ou une visite? |
| Mrs Jones | Je ne comprends pas, vous pouvez expliquer? |
| Secrétaire | Pour une consultation vous venez ici, pour une visite le médecin va chez vous. Vous êtes la patiente? |
| Mrs Jones | Non, c'est ma fille. Elle a beaucoup de fièvre ... |
| Secrétaire | Alors vous voulez une visite ... Ecoutez, le docteur est pris toute la journée mais il pourrait passer voir votre fille dans la soirée vers ... peut-être 19h.30. Qu'est-ce qu'elle a, votre fille? |
| Mrs Jones | Je ne sais pas, peut-être la grippe. Elle a très mal à la tête. |
| Secrétaire | Vous pouvez me donner votre nom et adresse? |
| Mrs Jones | Jones. J-O-N-E-S et j'habite appartement 2, 10 rue Legrand, à côté de la piscine. |
| Secrétaire | Bon, eh bien Mme Jones, le docteur Leroux passera voir votre fille vers 19h.30. |
| Mrs Jones | Merci beaucoup. Au revoir, Madame. |

| | |
|---|---|
| **est pris** | is busy (lit. is taken) |
| **passer voir** | come (go) and see |
| **la grippe** | flu |

## Activité 4

It's your turn to make an appointment at the dentist. Say your part.

| | |
|---|---|
| Secrétaire | Allô, allô |
| (a) You | *Say: I would like to make an appointment.* |
| Secrétaire | Oui très bien; c'est pour vous? |

| | |
|---|---|
| (b) You | *Say: No, it's for my son. We are English, on holiday here and he has had toothache since Tuesday.* |
| Secrétaire | Il a quel âge votre fils? |
| (c) You | *Say: he's 12.* |
| Secrétaire | Oui, je vois. Et quand peut-il venir? |
| (d) You | *Say: he can come today, this morning or this afternoon.* |
| Secrétaire | Bon; eh bien cet après-midi, à 3h45. Ça vous va? |
| (e) You | *Ask her to repeat the time.* |
| Secrétaire | Oui à 3h45. Votre nom s'il vous plaît? |
| (f) You | *Say your name and spell it.* |
| Secrétaire | Merci, Nous attendons donc votre fils à 3h45. Au revoir Monsieur/Madame. |

# Le téléphone en France
## *Phoning in France*

Vous pouvez téléphoner d'un bureau de poste (ils sont ouverts de 8h à 19h du lundi au vendredi et de 8h à 12h le samedi), d'un café ou de cabines téléphoniques. Les cabines marchent avec des pièces ou avec une télécarte que vous achetez dans un bar ou à la poste. Pour téléphoner avec une télécarte, il faut comprendre certaines instructions.

### ✔ Activité 5

The instructions on the left are what appears on the screen, in a sequential order, when using the phone card ➡ P 200. Can you find for each French instruction its English equivalent?

| | | | |
|---|---|---|---|
| (a) | décrochez | (i) | dial the number |
| (b) | introduisez carte | (ii) | wait |
| (c) | fermez le volet | (iii) | number being connected |
| (d) | patientez SVP | (iv) | insert card |
| (e) | numérotez | (v) | lift receiver |
| (f) | numéro appelle | (vi) | close the shutter |

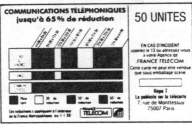

## ✔ Activité 6

Read the French notice below giving you the different telephone rates. Can you work out what **tarif** applied in the following cases?

(a) A woman phoning her parents on Sundays.
(b) A night watchman phoning his wife around midnight.
(c) A bank clerk phoning during working hours.
(d) A post office employee phoning over lunch time.

---

**A savoir:**
4 tarifs selon l'heure:
- le **rouge** au prix fort, appliqué en semaine de 8h à 12h.30 et de 13h.30 à 18h.
- le **blanc** donne droit à 30% de réduction entre 12h30-13h.30 et de 18h à 21h30.
- le **bleu,** c'est moitié prix de 21h30 à 22h30 et entre 6h et 8h en semaine, et le samedi après-midi et toute la journée dimanche.
  Enfin avec le **bleu nuit** tarif réduit de 65% entre 22h30 et 6h.

---

Using the phone in France may seem like a daunting experience but it doesn't need to be. Here are two useful tips when speaking on the phone.

1  Speak clearly and open your mouth wide, particularly when pronouncing the vowels **i, o, u, é**.

2  If you don't understand what is being said, don't be afraid to ask the person at the other end to repeat using one of the following expressions:

**Vous pouvez répéter, s'il vous plaît?**
**Vous pouvez parler plus lentement?**
**Je ne comprends pas.**
**Vous pouvez expliquer?**

## Activité 7

To practise the first tip given above, listen to Cloé and repeat after her some of the following sentences: (if you don't have the cassette, find out how to pronounce them looking at the Pronunciation Guide →P 5)

J'ai pris un rendez-vous/avec la secrétaire du Docteur Mireau.
Vous avez un médicament/pour le mal de tête?
Vous avez quelque chose d'autre?
J'ai perdu mes clefs.
Mes lunettes sont cassées.

## Au commissariat de police
## *At the police station*

Si vous perdez quelque chose dans une gare ou un aéroport, allez au **bureau des objects trouvés** (*lost property office*). Si on vous a volé quelque chose, il faut aller à la **gendarmerie** ou au **commissariat de police** (*police station*) pour expliquer; vous pouvez dire **on m'a volé...** . Ensuite il faut faire une **déclaration de vol** (*statement*), nécessaire pour les assurances.

## Activité 8

To familiarise yourself with some of the vocabulary you need to describe the kind of problems you may experience in France, listen to Michel's various mishaps and fill in the blanks using the correct items from the box. Even without the cassette, you may be able to work out what goes where.

(a) Hier matin, dans le métro, j'ai perdu mes ....... d'appartement.

(b) Après ça, à la banque, j'ai laissé mon ....... en or et mes .......

(c) A midi on m'a volé, au restaurant, mon ....... avec tout mon ....... et mes .......

(d) Au commissariat de police, hier soir, j'ai laissé mon ....... et ma .......

(e) Ce matin, je voulais téléphoner au commissariat de police mais mon ....... est cassé.

(f) Alors j'ai pris la voiture, mais je ne comprends pas, l'....... arrière ne fonctionne plus et les ....... ne marchent pas.

Mais qu'est-ce que je vais faire?

| | | |
|---|---|---|
| cartes de crédit | téléphone | freins |
| lunettes | argent | parapluie |
| clefs | carte d'identité | stylo |
| portefeuille | essuie-glace | |

# ——————— Dialogue 3 ———————

Can you give the make, colour and number plate of the stolen car?

Agent  Monsieur?

Homme  Je suis anglais, en vacances avec ma famille ... On m'a volé ma voiture.

Agent  Quand ça?

Homme  La nuit dernière.

Agent  Où **était** votre véhicule?

Homme  Ma voiture? Dans la rue Richelieu devant l'hôtel du Lion d'Or.

| Agent | Elle est comment votre voiture? |
|---|---|
| Homme | C'est une Volkswagen Polo rouge. |
| Agent | Quel est le numéro d'immatriculation? |
| Homme | Euh... D 546 YAP |
| Agent | Bon, nous allons essayer de la retrouver. **En attendant,** il faut faire une déclaration par écrit. Vous pouvez remplir cet imprimé? |
| Homme | Euh... maintenant? |
| Agent | Oui, tout de suite vous en avez besoin pour vos assurances en Angleterre; mais c'est facile c'est traduit en anglais. |

| **était** | was |
|---|---|
| **en attendant** | in the meantime |

## Activité 9

Read the dialogue again and try to spot the French version of the following phrases then write them out:

(a) my car was stolen ..........................................
(b) what car have you got? ..........................................
(c) what's the registration number? ..........................................
(d) write a statement ..........................................
(e) fill in this printed form ..........................................
(f) you need it for your insurance ..........................................

## Activité 10

In this last exercise, following the examples given, practise saying who lost what, where, and what it looked like. Revise how to say *my, your, his*, etc →P. 41

**J'ai perdu ma montre dans le train. Elle est en or.**
*I have lost my watch on the train. It's gold.*

**Mon amie a perdu son sac à main dans le bus. Il est en cuir, il est marron.**
*My friend has lost her handbag on the bus. It's leather and it's brown.*

| who | what | where | description |
|---|---|---|---|
| (a) you | your pen | office | gold |
| (b) my brother | his suitcase | train | leather, brown |
| (c) your sister | her purse | park | leather, white |
| (d) his father | his passport | bank | blue |
| (e) a friend | his umbrella | bus | black, very old |

## ✅ Petit test on Unit 19

How would you say:

1 I would like something for headaches.
2 I would like to make an appointment.
3 I've got a sore throat.
4 My handbag was stolen in the cinema.
5 My glasses are broken.

**Congratulations!** You have completed *Teach Yourself Beginner's French* and are now a competent speaker of basic French. You should be able to handle most everyday situations on a visit to France and to communicate with French people sufficiently to make friends. If you would like to extend your ability so that you can develop your confidence, fluency and scope in the language, whether for social or business purposes, why not take your French a step further with the full *Teach Yourself French* course or *Teach Yourself Business French?*

# Réponses
## *Answers*

## Unit 1

### Activités

1 (a) Bonjour Madame (b) Bonjour Monsieur (c) Bonsoir Mademoiselle (d) Bonjour Messieurs-dames (e) Bonne nuit, Monsieur (f) Bonsoir Messieurs-dames 2 Bonsoir Monsieur 3 (c) 4 Bonne nuit 5 Comment ça va? Très bien merci. 6 (a) s'il vous plaît (b) ça va (c) au revoir (d) madame (e) bonsoir (f) non merci 7 (a)(iii), (b)(ii), (c)(iii), (d)(iii)

### Petit test

1 Bonjour, comment ça va? 2 Parlez plus lentement, s'il vous plaît 3 Pardon 4 D'accord

## Unit 2

### Essayez

Bonjour Madame. Je voudrais une baguette, s'il vous plaît.

### Dialogue

Beer, wine and mineral waters; no, she doesn't get any beer.

### Activités

1 (a) un café (b) une bière (c) un journal (d) des bouteilles (e) un franc (f) des timbres 2 une chambre, un café, un journal 3 (a) Je voudrais quatre cartes, s'il vous plaît (b) Vous avez quatre timbres pour l'Angleterre? (c) Et de l'aspirine, s'il vous plaît? (d) C'est combien? 4 trois 5 (a)(ii), (b)(iv), (c)(iii), (d)(i) 6 (a) Messieurs-dames (b) café (c) bouteille (d) voudrais (e) addition 7 (a) cinq (b) neuf (c) dix (d) neuf (e) deux (f) quatre (g) neuf (h) huit

### Petit test

1 Très bien merci 2 Speak more slowly 3 Vous avez de l'aspirine, s'il vous plaît? Merci, au revoir 4 la gare

## Unit 3

### Essayez

Je voudrais deux bouteilles d'eau minérale et un kilo d'oranges.

### Dialogue

Yes, as a secretary; 3 children – a girl and 2 boys; Jane is not married, she has a boyfriend.

### Pratiques:

travaille, travailles, travaille, travaillons, travaillez, travaillent

### Activités

1 (a) 13 (b) 18 (c) 4 (d) 12 (e) 7 (f) 19 (g) 5 (h) 15 (i) 12 (j) 9 2 (a) treize (b) quinze (c) vingt (d) treize (e) dix-neuf (f) onze (g) cinq (h) six (i) quatre (j) douze 3 (a) est (b) ont (c) Elles (d) enfants, un (e) n'a pas (f) n'est pas (g) dix (h) a, ans 4 (a) n'ai pas de timbres (b) n'a pas de café (c) n'est pas marié (d) n'est pas secrétaire (e) n'ai pas de chambre (f) n'est pas d'enfants (g) n'est pas dans le nord de l'Angleterre (h) ne parle pas français (i) n'a pas 18 ans 5 (a) Je m'appelle Anne (b) Non, je suis mariée (c) Oui, j'ai deux enfants (d) Une fille et un garçon (e) Ils ont douze et dix (f) J'habite Chaville (g) Oui, je suis secrétaire 6 (a) Vous êtes marié? (b) Vous avez des enfants? (c) Vous travaillez? (d) Vous habitez Paris? (e) Vous avez des frères et soeurs? (f) Ils ont quel âge? (g) Vous êtes français? (h) Vous parlez anglais? 7 (a)(iv), (b)(iii), (c)(i), (d)(ii), (e)(vii), (f)(v), (g)(vi)

### Petit test

1 Parlez plus lentement, s'il vous plaît 2 (b) 3 I don't understand 4 Je voudrais une bouteille de vin, s'il vous plaît 5 C'est combien? 6 (a) Je m'appelle (b) Je ne suis pas marié(e) (c) J'habite (à) Brighton

## Unit 4
### Essayez
Vous parlez anglais? Vous êtes marié(e)?
Vous avez des enfants? Des filles ou des
garçons? Vous travaillez? Vous habitez à
… ? Je m'appelle … et vous?

### Dialogue
Yes: Yes: Yes: 3 children.

### Activités
**1** (a) (v) (b) (i) (c) (vii) (d) (viii) (e) (iii) (f)
(ii) (g) (vi) (h) (iv) **2** (Note that there are
alternative ways of asking these questions.) (a) Il y a un restaurant dans l'hôtel?
(b) Il y a une pharmacie près d'ici? (c) Il y a
des magasins près d'ici? (d) La banque est
ouverte? (e) Il y a un train direct pour
Paris? (f) La gare, c'est loin? (g) Les
toilettes sont où? **3** (a) Il y a une pharmacie mais il n'y a pas d'aspirine (b) Il y a une
pâtisserie mais il n'y a pas de croissants (c)
Il y a une gare mais il n'y a pas de trains (d)
Il y a un arrêt d'autobus mais il n'y a pas de
bus (e) Il y a un bar mais il n'y a pas de
bière (f) Il y a une cabine téléphonique mais
il n'y a pas de téléphone **4** (a) Vous êtes
en vacances? (b) Vous êtes marié? (c)
Vous avez des enfants? (d) Vous habitez
Londres? (e) Vous travaillez? **5** (a) combien (b) où (c) quand (d) où (e) où (f)
comment **6** (a) 49F50 (b) 3F75 (c) 8F60
(d) 60 centimes (e) 56F15 (f) 68F00

### Petit test
**1** Vous vous appelez comment? **2** Vous
travaillez? **3** Vous habitez où? J'habite
dans la banlieue de Londres **4** J'ai …
ans **5** Il y a une banque près d'ici au bout
de la rue.

## Unit 5
### Essayez
Vous avez un plan, s'il vous plaît? Il y a une
banque et une cabine téléphonique près
d'ici? *You can find more questions to ask in*
*Mots-clefs.*

### Dialogue
8.30am and 5.30pm. School canteen.

### Activités
**2** (a) prends (b) commencent (c) arrive (d)
apprend (e) déjeune (f) prenez (g) fais (h)
est (i) finit (j) faites (k) attendons (l)
comprennent **3** (a)(iii), (b)(vii), (c)(v),
(d)(i), (e)(ii), (f)(iv), (g)(vi) **4** f, e, a, c, g,
d, h, b **5** prends, prennent, commence,
travaille, déjeune, finit, fait, regardent **6**
le 1er mai, le 10 juin, le 3 février, le 13
octobre, le 21 mars, le 30 septembre, le 15
juillet, le 6 août **7** (a) mercredi (b) vendredi (c) dimanche (d) lundi (e) jeudi (f)
samedi (g) mardi **8** neuf heures dix, onze
heures quarante, treize heures trente, dix-
huit heures vingt-cinq, vingt-trois heures
cinquante **9** (a) 2.35pm (b) 12.15pm (c)
9.10am (d) 11.45pm (e) 4.25am (f) 6.30pm

### Petit test
**1** dimanche, samedi, vendredi, jeudi, mercredi, mardi, lundi **2** Quand est-ce que la
banque ferme? **3** Il y a un train pour
Lille? **4** Est-ce que je peux prendre le
petit déjeuner à l'hôtel? **5** (Nous sommes
le …) Aujourd'hui c'est le … Il est …

## Unit 6
### Essayez
**1** Vous pouvez parler plus lentement?
Vous pouvez répéter, s'il vous plaît? **2**
*Use the dialogue and Mots-clefs of Unit 5*

### Dialogue
As you leave the house turn left, go to the
end of rue Vaugirard, turn right into rue
Vincennes and the park is 200 metres
on your left. It takes approximately 25
minutes.

### Activités
**1** (a) Pour aller à la piscine? (b) Pour aller à
la gare? (c) Pour aller à l'église St Paul? (d)
Pour aller au musée? (e) Pour aller à
l'office du tourisme? **2** (a) C (b) E (c) A
(d) D (e) B **4** à Brighton, en France,
l'Allemagne, à Berlin, à Bonn, au Danemark, aux Etats-Unis, au Japon, à
Londres **5** Allemagne Angleterre Belgi-
que Danemark Espagne France Italie Nor-
vège Portugal Suède Suisse **7** (a) en face
du (b) à côté de la (c) au coin de (d) entre
(e) au bout de (f) grands magasins (g) bar
(h) pâtisserie (i) dans la rue (j) sur la place

— **206** —

# Unit 7

**Essayez**

1 dans  2 sur  3 entre  4 à côté du  5 sous  6 devant  7 derrière

**Dialogue**

A silk scarf, 200F: 350F and 250F, small with a scene of the Champs-Elysées.

**Activités**

1 cet, ces, ce, ces, ce, cet, cette, cette  2 Mme Durand a 35 ans. Elle a les cheveux blonds et longs. Elle a les yeux verts. Elle fait 1,70 et pèse 65 kg. Elle porte des lunettes rouges. Elle porte un ensemble vert uni, des chaussures légères et une chemise blanche. Jane a 23 ans. Elle a les cheveux châtains et courts. Ses yeux sont bleus (Elle a les yeux bleus). Elle fait 1,62 et pèse 55 kg. Elle porte un jean bleu pâle et un pullover blanc. Elle a (porte) des bottes blanches.  3 (a) une boîte de petits pois français (b) une tarte aux pommes (c) un baba au rhum (d) une glace à la vanille (e) un sorbet au citron (f) un grand verre de vin rouge (g) un café au lait sans sucre (h) un poulet à 45 francs (i) un petit café noir (j) un sandwich au fromage (k) une bouteille de lait.  4 (a) Chère (b) famille (c) tout (d) sympathique (e) bonnes (f) confortable (g) grande (h) longues (i) jours (j) meilleure (k) anglaise (l) mieux (m) prochaine  5 (a) un grand café noir (b) deux petites bières (c) et un petit crème (d) non, deux petites bières et un grand café noir (e) vous avez des croissants? (f) j'en voudrais quatre

**Petit test**

1 (a) au bout de la rue (b) prenez la route pour Lille  2 (b)  3 (a)  4 vous avez autre chose? C'est de quelle couleur? Je vais prendre le plus petit

# Unit 8

**Essayez**

Je cherche quelque chose pour ouvrir les bouteilles de vin.

**Dialogue**

Cooking French dishes. Squash, swimming, wind-surfing. Beef stew with wine and chicken in wine. Twice a week.

**Activités**

1 (a) Comment vous appelez-vous? Je m'appelle Roger Burru. (b) Quel âge avez-vous? J'ai 35 ans. (c) Vous êtes marié? Oui, je suis marié. (d) Vous avez des enfants? Non, je n'ai pas d'enfants. (e) Qu'est-ce que vous faites dans la vie? Je suis professeur. (f) Depuis quand? Depuis 10 ans. (g) Où habitez-vous? J'habite Lille. (h) Qu'est-ce que vous faites comme sports? Je fais de la natation. (i) Qu'est-ce que vous avez comme loisirs? J'aime beaucoup faire la cuisine.  2 (e)(c)(a) adore, (d)(g) aime beaucoup, (f)(h) n'aime pas, (b) déteste  3 (b) le prends (c) le connaissez (d) les a (e) l'ai (f) l'aiment (g) la fais (h) l'attendons (i) la regarde (j) les écoutons  4 (a)(viii), (b)(vii), (c)(iv), (d)(ii), (e)(ix), (f)(x), (g)(iii), (h)(vi), (i)(v), (j)(i)  5 (a) F (b) F (c) V (d) V (e) V (f) F (g) V (h) V (i) F (j) F (k) V (l) F

**Petit test**

1 Je joue au squash mieux que Fabrice  2 La France est plus grande que l'Angleterre  3 Elle a des lunettes et des cheveux longs  4 Je cherche quelque chose pour réparer ma voiture  5 J'aime le squash mais je préfère jouer au tennis  6 j'aime beaucoup la cuisine française

# Unit 9

**Essayez**

1 Vous pouvez répéter, s'il vous plaît  2 Vous pouvez parler plus lentement s'il vous plaît?

**Activités**

1 (a)(v), (b)(vii), (c)(ix), (d)(vi), (e)(iii), (f)(viii), (g)(ii), (h)(iv). (i)(i)  2 (a)(iv), (b)(v), (c)(i), (d)(vi), (e)(ii), (f)(iii)  3 (a) C (b) F (c) B (d) D (e) A (f) E; (i) 7 (ii) add pepper and salt (iii) 30g. of butter (iv) when the butter is hot (v) a fork

**Pratique:** It is strictly forbidden to take photographs using a tripod or flash; to damage the sculptures or the vases; to pick flowers or fruit; to climb on the sculptures; to walk on the lawn or to climb on the seats; to lunch outside the area reserved for the cafeteria; to bring animals into the museum's grounds; to ride a bicycle; to play ball games; to drop rubbish except in the litter baskets.

**Grand Test**
1 (a) 2 (b) 3 (b) 4 (c)(d) 5 (b)(e) 6 (b) 7 (b) 8 (b)(f) 9 (a)(e) 10 (c) 11 (a)(d) 12 (b)(d) 13 (c)(f) 14 (b)(e) 15 (a)

# *Unit 10*
**Activités 1, 2, 3, 4 could have alternative answers to the ones given below:**

## Essayez
1 Out of order 2 Qu'est-ce qu'il faut faire pour téléphoner en Angleterre.

## Dialogue
4 weeks; to the seaside and to the mountains; swimming, play tennis, go for long walks and see regional historic monuments.

## Pratiquez
Je m'habille, tu t'habilles, il/elle/on s'habille, nous nous habillons, vous vous habillez, ils s'habillent.

## Activités
1 (a) D'abord je me lève à 7 heures (b) puis je me lave (c) ensuite je prends le petit déjeuner (d) A 8h30 j'emmène les enfants à l'école (e) ensuite je fais des courses (f) A midi je prépare le déjeuner (g) L'après-midi, je joue au tennis (h) ou je vais chez mes amis (i) ou je vais au cinéma (j) Le soir, je regarde la télévision (k) ou j'écoute la radio (l) enfin je me couche à 11 heures. 2 (a) ...il/elle se lève ... (b) ... il/elle se lave ... (c) ...il/elle prend... (d) il/elle emmène... (e) ...il/elle va... (f) ...il/elle rentre, prépare ... (g) il/elle joue ... (h) ...il/elle va chez ses amis... (i) il/elle va ... (j) il/elle regarde ... (k) il/elle écoute ... (l) il/elle se couche ... 3 *Robert:* (a) en août (b) 3 semaines (c) à Oxford en Angleterre (d) Je vais apprendre l'anglais, visiter des monuments historiques, voir des amis, sortir le soir,

jouer au tennis. *Jeanine:* (a) le 21 juin (b) 10 jours (c) à Anglet près de Biarritz dans le sud de la France (d) Je vais me baigner, lire beaucoup, regarder un peu la télévision, faire de longues promenades, me coucher tôt. 4 (a) Vous allez partir quand en vacances? (b) Vous allez partir... (c) Où allez-vous aller? (d) Comment allez-vous passer vos vacances? 5 (a) beaucoup (b) mari (c) Grande-Bretagne (d) finit (e) samedi (f) après-midi (g) rester (h) jours (i) visiter (j) habitent (k) besoin (l) prendre 6 (a) téléphoner à Marc (b) aller chez le dentiste (c) aller à la banque (d) faire des courses pour acheter 2 steaks, une bouteille de vin et une glace à la fraise (e) écrire une lettre à ma mère (f) poster la lettre (g) jouer au tennis (h) faire la cuisine (i) inviter Anne à dîner

**Grand test**
1 (b)(d) 2 (a)(f) 3 (b)(f) 4 (a)(d) 5 (c)(f) 6 (c)(d) 7 (a)(e) 8 (a)(d) 9 (c)(e) 10 (b)(f) 11 (a)(e) 12 (b)(f) 13 (a)(f) 14 (a)(e)

# *Unit 11*
## Activités
1 (a) 19/20 hours (b) shut (c) lundi (d) patisseries charcuteries 3 (a), (c) boucherie, (d)(e)(g) épicerie, (b) boulangerie, (f) charcuterie 4 (c), (f), (h), (a), (e), (d), (g), (i), (b) 5 (b), (d), (g), (l) 7 (a) Je cherche une jupe noire (b) vous faites quelle taille? (c) quelque chose de moins cher (d) je vais essayer (e) la jupe à 250 francs (f) elle vous va bien? 8 (a) Je voudrais un journal, s'il vous plaît. Qu'est-ce que vous avez comme journaux anglais? (b) Je vais prendre le Times et ces trois cartes postales. C'est combien un timbre pour l'Angleterre? (c) Je vais prendre huit timbres (d) Je vais aussi acheter le magazine 'Elle' pour ma femme 9 (a) a pullover (b) white/pale yellow (c) it's too big (d) he doesn't like the colour (e) 350F

**Petit test**
1 J'ai besoin de kleenex 2 Je voudrais quelque chose de plus grand, s'il vous plaît 3 Vous avez autre chose? 4 C'est tout 5 Vous acceptez les cartes de crédit?

## Unit 12
### Activités

1 (a) le guide rouge Michelin (b) yes (c) no (d) book your accommodation (e) no  2 All possible answers are given: (a) un bidet, une baignoire, un WC dans la chambre, un téléphone intérieur, un téléphone extérieur, une radio, une TV, un bar privé. (b) un téléphone intérieur, un WC dans la chambre, une baignoire, un bidet (c) un ascenseur, un téléphone intérieur, un WC dans la chambre, une baignoire, un bidet, une douche, l'eau courante chaude et froide au lavabo.  3 (a) Vous avez une liste d'hôtels? (b) Pouvez-vous me réserver une chambre? (c) Vous choisissez quel hôtel? (d) Dans le 16ème arrondissement (e) J'espère que l'hôtel ne sera pas complet (f) Il y aura de la place  4 (a) F (b) F (c) V (d) V (e) F (f) V (g) V  5 Bonsoir, vous avez une chambre, s'il vous plaît? Non, une chambre double à deux lits et avec salle de bains. C'est pour trois nuits. C'est combien? Est-ce que le petit déjeuner est compris? A quelle heure servez-vous le petit déjeuner? On peut prendre un repas dans l'hôtel?  6 (a) Le radiateur ne marche pas (b) Il n'y a pas de savon (c) Il n'y a pas d'eau chaude (d) La lampe ne marche pas (e) Il n'y a pas de serviettes (f) La douche ne marche pas (g) La télévision ne marche pas (h) Il n'y a pas de couvertures  8 (a) F (b) V (c) F (d) F (e) F (f) V

### Petit test

1 Je cherche un hôtel à deux étoiles  2 Vous pouvez me réserver une chambre, s'il vous plaît?  3 Le petit déjeuner est compris?  4 Il n'y a pas de téléphone dans la chambre  5 Il y a un camping près d'ici?

## Unit 13
### Activités

1 (a) cheap (b) meat with vegetable or noodles (c) outside the town (d) drink is included in the price (e) a limited range of dishes (f) today's special (g) crêperie (h) le menu touristique  2 (c) (e) (g)  (a)  3 (a) Je voudrais un croque-monsieur (b) Vous avez des omelettes? (c) Qu'est-ce que c'est 'parmentier'? (d) Je vais prendre

l'omelette parmentier; (e) Qu'est-ce que vous avez comme jus de fruit? (f) Je voudrais un jus d'ananas et l'addition, s'il vous plaît.  5 (a) Qu'est-ce que c'est une blanquette de veau? (b) Je n'aime pas les viandes en sauce (c) Je préfère les grillades (d) Je voudrais un steak bien cuit (e) Comme légumes, je vais prendre des haricots verts (f) Un demi-litre de vin rouge (h) Comme dessert, je vais prendre une crème au caramel  6 (a) Pour commencer je vais prendre un filet de hareng (b) Je vais prendre un avocat coktail (c) Qu'est-ce que c'est le cassoulet? (d) Je n'aime pas les haricots. Je vais prendre une grillade du jour avec frites (e) A point. Je voudrais aussi une bouteille de Sauvignon (f) Je voudrais du pain, s'il vous plaît.  7 (a) Tuesday (b) mid-August – mid-September (c) the menus (d) yes (e) yes (f) yes

### Petit test

1 (a) Où est le restaurant le plus proche? (b) Je cherche quelque chose de moins cher (c) Vous avez autre chose?  2 (a)  3 (a) Il n'y a plus de sandwich au fromage (b) Comme dessert, je vais prendre une glace à la vanille (c) Qu'est-ce que vous avez comme boissons?

## Unit 14
### Activités

1 (a) V (b) F (c) F (d) F (e) V (f) V  2 (a) direction (b) prenez (c) changer (d) Porte de Clignancourt (e) descendez  3 You get the Pont de Neuilly line and change at Châtelet. Then you get the Porte d'Orléans line and get off at Raspail.  4 (a)(ii), (b)(i), (c)(iii)  5 (a) C'est quelle ligne pour aller au musée d'Orsay? (b) C'est direct? (c) C'est loin à pied? (d) Le bus part à quelle heure? (e) Où est-ce que je peux acheter un ticket? (f) Je voudrais acheter un aller-retour pour les Invalides. (g) Je vais prendre un carnet.  6 (a)(vii), (b)(v), (c)(iv), (d)(ii), (e)(vi), (f)(i), (g)(iii)  7 Je voudrais aller à Grenoble. Je voudrais un aller-retour, s'il vous plaît. Je voudrais voyager le matin. En première. Non. Il faut changer? Il y a une voiture-restaurant?

### Petit test

1 Je voudrais un sandwich au fromage  2

Qu'est-ce que vous avez à boire? **3** Je voudrais un carnet (de tickets) **4** A quelle heure part le prochain train pour Paris?

# Unit 15
## Activités
**1** (a) Je voudrais un plan de la ville (b) Qu'est-ce qu'il y a à voir? (c) Qu'est-ce qu'il y a à faire pour les enfants? (d) Il y a une piscine couverte? (e) Pour aller au Parc Floral, il y a un bus? **2** (a) 9h – 18h (b) 14F (c) Yes (d) 10F (e) 20 minutes (f) 1h30 (g) No (h) 7F **3** C'est combien l'entrée? Neuf ans. Il faut payer pour le mini-golf? On peut piqueniquer? A quelle heure ferme le parc? **4** (a) The Arc de Triomphe and the Panthéon (b) Sunday (c) The Picasso Museum (d) The Panthéon (e) No **5** (a) 7.15am (b) one hour (c) have lunch, visit the Hospices, the wine museum and the wine cellar (d) 400F **6** (a) Nous voulons faire l'excursion de la route des vins de Bourgogne (b) Nous voulons deux places pour le 22 juillet. (c) Le car part d'ici? (d) Vous pouvez répéter, s'il vous plaît? Merci. A quelle heure part le car? (f) On peut acheter du vin dans la cave? **7** (a) 23 septembre (b) 7h30 (c) pour le déjeuner (d) l'abbaye, le cloître, les remparts (e) vers 23 heures

## Petit test
**1** Je voudrais un plan de ville, s'il vous plaît **2** Est-ce que le musée ferme entre midi et deux heures? **3** Il y a une visite guidée?

# Unit 16
## Activités
**1** (a) programme (b) horaires (c) office du tourisme (d) Pariscope (e) l'Officiel des Spectacles (f) agence de location **2** (a) F (b) F (c) F (d) V (e) V (f) V **3** (a)(iv), (b)(v), (c)(iii), (d)(i), (e)(ii) **4** (a) Sunday (b) two (c) around 9.00 pm. (d) Dinner by candlelight (e) Franco-spanish (f) 2 am. (g) 350F **5** (a) Je voudrais des places pour samedi prochain (b) Ca finit à quelle heure, le concert (c) C'est combien la place? (d) C'est tarif réduit (e) Ma soeur doit payer? **6** (a) Opéra (b) Carte Bleue (French equivalent to Visa Card) (c) 38F

(d) Monday (e) 13h35, 16h15, 18h55 **7** (a) Où est-ce qu'on peut jouer au tennis? (b) Où est-ce qu'on réserve le court? (c) C'est combien l'heure? (d) On peut louer une raquette? (e) Vous pouvez me donner l'adresse du Club, s'il vous plaît? **8** (a) (i) yes (ii) no; (b) (i) yes (ii) no; (c) (i) no (ii) yes (d) (i) yes (ii) no (e) (i) table tennis (ii) board-games

## Petit test
**1** (a) date-stamp (b) exit (c) connection (d) left luggage (e) platform (f) ticket office **2** (a) un carnet (de tickets), s'il vous plaît (b) un aller-retour svp (c) un horaire svp (d) l'arrêt d'autobus svp? (e) le bureau de renseignements svp? (f) un aller (simple) svp? **3** (c) **4** (c) **5** (a) **6** place, tarif, boîte de nuit, ambiance, spectacles

# Unit 17
## Activités
**1** (a) yes (b) 10–15km (c) une carte (d) route nationale **2** (a) juin (b) août (c) le 7 juillet et le 9 septembre **3** (d), (b), (f), (c), (a), (e) **4** (a) C'est quelle route pour Paris s'il vous plaît? (b) C'est cher l'autoroute? (c) Où est la (route) nationale 10? (d) La (route) nationale 10 est indiquée? (e) Bon, il faut prendre la nationale 751 direction Loches jusqu'aux feux. Aux feux, je prends à gauche, direction Paris **5** (a) stationnement interdit (b) défense de stationner (c) amende (d) piétonne (e) d'enlèvement (f) police (g) parking gratuit (h) parking payant (i) horodateur (j) parcmètre **6** (a)(iv), (b)(vii), (c)(i), (d)(vi), (e)(iii), (f)(ii), (g)(v) **7** pompiste (a) (c) (f); client (b) (d) (e) **8** (a) Bonjour, je voudrais du super, s'il vous plaît (b) Non, pour 180F (c) Vous pouvez vérifier l'huile? (d) Un litre (e) Non, merci, ça va **9** (a) Vous pouvez m'aider, je suis en panne (b) Je ne sais pas, le moteur ne marche pas (c) Je suis entre Orléans et Blois sur l'autoroute A10 (d) direction de Tours (e) J'ai une voiture anglaise: une Vauxhall Astra bleue. Vous arrivez quand? **10** (a) B (b) A (c) D (d) C (e) E (f) F (g) H (h) G **11** (a) le pneu est crevé (b) la batterie est à plat (c) le pare-brise est cassé (d) les freins ne marchent pas (e) le moteur chauffe

## Unit 18
### Activités

1 (a) Où est la banque la plus proche? (b) A quelle heure est-ce que la banque ouvre aujourd'hui? (c) A quelle heure est-ce que la banque ferme? 2 (a) Vous pouvez changer 10F svp? (b) Il me faut des pièces de 1F (c) No change given 3 (a) Pardon Monsieur, vous avez de la monnaie pour le téléphone, s'il vous plaît? (b) Je n'ai qu'une pièce de 10F et il me faut des pièces de 1F. (c) Qu'est-ce que c'est une télécarte? (d) Où est-ce que je peux acheter une télécarte? 4 (a) changer (b) pièce (c) signer (d) écrire (e) à combien (f) payer 5 (a) Je voudrais changer des dollars. (b) Des dollars américains. (c) Des billets. (d) 100 dollars; c'est à combien le dollar? (e) Vous êtes ouvert le dimanche? 6 (a) after breakfast (b) 14 (c) no (d) drinks from the mini-bar (e) 446F (f) yes 7 (a) 5F40 (b) 7F22 (c) 0F50 (d) 19F75 (e) 22F (f) 89F56 (g) 172F (h) 315F40 (i) 632F15 (j) 918F30

### Petit test

1 Il y a un parking près d'ici? 2 Il me faut quatre pièces de 1 franc pour the parcmètre 3 Vous pouvez m'aider, s'il vous plaît? Je suis en panne 4 Il me faut un litre d'huile 5 Vous avez de la monnaie? 6 Vous acceptez les cartes de crédit? 7 Je voudrais régler ma note 8 Vous pouvez vérifier la pression des pneus, s'il vous plaît? 9 Vous pouvez faire le plein, s'il vous plaît? 10 Je voudrais changer cinquante livres en francs.

## Unit 19
### Activités

1 (a) (ii)(iv) (b) No (c) (iii) two every four hours and (iv) one when needed 2 (a) Ma fille a mal aux dents. (b) Oui, un peu. (c) Depuis hier. (d) Merci; vous avez quelque chose pour les piqûres d'insectes. (e) Je vais la prendre; c'est combien? 3 (a) to make an appointment (b) her daughter (c) yes, high temperature; (d) a bad headache (e) 19.30 4 (a) Je voudrais prendre rendez-vous (b) Non, c'est pour mon fils. Nous sommes Anglais, en vacances ici et il a mal aux dents depuis mardi. (c) Il a 12

ans. (d) Il peut venir aujourd'hui, ce matin ou cet après-midi. (e) Vous pouvez répéter l'heure, s'il vous plaît? (f) Mon nom est... 5 (a)(v), (b)(iv), (c)(vi), (d)(ii), (e)(i), (f)(iii) 6 (a) le bleu (b) le bleu nuit (c) le rouge (d) le blanc 8 (a) clefs (b) stylo, lunettes (c) portefeuille, argent, cartes de crédit (d) parapluie, carte d'identité (e) téléphone (f) essuie-glace, freins 9 (a) on m'a volé ma voiture (b) elle est comment votre voiture? (c) quel est le numéro d'immatriculation (d) faire une déclaration (e) remplir cet imprimé (f) vous en avez besoin pour vos assurances 10 (a) J'ai perdu mon stylo dans le bureau. Il est en or. (b) Mon frère a perdu sa valise dans le train. Elle est en cuir. Elle est marron (c) Ma soeur a perdu son porte-monnaie dans le parc. Il est en cuir. Il est blanc (d) Son père a perdu son passeport dans la banque. Il est bleu (e) Un ami a perdu son parapluie dans le bus. Il est noir. Il est très vieux.

### Petit test

1 Je voudrais quelque chose pour le mal à la tête 2 Je voudrais prendre rendez-vous 3 J'ai mal à la gorge 4 On m'a volé mon sac au cinéma 5 Mes lunettes sont cassées.

# Les chiffres  *Numbers*

| | | |
|---|---|---|
| 0 zéro | 21 vingt et un | 70 soixante-dix |
| 1 un | 22 vingt-deux | 71 soixante et onze |
| 2 deux | 23 vingt-trois | 72 soixante-douze, |
| 3 trois | 24 vingt-quatre | etc. |
| 4 quatre | 25 vingt-cinq | 80 quatre-vingts |
| 5 cinq | 26 vingt-six | 81 quatre-vingt-un |
| 6 six | 27 vingt-sept | 82 quatre-vingt-deux, |
| 7 sept | 28 vingt-huit | etc. |
| 8 huit | 29 vingt-neuf | 90 quatre-vingt-dix |
| 9 neuf | 30 trente | 91 quatre-vingt-onze |
| 10 dix | 31 trente et un | 92 quatre-vingt- |
| 11 onze | 32 trente-deux, etc. | douze, etc. |
| 12 douze | 40 quarante | 100 cent |
| 13 treize | 41 quarante et un | 101 cent un |
| 14 quatorze | 42 quarante-deux, etc. | 102 cent deux, etc. |
| 15 quinze | 50 cinquante | 200 deux cents |
| 16 seize | 51 cinquante et un | 210 deux cent dix |
| 17 dix-sept | 52 cinquante-deux, etc. | 300 trois cents |
| 18 dix-huit | 60 soixante | 331 trois cent trente et |
| 19 dix-neuf | 61 soixante et un | un |
| 20 vingt | 62 soixante-deux, etc. | |

| | | | |
|---|---|---|---|
| 1000 | mille | 1,000,000 | un million |
| 2000 | deux mille | 2,000,000 | deux millions |

# VOCABULARY
## French–English

à  *to, in*
abord  *see* d'abord
accord  *see* d'accord
abricot (m)  *apricot*
achat (m)  *shopping;* faire des
  achats  *to do some shopping*
acheter  *to buy*
addition  (f)  *bill, sum*
adorer  *to adore, to love*
adresse (f)  *address*
affaires (f pl)  *business;* homme
  d'affaires  *businessman*
âge (m)  *age*
agence de voyages (f)  *travel
  agency*
agence de location (f)  *booking
  office, box office*
aider  *to help*
aimer  *to like, to love*
aire (f) de piquenique  *picnic area*
alcool (m)  *spirit*
alimentation (f)  *grocer's shop*
aller  *to go*
aller (m) simple  *single ticket*
aller-retour (m)  *return ticket*
allô  *hello (on phone)*
alors  *well, then*
ambiance (f)  *atmosphere*
ami (m), amie (f)  *friend*
amende (f)  *fine*
an (m)  *year*
ancien(ne)  *ancient*
anglais (e)  *English (often used for
  British)*
Angleterre (f)  *England*

année (f)  *year*
après  *after*
après-midi (m)  *afternoon*
apprécier  *to appreciate*
août  *August*
apparaître  *to appear*
s'appeler  *lit. to be called*
  je m'appelle  *my name is*
apprendre  *to learn*
argent (m)  *money*
arrêt (m)  *stop*
arrivée (f)  *arrival*
arriver  *to arrive*
ascenseur (m)  *lift*
aspirine (f) effervescente  *soluble
  aspirin*
assez  *enough, fairly*
assiette (f)  *plate*
attendre  *to wait for*
aujourd'hui  *today*
au revoir  *goodbye*
aussi  *also, too, as well*
autobus (m)  *bus;* en autobus
  *by bus*
autocar (m)  *coach;* en autocar
  *by coach*
automne (m)  *autumn;*
  en automne  *in autumn*
autoroute (f)  *motorway*
autre  *other;* autre chose
  *something else*
avec  *with*
avion (m)  *aeroplane*
avoir  *to have*
avril  *April*

se baigner *to go for a swim*
baguette (f) *'French stick'*
*(bread)*
balle (f) *ball*
banlieue (f) *suburb*
banque (f) *bank*
bar (m) *bar*
bas(se) *low*
bas (m) *bottom, lower part*
bâtiment (m) *building*
battre *to beat*
beau (belle) *handsome, beautiful*
beaucoup (de) *much, a lot*
belle *see* beau
besoin (m) *need;* avoir besoin
*to need*
beurre (m) *butter*
bien *well;* bien sûr *certainly*
bientôt *soon;* à bientôt *see you
soon*
bière (f) *beer*
billet (m) *ticket, (bank) note*
blanc (blanche) *white*
bleu(e) *blue;* bleu marine *navy
blue;* bleu pâle *pale blue*
blond(e) *blond*
boeuf (m) *beef, ox*
boire *to drink*
boîte (f) *box, can, tin*
boîte aux lettres *letter box*
boîte (f) (de nuit) *disco, night club*
boisson (f) *drink*
bol (m) *bowl*
bon(ne) *good;* bon marché
*cheap*
bonjour *good day, hello*
bonsoir *good evening*
botte (f) *boot*
boucherie (f) *butcher's*
bouchon (m) *cork, bottleneck*
boulangerie (f) *baker's*
boulevard (m) *boulevard*
bout (m) *end;* au bout de *at the
end of*

bouteille (f) *bottle*
brasserie (f) *pub-restaurant*
briller *to shine*
brouillard (m) *fog*
bruit (m) *noise*
brun (brune) *brown (hair,
complexion)*
bureau (m) de location *box office*
bureau (m) de renseignements
*information office*
bureau (m) des réservations
*booking office*
bus (m) *see* autobus

cabine téléphonique (f) *telephone
box*
cabinet de toilette (m) *small room
containing wash basin and bidet*
cadeau (m) *present*
café (m) *coffee, café;* café au lait
(m) *white coffee;* café
crème *coffee served with
cream*
caisse (f) *cash desk, cashier's,
ticket office*
ça *that, it;* ça va? *how are
things?;* ça va *things are OK*
cabine (f) d'essayage *fitting room*
campagne (f) *country;* à la
campagne *in (to) the country*
camping (m) *camping, campsite*
car (m) *see* autocar
carnet (m) *book (of tickets), 10
metro tickets*
carrefour (m) *crossroads*
carte (f) *map, card, menu;*
carte bancaire *banker's card;*
carte d'abonnement *season
ticket;*
carte de crédit *credit card;*
carte d'identité *identity card;*
carte postale (f) *post-card;*
à la carte *menu*

cassé(e)  *broken*
ce, cet, cette  *this, that (adjective)*
ceci  *see* ce
célèbre  *famous*
célibataire (m and f)  *single, bachelor*
cent  *a hundred*
centime (m)  *centime*
centre (m)  *centre;* au centre de  *in the centre of;* centre ville  *town centre*
centre commercial (m)  *shopping centre*
certain(e)  *certain*
certainement  *certainly*
ces  *these, those*
c'est  *it is, this is*
c'est ça  *that's it*
cet, cette  *see* ce
chambre (f)  *(bed)room*
champignon (m)  *mushroom*
chance (f)  *luck*
changer  *to change*
changeur (m) de monnaie  *coin changing machine*
charcuterie (f)  *selling cooked meats*
chaud(e)  *hot;* avoir chaud  *to be hot*
chauffer  *to heat up*
chaussure (f)  *shoe*
chemise (f)  *shirt*
chèque de voyage (m)  *see* traveller
cher (chère)  *expensive, dear*
chercher  *to look for;* aller chercher  *to go and fetch*
cheveux (m pl)  *hair*
chez  *at the home of;* chez moi  *at my house, at home*
choisir  *to choose*
choix (m)  *choice*
chose (f)  *thing*

chocolat (m)  *eating or drinking chocolate*
cinq  *five*
cinquante  *fifty*
circulation (f)  *traffic*
citron (m)  *lemon*
classe (f)  *class*
classique  *classical*
clef (f)  *key*
coin (m)  *corner*
combien (de)?  *how much? how many?*
commander  *to order*
comme  *as, like, in the way of*
commencer  *to start, to begin*
comment  *how, how to, what*
complet(ète)  *full*
composer  *to dial (a telephone number)*
composter  *to date-stamp (a ticket)*
comprendre  *to understand*
comprimé (m)  *tablet*
compris  *understood, included*
connaître  *to know (a person or a place)*
connu(e)  *known*
conseiller  *to advise*
consigne (f)  *left luggage;* consigne automatique  *luggage lockers*
content(e)  *pleased*
continuer  *to continue*
copain/copine  *(boy, girl) friend*
correspondance (f)  *connection*
côté (m)  *side;* à côté de  *next to;* de l'autre côté  *on the other side*
costume (m)  *suit for men*
couchette (f)  *couchette*
se coucher  *to go to bed*
couleur (f)  *colour*
coup (m) de fil  *telephone call*

cours (m) particulier  *private lesson*
cours (m) de change  *exchange rate*
courses (f pl)  *shopping*
court(e)  *short*
court (m) de tennis  *tennis court*
coûter  *to cost*
couverture (f)  *blanket, cover*
cravate (f)  *tie*
crème (f)  *cream*
crêperie (f)  *pancake house*
croire  *to believe*
croissant (m)  *croissant*
croque-monsieur (m)  *toasted cheese sandwich with ham*
en cuir  *in leather*
cuisine (f)  *kitchen, cooking*
cuit(e)  *cooked*

d'abord  *firstly*
d'accord  *O.K., agreed*
dans  *in, into*
danser  *to dance*
date (f)  *date*
de  *of, from*
décembre  *December*
décider  *to decide*
décrocher l'appareil  *to lift the receiver*
déjeuner  *to lunch, lunch;* petit déjeuner (m)  *breakfast*
demain  *tomorrow*
demi(e)  *half*
    demi-kilo (m)  *half a kilogram*
    demi-heure (f)  *half an hour*
dent (f)  *tooth*
dentifrice (m)  *toothpaste*
dépannage: le service de dépannage  *breakdown service*
dépendre de  *to depend on*
depuis  *since;* je suis marié depuis 10 ans  *I've been married for 10 years*

déranger  *to disturb, to inconvenience;* en dérangement  *out of order*
dernier(e)  *last*
descendre  *to go down*
désirer  *to wish for*
détester  *to hate*
deux  *two*
deuxième  *second*
devoir  *must, should, ought*
différent(e)  *different*
dimanche  *Sunday*
diminuer  *to decrease*
dîner (m)  *dinner, to have dinner*
dire  *to say*
direct(e)  *direct*
directement  *directly*
direction (f)  *direction*
disque (m)  *record*
dix  *ten*
dix-huit  *eighteen*
dix-neuf  *nineteen*
dix-sept  *seventeen*
doit, ça doit  *see* devoir
donner  *to give*
dormir  *to sleep*
douche (f)  *shower*
douze  *twelve*
droit(e)  *straight;* tout droit  *straight on*
à droite  *right (hand);* avoir droit  *to be entitled*

eau (f)  *water*
    eau minérale (f)  *mineral water*
école (f)  *school*
écouter  *to listen*
église (f)  *church*
élève (m and f)  *pupil*
écrire  *to write*
par écrit  *in writing*
emmener  *to take (someone somewhere)*

emplacement (m)   *pitch*
en   *in, on, of it, of them*
enfant (m and f)   *child*
ensemble   *together*
ensemble (m)   *outfit, suit (woman)*
ensuite   *then*
entre   *between*
entrée (f)   *way in, admission charge*
environ   *about*
environs (m pl)   *surroundings*
envoyer   *to send*
équitation (f)   *riding*
erreur (f)   *mistake*
espérer   *to hope*
essayer   *to try*
essence (f)   *petrol*
essuie-glace (m)   *windscreen wiper*
est (m)   *east*
et   *and*
étage (m)   *floor*
été (m)   *summer;* en été   *in summer*
étoile (f)   *star*
être   *to be*
eux   *them (people)*
éviter   *to avoid*
excursion (f)   *excursion, trip;* faire une excursion   *to go on an excursion*
excuser   *to excuse*
expliquer   *explain*
en face (de)   *facing*


facile   *easy*
faim (f)   *hunger;* avoir faim   *to be hungry*
faire   *to do, to make*
famille (f)   *family*
il faut   *it is necessary, one has to*
il faudra   *it will be necessary*

faux (fausse)   *false*
favori (favorite)   *favourite*
femme (f)   *wife, woman*
fenêtre (f)   *window*
fermé(e)   *closed*
fermer   *to close*
fête (f)   *feast-day, celebration*
feux (m pl) (rouges)   *traffic lights*
février   *February*
fièvre (f)   *fever, temperature*
fille (f)   *daughter, girl*
fils (m)   *son*
finalement   *finally*
finir   *to finish*
fleur (f)   *flower*
fois (f)   *time;* une fois   *once*
fondre   *to melt*
forme (f)   *shape*
formidable   *great*
foulard (m)   *scarf*
fourchette (f)   *fork*
fraise (f)   *strawberry*
franc (m)   *franc*
français(e)   *French*
France (f)   *France*
frère (m)   *brother*
frein (m)   *brake*
frite (f)   *chip; (adjective) fried*
froid(e)   *cold;* avoir froid   *to be cold*
fromage (m)   *cheese*
fruit (m)   *fruit*

garçon (m)   *boy, waiter*
garder   *to keep*
gare (f)   *station;* gare routière (f)   *bus, coach station;* gare SNCF (f)   *railway station*
garer   *to park*
garni(e)   *served with vegetables, salads etc*
à gauche   *left*
généralement   *generally*
glace (f)   *ice-cream*

gonflage (m) des pneus  *pumping up the tyres*
gorge (f)  *throat*
gourmet (m)  *gourmet*
grand(e)  *big, tall*
Grande-Bretagne (f)  *Great Britain*
gratuit(e)  *free*
grillade (f)  *grilled meat*
grippe (f)  *flu*
gros (grosse)  *fat, large*
guichet (m)  *ticket office*

(s')habiller  *to dress*
habiter  *to live*
haricot (m)  *bean;* haricot vert  *green bean*
heure (f)  *hour;* quelle heure est-il?  *what time is it?*
hiver (m)  *winter;* en hiver  *in winter*
homme (m)  *man;* homme d'affaires  *businessman*
hôpital (m)  *hospital*
horaire (m)  *timetable*
hôtel (m)  *hotel*
  hôtel de ville (m)  *town hall*
hors  *outside;* hors-d'oeuvre  *starter;* hors de service  *out of service*
huile (f)  *oil*
huit  *eight*

ici  *here*
île (f)  *island;* île de France  *Paris area*
indicatif (m)  *dialling code*
indiquer  *indicate*
ingénieur (m)  *engineer*
intéressant(e)  *interesting*
introduire  *to insert*
inviter  *to invite*
inscription (f)  *enrolment*

jamais  *never*

jambon (m)  *ham*
janvier  *January*
jardin (m)  *garden*
jardinage (m)  *gardening*
jaune  *yellow*
jean (m) or jeans (m pl)  *jeans*
jeu (m)  *game;* jeu de société  *parlour game*
jeudi  *Thursday*
jeune  *young*
joli(e)  *pretty*
jouer  *to play*
jour (m)  *day;* jour férié  *bank holiday*
journal (m)  *newspaper*
journée (f)  *day, day-time*
joyeux(se)  *joyful, merry*
juillet  *July*
juin  *June*
jupe (f)  *skirt*
jus (m) de fruit  *fruit juice;*
jusqu'à  *until, as far as*

kilo(gramme) (m)  *kilogram*

la  *the, her, it*
là(-bas)  *(over) there*
lait (m)  *milk*
laisser  *to leave;* laissé  *left*
large  *wide, big*
(se) laver  *to wash*
le  *the, him, it*
léger (légère)  *light*
légume (m)  *vegetable*
lentement  *slowly*
lettre (f)  *letter*
leur(s)  *their, to them*
se lever  *to get up*
libre  *free (but for free of charge use* gratuit*);* libre service (m)  *small supermarket*
ligne (f)  *number (bus), line (métro)*
lire  *to read*
lit (m)  *bed;* à deux lits  *twin-*

bedded; le grand lit *double bed*
litre (m) *litre*
livre (m) *book;* (f) *pound*
location (f) *hire*
loin *far*
loisir (m) *hobby*
long (longue) *long*
louer *to let, to hire, to book*
lourd(e) *heavy*
lui *to him, to her, he, as for him*
lundi *Monday*
lunettes (f pl) *glasses*

Madame *Madam, Mrs*
Mademoiselle *Miss*
magasin (m) *shop;* grand
  magasin *department store*
*mai May*
maintenant *now*
mais *but*
maison (f) *house;* à la maison *at
  home*
mal *badly;* avoir mal *to have a
  pain;* mal (m) au dos *backache*
malheureusement *unfortunately*
manger *to eat*
manquer *to be lacking, missing*
marché (m) *market;* bon
  marché *cheap*
marcher *to walk, to work (for a
  machine)*
mardi *Tuesday*
mari (m) *husband*
marié(e) *married*
marron *brown*
mars *March*
matin (m) *morning*
mauvais(e) *bad*
médecin (m) *doctor, physician*
médicament (m) *medicine*
meilleur(e) *better*
mélange (m) *mixture,*
  mélanger *to mix*
même *same, even*

menu (m) *set meal*
mer (f) *sea;* au bord de la
  mer *at the seaside, by the sea*
mère (f) *mother*
merci *thank you*
mercredi *Wednesday*
mesurer *to measure*
Messieurs-dames *ladies and
  gentlemen*
métro (m) *underground*
mettre *to put*
midi *midday, lunch-time*
mieux *better*
milieu (m) *middle, milieu*
mille *a thousand*
mince *thin*
minuit *midnight*
moi *me, I*
moins *less*
mois (m) *month*
moitié (f) *half*
mon, ma, mes *my*
monument (m) *monument*
monde (m) *world;* tout le
  monde *everybody*
monnaie (f) *small change*
Monsieur *Sir, Mr.*
montagne (f) *mountain;* à la
  montagne *in, to the mountains*
monter *to go up*
montre (f) *watch*
montrer *to show*
morceau (m) *piece*
moteur (m) *engine*
motif (m) *pattern, design*
moyen(ne) *medium, average*
musée (m) *museum*

natation (f) *swimming*
neiger *to snow*
neuf *nine*
neuf (neuve) *new*
niveau (m) *level*
Noël (m) *Christmas*

noir(e)   *black*
nom (m)   *name*
non   *no*
nord (m)   *north*
note (f)   *bill (hotel, telephone)*
notre, nos   *our*
nouveau (elle)   *new;* à
   nouveau   *again*
novembre   *November*
nuit (f)   *night*
numéro (m)   *number,* numéro
   d'immatriculation   *number plate*

occupé(e)   *busy*
s'occuper   *to deal with, to attend
   to*
octobre   *October*
office du tourisme (m)   *tourist
   office*
oeil (m)   *eye*
oeuf (m)   *egg*
omelette (f)   *omelet*
on   *one (used also for 'we' and 'I')*
onze   *eleven*
en or   *made of gold*
ou   *or;* ou … ou   *either … or*
où   *where*
ouest (m)   *west*
oui   *yes*
ouvert(e)   *open*
ouvrir   *to open*

pain (m)   *bread*
panne (f)   *breakdown*
panneau (m)   *sign*
pantalon (m)   *trousers*
paquet (m)   *packet*
paquet-cadeau (m)   *gift-package*
parcmètre (m)   *parking meter*
pardon   *pardon, sorry, excuse me*
parfum (m)   *perfume, flavour (ice-
   cream)*
parking (m)   *car park*
parler   *to speak*
en particulier   *particularly*

partir   *to go*
à partir de   *from, as*
pas   *not;* pas du tout   *not at all*
passer   *to pass*
pâté (m)   *pâté;* pâté de
   campagne   *country pâté*
patisserie (f)   *a cake shop, pastry,
   cake*
payer   *to pay*
pays (m)   *country, area*
à péage   *toll payable*
pendant   *during*
penser   *to think*
perdre   *to lose;* perdu   *lost*
père (m)   *father*
personne (f)   *person;* personne
   (+ne)   *nobody*
peser   *to weigh*
pétanque (f)   *petanque (kind of
   bowls)*
petit(e)   *small;* petit
   déjeuner   *breakfast*
(un) peu   *(a) little, few*
pharmacie (f)   *chemist's*
pharmacien(ne)   *chemist*
pied (m)   *foot;* à pied   *on foot*
pièce (f)   *room, coin;* pièce
   d'identité   *identification*
piquenique (m)   *picnic*
piscine (f) (couverte)   *(indoor)
   swimming pool*
plan (m) (de la ville)   *(town) map*
place (f)   *square, space, seat*
plaisir (m)   *pleasure;* faire
   plaisir   *to please;* avec
   plaisir   *with pleasure*
planche à voile (f)   *windsurfing
   board*
plat (m)   *dish, course*
plein(e)   *full;* le plein, s'il vous
   plaît   *(at the garage) fill it up,
   please*
il pleut   *it is raining*
sans plomb (m)   *lead-free petrol*

(la) plupart *most*

plus *more, plus*
  plus ... que *more than*
  en plus *in addition, extra*
  ne ... plus *no longer, no more*

pneu (m) *tyre*

poêle (f) *frying pan*

poids (m) *weight*

à point *medium done (meat)*

pois, petits pois (m pl) *peas*

poisson (m) *fish*

pointure (f) *size shoes*

poivre (m) *pepper;* poivrer *to pepper*

pomme (f) *apple;* pomme de terre (f) *potato;* pommes frites (f pl) *chips*

pompiste (m) *pump attendant*

pont (m) *bridge*

portefeuille (m) *wallet*

porte-monnaie (m) *purse*

porter *to carry, to wear*

poste (f) *post, post office*

pourboire (m) *tip*

poulet (m) *chicken*

pour *for, in order to*

pouvoir *can, be able to;* vous pouvez *you can*

pratique *practical, convenient*

pratiquer *to practise, to do*

préférer *to prefer*

premier(ière) *first*

prendre *to take;* pris *taken*

près (de) *near;*
  près d'ici *near by*

pression (f) *pressure (tyre); draught (beer)*

presque *nearly*

printemps (m) *spring;* au printemps *in spring*

prix (m) *price*

prochain(e) *next*

proche *near*

professeur (m and f) *teacher*

profession (f) *profession*

promenade (f) (à pied) *walk*

se promener (à pied) *to go for a walk*

puis *then*

pull(over) (m) *pullover*

quai (m) *platform*

quand? *when?*

quarante *forty*

quatorze *fourteen*

quatre *four*

quatre-vingts *eighty*

quatre-vingt-dix *ninety*

quel(le)? *which?, what?*

quelque(s) *some (a few);* quelque chose *something*

quelqu'un *someone*

quelquefois *sometimes*

que *that, than*

(ne) ... que *only*

qu'est-ce que *what*

qui *who, which*

quinze *fifteen*

quinzaine (f) *fifteen or so*

quitter *to leave*

quoi? *what?*

raide *straight (hair)*

randonnée (f) *hike*

rapide *rapid*

raquette (f) *racket*

régler *to settle (bill)*

regretter *to be sorry*

regarder *to watch*

remplir *to fill in*

rendez-vous (m) *appointment*

rendre *to give back*

rendre visite *to pay a visit*

renseignement (m) *(piece of) information*

se renseigner *to inquire*

rentrer *to go back, to go home*

réparer *to repair*

repas (m)  *meal*
répéter  *to repeat*
se reposer  *to rest*
RER  *fast extension of the underground in the suburbs*
restaurant (m)  *restaurant*
réserver  *to reserve, to book*
rester  *to stay*
retourner  *to go back, to return*
rien  *nothing;* de rien  *don't mention it*
robe (f)  *dress*
rouge  *red*
route (f)  *road*
rue (f)  *street*

sac à main (m)  *handbag*
saignant(e)  *bleeding, rare (meat)*
saison (f)  *season;* hors saison  *out of season;* en pleine saison  *in high season*
saler  *to salt*
salle (f)  *hall, auditorium, room;* salle de bains  *bathroom;* salle à manger  *dining room*
sandwich (m)  *sandwich*
sans  *without*
saucisson (m)  *kind of salami*
savoir  *to know (a fact or how to do something e.g.* je sais faire la cuisine  *I know how to cook)*
savon (m)  *soap*
scène (f)  *scene*
séance (f)  *session*
secrétaire (m and f)  *secretary*
seize  *sixteen*
sel (m)  *salt*
selon  *according to*
semaine (f)  *week*
sept  *seven*
septembre  *September*
servir  *to serve*
serviette (f)  *towel, napkin*

serviette de toilette  *hand-towel*
shampooing (m)  *shampoo*
s'il vous plaît  *please*
situé(e)  *situated*
six  *six*
SNCF  *French railways*
soeur (f)  *sister*
soie (f)  *silk;* de soie  *made of silk*
soif (f)  *thirst;* avoir soif  *to be thirsty*
soir (m)  *evening*
soirée (f)  *evening, evening entertainment*
soixante  *sixty*
soixante-dix  *seventy*
en solde  *on sale*
soleil (m)  *sun*
son, sa, ses  *his, her, its*
sortie (f)  *exit*
sortir  *to go out*
souffrir  *to suffer*
souvenir (m)  *souvenir, memory*
souvent  *often*
spectacle (m)  *show*
sport (m)  *sport*
station (f) de métro  *underground station*
station-service (f)  *petrol station*
stationnement (m) (interdit)  *(no) parking*
stationner  *to park*
stylo (m)  *pen*
sucre (m)  *sugar,* sucreries (f pl)  *sweet things*
sud (m)  *south*
suivre  *to follow*
super (m)  *four-star petrol*
supermarché (m)  *supermarket*
sur  *on*
surtout  *mainly, especially*
svp (s'il vous plaît)  *please*
sympathique  *friendly, pleasant*

syndicat d'initiative (m)   *tourist office*

tabac (m)   *tobacconist's-cum-newsagent's*
taille (f)   *size, waist*
tarif (m)   *price list, rate;* tarif réduit   *reduced rate*
tarte (f)   *pie*
taxi (m)   *taxi*
tête (f)   *head*
téléphone (m)   *telephone*
téléphoner (à)   *to phone*
temps (m)   *time, weather*
T.G.V.   *high speed train*
thé (m)   *tea*
ticket (m)   *ticket*
timbre (m)   *stamp*
tir-à-l'arc (m)   *archery*
tire-bouchon (m)   *corkscrew*
toi   *you (familiar)*
toilette (f) faire sa toilette   *to wash and dress;* les toilettes   *lavatory*
ton, ta, tes   *your*
tonalité (f)   *dialling tone*
toujours   *always*
touriste (m and f)   *tourist*
tourner   *to turn*
tout(e) tous   *all*
  tout de suite   *immediately*
  tout droit   *straight ahead*
  tout le monde   *everybody*
  tous les deux   *both of them*
  tous les jours   *every day*
train (m)   *train*
  en train   *by train*
trajet (m)   *journey*
tranche (f)   *slice*
travail (m)   *work, job*
travailler   *to work*
traveller (m)   *travellers' cheque*
traverser   *to cross*

treize   *thirteen*
trente   *thirty*
très   *very*
trois   *three*
troisième   *third*
se tromper   *to make a mistake*
trop   *too, too much, too many*
trouver   *to find;* se trouver   *to be (situated)*
TTC   *all taxes included*

un(e)   *a, an, one*
uni(e)   *plain*

va, vas see aller
vacances (f pl)   *holiday(s)*
valise (f)   *suitcase*
vanille (f)   *vanilla*
vase (m)   *vase*
il vaut   *it costs, it is worth*
veau (m)   *veal*
vélo (m)   *bicycle*
vendeur (m), vendeuse (f)   *sales assistant*
vendredi   *Friday*
vent (m)   *wind*
ventre (m)   *stomach*
vérifier   *to check*
verre (m)   *glass*
vers   *towards*
verser   *to pour*
vert(e)   *green*
vêtement (m)   *garment*
viande (f)   *meat*
vie (f)   *life, cost of living*
vieux (vieil, vieille)   *old*
ville (f)   *town*
vin (m)   *wine*
vingt   *twenty*
vite   *quickly*
vitesse (f)   *speed*
visite (f) guidée   *guided tour*
visiter   *to visit (a place)*
voie (f)   *track*

voilà   *there is, here is, there you are*
voir   *to see*
voiture (f)   *car;* voiture-restaurant   *restaurant-car;* en voiture   *by car*
voler   *to steal;* volé   *stolen*
votre, vos   *your*
je voudrais   *I'd like*
vouloir   *to want;* vous voulez   *you want*
voyager   *to travel*
vrai(e)   *true*
V.T.T.   *mountain biking*

WC (m) (pronounced vé-cé)   *toilet*
week-end (m)   *week-end*

y   *there, to it*
yaourt (m)   *yoghurt*
yeux *see* oeil

zéro   *zero*

# VOCABULARY
## English–French

*a* un, une
*about* environ
*address* l'adresse (f)
*admission charge* l'entrée (f)
*after* après
*afternoon* après-midi (m)
*again* encore, de nouveau
*age* l'âge (m)
*agency* l'agence (f); *travel agency* l'agence (f) de voyages
*all* tout, toute, tous, toutes
*also* aussi
*always* toujours
*and* et
*appear* apparaître
*apple* la pomme
*appointment* le rendez-vous
*April* avril
*arrival* l'arrivée (f)
*arrive* arriver
*as* comme
*aspirin* l'aspirine (f)
*at* à, chez; *at the corner* au coin; *at home* à la maison
*August* août
*autumn* l'automne; *in autumn* en automne

*bad* mauvais(e); *badly* mal
*baker's* la boulangerie
*bank* la banque; *bank holiday* le jour férié
*bath* le bain; *to have a bath* prendre un bain; *bathroom* salle de bains
*be* être

*be able to* pouvoir
*bean* l'haricot (m)
*beautiful* beau, belle
*bed* le lit; *double bed* le grand lit; *twin-bedded* à deux lits
*beer* la bière; *draught (beer)* la pression
*before* avant
*behind* derrière
*believe* croire
*better* meilleur (e), mieux
*between* entre
*bicycle* le vélo
*big* grand(e)
*bill (food, drinks)* l'addition
*bill (hotel)* la note
*black* noir(e)
*blue* bleu(e)
*book* le livre
*book* louer; *booking office* l'agence de location
*bottle* la bouteille
*box* la boîte; *box office* le bureau de location
*boy* le garçon
*bread* le pain
*break* casser; *broken* cassé(e)
*breakdown* la panne; *breakdown service* le service de dépannage
*breakfast* le petit déjeuner
*bridge* le pont
*brother* le frère
*brown* marron
*bus* l'autobus (m), le bus; *bus stop* l'arrêt (m) d'autobus

*busy* occupé(e)

*but* mais

*butcher's* la boucherie

*butter* le beurre

*buy* acheter


*cake, cake shop* une pâtisserie

*camping, campsite* le camping

*can* peux, peut, pouvez

*car park* le parking

*car* la voiture; *by car* en voiture

*carry* porter

*cash desk, cashier's* la caisse

*catch* prendre

*certainly* bien sûr

*change* changer

*change (small)* la monnaie

*cheap* bon marché;
   *cheaper* meilleur marché

*check* vérifier

*cheese* le fromage

*chemist* le pharmacien, la
   pharmacienne

*chemist's* la pharmacie

*chicken* le poulet

*child* l'enfant (m and f)

*chips* les frites

*choose* choisir

*church* l'église (f)

*close* fermer; *closed* fermé(e)

*clothes* les vêtements

*coach* l'autocar (m), le car

*coffee (black)* le café

*coin* la pièce

*cold* froid(e); *to be cold* avoir
   froid

*colour* la couleur

*come* venir; *come
   home* rentrer

*cook* faire la cuisine

*cooking* la cuisine

*corkscrew* le tire-bouchon

*cost* coûter

*country* le pays


*course* le plat

*credit card* la carte de crédit

*cross* traverser


*dance* danser

*daughter* la fille

*day* le jour; *the whole day* toute
   la journée

*dear* cher, chère

*December* décembre

*dinner* le dîner

*dish* le plat

*do* faire

*doctor* le médecin

*dress* la robe, s'habiller

*drink* boire; la boisson

*during* pendant


*easy* facile

*eat* manger

*egg* l'oeuf (m)

*end* le bout; *at the end* au bout

*engine* le moteur

*England* l'Angleterre (f)

*English* anglais(e)

*Englishman* l'Anglais;
   *Englishwoman* l'Anglaise

*enough* assez

*evening* le soir, la soirée

*every* tout, toute

*everyday* tous les jours;·
   *everybody* tout le monde

*everything* tout

*excuse me* pardon

*exit* la sortie

*expensive* cher, chère

*eye* l'oeil (m)


*false* faux, fausse

*family* la famille

*far* loin

*fat* gross(e)

*father* le père

*February* février

*fill in*   remplir; *fill it up (with petrol)*   faire le plein
*find*   trouver
*finish*   finir
*first*   premier, première
*firstly*   d'abord
*fish*   le poisson
*floor*   l'étage (m)
*follow*   suivre
*foot*   le pied; *on foot*   à pied
*for*   pour
*France*   la France
*free (costing nothing)*   gratuit(e)
*French*   français(e)
*Frenchman*   le Français, *Frenchwoman*   la Française
*French railways*   S.N.C.F
*Friday*   vendredi
*friend*   l'ami (m), l'amie (f)
*friendly*   sympatique
*from*   de, à partir de
*fruit juice*   le jus de fruit
*full*   complet, complète, plein(e)

*gardening*   le jardinage
*get up*   se lever
*girl*   la fille
*give*   donner
*glasses*   les lunettes (f pl)
*go*   aller, partir, *to go up*   monter; *to go down*   descendre
*go and get*   aller chercher
*go out*   sortir; *go home*   rentrer à la maison
*good*   bon, bonne
*good evening*   bonsoir
*goodbye*   au revoir
*good night*   bonne nuit
*Great Britain*   la Grande-Bretagne
*green*   vert(e)
*grocer's shop*   l'alimentation (f)

*hair*   les cheveux (m pl)

*half*   demi(e); *half an hour*   demi-heure
*ham*   le jambon
*handbag*   le sac à main
*hate*   détester
*have*   avoir
*head*   la tête
*headache*   le mal à la tête
*hear*   entendre
*heavy*   lourd(e)
*hello*   bonjour, allô (*on the phone*)
*help*   aider
*here*   ici
*here is*   voilà
*hike*   la randonnée
*hire, hiring*   louer, la location
*hobby*   le loisir
*holiday(s)*   les vacances (f pl)
*home, at home*   à la maison; *at my home*   chez moi
*hope*   espérer
*hospital*   l'hôpital (m)
*hot*   avoir chaud(e); *to be hot*   avoir chaud
*hotel*   l'hôtel (m)
*hour*   l'heure (f)
*house*   la maison
*how*   comment
*how much/how many*   combien
*hundred (a)*   cent
*hunger*   la faim; *to be hungry*   avoir faim
*husband*   le mari

*I*   je, moi
*ice-cream*   la glace
*identification*   la pièce d'identité
*ill*   malade
*immediately*   tout de suite
*in, into*   à, en, dans
*in front of*   devant
*information (piece of)*   le renseignement

*information office* le bureau de renseignements
*inquire* se renseigner
*insert* introduire
*interesting* intéressant(e)
*invite* inviter
*it's* c'est, il est, elle est

*January* janvier
*jeans* le jean, les jeans
*journey* le trajet
*July* juillet
*June* juin

*key* la clef
*know* savoir, connaître

*ladies and gentlemen* Messieurs-dames
*large* gros(se), grand(e)
*last* dernier, dernière
*learn* apprendre
*leave* quitter
*left, on the left* à gauche
*left luggage* la consigne
*lemon* le citron
*less* moins
*letter box* la boîte aux lettres
*letter* la lettre
*lift* l'ascenseur (m)
*like* aimer
*like* comme
*line (underground)* la ligne
*listen* écouter
*litre* le litre
*little* petit(e); *(a) little* (un) peu
*live* habiter
*long* long, longue
*look for* chercher
*lose* perdre; *lost* perdu(e)
*lot, a lot (of)* beaucoup (de)
*love* aimer
*lunch* le déjeuner

*Madam, Mrs* Madame, Mme
*make* faire

*man* l'homme (m)
*many* beaucoup
*map* la carte; *map (town)* le plan (de la ville)
*March* mars
*market* le marché
*married* marié(e)
*May* mai
*me* moi
*meal* le repas
*measure* mesurer
*meat* la viande; *well done* bien cuit(e); *medium* à point
*medicine* le médicament
*menu* à la carte
*midday* midi
*middle* milieu; *in the middle* au milieu
*midnight* minuit
*milk* le lait
*Miss* Mademoiselle
*Monday* lundi
*money* l'argent (m)
*month* le mois
*more* plus; *no ... more* ne ... plus
*morning* le matin, la matinée
*mother* la mère
*motorway* l'autoroute (f)
*mountain* la montagne; *in/to the mountains* à la montagne
*much* beaucoup
*museum* le musée
*must; one must* il faut + infinitive

*name* le nom
*near* près (de)
*nearby* près de; *near here* près d'ici
*nearly* presque
*need* avoir besoin
*never* jamais
*new* neuf, neuve, nouveau, nouvelle
*newspaper* le journal

*next*  prochain(e)
*next to*  à côté de
*night*  la nuit
*night club*  la boîte (de nuit)
*no*  non
*nothing*  rien
*November*  novembre
*now*  maintenant
*number*  le numéro;
  *(bus) number*  la ligne

*October*  octobre
*of, off*  de
*often*  souvent
*oil*  l'huile (f)
*O.K.*  d'accord
*old*  vieux, vieil, vieille
*omelet*  l'omelette (f)
*on*  sur, à, en; *on foot*  à pied
*once*  une fois
*one*  un, une, on
*only*  seulement
*open*  ouvrir; *opened*  ouvert(e)
*opposite*  en face de
*or*  ou
*order*  commander
*other*  autre
*out of*  hors de

*packet*  le paquet
*pain*  la douleur; *to have a
  pain*  avoir mal
*park*  garer
*parking meter*  le parcmètre
*particularly*  particulièrement
*pay*  payer
*peas*  les petits pois
*pepper*  le poivre
*person*  la personne
*petrol*  l'essence (f); *petrol
  station*  la station-service
*petrol: 4 star*  le super;
  *lead free*  le sans plomb
*picnic*  le piquenique; *to have a
  picnic*  faire un piquenique

*pie*  la tarte
*piece*  le morceau
*platform*  le quai
*play*  jouer
*please*  s'il vous plaît
*pleased*  content(e)
*post-card*  la carte postale
*post; post office*  la poste
*potato*  la pomme de terre
*pound (sterling)*  la livre (sterling)
*prefer*  préférer
*pressure (tyre)*  la pression
*pretty*  joli(e)
*price*  le prix
*price list*  le tarif
*pullover*  le pull(over)
*pump attendant*  le pompiste
*purse*  le porte-monnaie
*put*  mettre

*quick*  rapide; *quickly*  vite

*rain*  la pluie; *it's raining*  il pleut
*rare (meat)*  saignant(e)
*read*  lire
*record*  le disque
*red*  rouge
*repair*  réparer
*repeat*  répéter
*reserve*  réserver
*rest*  se reposer
*right, on the right*  à droite
*road*  la route
*room*  la pièce; la salle
*room*  la salle; *bathroom*  salle de
  bains; *dining room*  la salle à
  manger

*sale (on)*  en solde
*sales assistant*  le vendeur, la
  vendeuse
*salt*  le sel
*same*  même
*sandwich*  le sandwich

*Saturday* samedi

*say* dire

*school* l'école (f)

*sea* la mer; *by the sea* au bord de la mer

*season* la saison; *out of ...* hors ...; *in high ...* en pleine ...

*seat* la place

*secretary* le/la secrétaire

*see* voir

*send* envoyer

*September* septembre

*serve* servir

*shampoo* le shampooing

*shine* briller; *the sun shines* le soleil brille

*shirt* la chemise

*shoe* la chaussure; *shoe size* la pointure

*shop* le magasin

*shopping* les courses; *to do some shopping* faire les courses

*shopping centre* le centre commercial

*show* montrer

*show* le spectacle

*shower* la douche; *to have a shower* prendre une douche

*sign* le panneau

*since* depuis

*single/bachelor* célibataire

*Sir, Mr.* Monsieur, M.

*sister* la soeur

*situated* situé(e)

*size* la taille

*skirt* la jupe

*sleep* dormir

*slice* la tranche

*slow* lent; *slowly* lentement

*small* petit(e)

*snow* neiger

*soap* le savon

*some* quelque(s)

*someone* quelqu'un

*something* quelque chose

*something else* quelque chose d'autre

*sometimes* quelquefois

*son* le fils

*soon* bientôt

*sorry* pardon

*speak* parler

*spend (time)* passer

*sport* le sport; *to do a sport* pratiquer un sport

*spring* le printemps; *in spring* au printemps

*square* la place

*stamp* le timbre

*star* l'étoile (f)

*start* commencer

*station (rail)* la gare (SNCF); *bus/coach station* la gare routière; *underground station* la station

*straight* raide, droit(e)

*straight on* tout droit

*street* la rue

*suburbs* la banlieue

*sugar* le sucre

*suitcase* la valise

*summer* l'été (m)

*sun* le soleil

*Sunday* dimanche

*supermarket* le supermarché

*surroundings* les environs (m pl)

*swim* nager

*swimming* la natation; *swimming pool* la piscine

*take, taken* prendre, pris

*tall* grand(e)

*taxi* le taxi

*tea* le thé

*teacher* le/la professeur

*tell* dire

*telephone* téléphoner, le téléphone

telephone box   la cabine
  téléphonique
than   que
thank you   merci
that's all   c'est tout
the   le, la, les
then   ensuite, puis, alors
there   y
these, those   ces
thin   mince
thing   la chose
think   penser
thirst   la soif; to be thirsty
  avoir soif
this is   c'est
this, that   ce, cet, cette
thousand   mille
throat   la gorge
Thursday   jeudi
ticket   le billet, le ticket
ticket office   le guichet
time   l'heure (f); what time
  is it?   quelle heure est-il?
time   le temps; spend
  time   passer le temps
timetable   l'horaire (m)
tip   le pourboire
to   à, en, pour, jusqu'à
tobacconist's/newsagent's
  le tabac
today   aujourd'hui
together   ensemble
toilet   les toilettes (f pl)
toll payable   à péage
tomorrow   demain
too; too much; too many   trop
tooth   la dent; toothpaste
  le dentifrice
tour   la visite; guided tour
  la visite guidée
tourist   le/la touriste
tourist office   l'office (m) du
  tourisme, le syndicat d'initiative
towards   vers

towel   la serviette
town   la ville
traffic   la circulation
train   le train; by train   en train;
  on the train   dans le train
travel   voyager, le voyage
travellers' cheque   le traveller
trip   l'excursion (f)
trousers   le pantalon
true   vrai
try   essayer
Tuesday   mardi
turn   tourner
tyre   le pneu

underground   le métro
understand   comprendre
until   jusqu'à

very   très
visit   visiter

wait   attendre
walk   marcher; a walk
  une promenade; to go for a walk
  se promener
wallet   le portefeuille
wash (oneself)   (se) laver
watch   regarder; la montre
water (mineral)   eau minérale
wear   porter
weather   le temps
Wednesday   mercredi
week   la semaine
weigh   peser
well   bien
what   quel(le); qu'est-ce que; quoi
when   quand
where   où
which   quel(le)
white   blanc, blanche
white coffee;   le café crème
who   qui
wife   la femme
windsurf board   la planche à voile

*wine*   le vin
*winter*   l'hiver (m); *in winter*
  en hiver
*wish*   désirer
*with*   avec
*without*   sans
*woman*   la femme
*work*   travailler, marcher
  (machine)
*work*   le travail
*write*   écrire

*year*   l'an (m), l'année (f)
*yellow*   jaune
*yes*   oui
*yoghurt*   yaourt
*you*   tu, toi
*young*   jeune

# Index

accents p.5

adjectives p.30, 74

**à**
    preceding the name of a place p.61
    to describe special features p.74

age p.31

**aller** p.60
    + à p.59
    + infinitive p.105

**au, à la, à l', aux** p.61

**avoir** p.21, 30
    constructions with avoir p.31, 104

**beaucoup de** p.73

**besoin de** p.104

capital letters p.31, 106

**ce, cet, cette, ces** p.73

**ce que** p.85

**c'est** .......? p.22, 40, 41

**combien** p.22, 41

**comment** p.41

**connaître** p.86

consonants p.6

countries, article with p.61

dates p.50

days p.46

**de** p.21, 73

**depuis** p.39

**du, de la, de l', des** p. 21, 62

**en**
    meaning one, some, of it, of them p.40
    preceding the name of a country p.61

-**er** verbs p.29

**est-ce que** p.49

**être** p.30

**faire** p.52, 84, 86

**faut** (il) p.60, 95

feminine p.20

**il y a** p.40

**il y en a/il n'y en a pas** p.40

infinitive p.29, 95

instructions p.95

-**ir** verbs p.50

**jouer** à p.84

**jouer de** p.84

**le, la, l', les** p.20, 85

**leur (s)** p.41

liaison p.7

masculine p.20

**me** p.94

**meilleur** p.76

**mieux** p.76

**moins** p.76

**mon, ma, mes** p.41

months p.47

nationality p.30, 31

**ne ... pas** p.30

**ne ... jamais** p.86

**ne ... plus** p.86

**ne ... que** p.86

**ne ... rien** p.86

**notre, nos** p.41

nouns p.20

numbers p.212

**on** p.29

one p.22, 29

**où** p.41

**partir** p.60

plural p.20

**plus** p.76

**pour** p.105

**pouvoir** p.49, 94

**premier, deuxième** etc p.62

**prendre** p.52

pronouns p.85

**quand** p.41

**quel, quelle** p.31, 61

**qu'est-ce que** p.49, 95

questions

   by intonation p.12, 21, 40, 49

   by inversion p.49

   using est-ce que p.49

**-re** verbs p.50

reflexive verbs p.104

**s'appeller** p.104

**savoir** p.86

**son, sa, ses** p.41

**sortir** p.106

time p.51

**ton, ta, tes** p.41

**un, une** p.20, 22

**venir** p.106

verbs p.29

   + infinitive p.48, 49, 84, 86, 94, 95, 105

**votre, vos** p.41

**voudrais** p.48

**vouloir** p.94

vowels p.5

weather p.86

with p.74

without p.74

**y** p.105